IT'S A

PROCESS!

By

Veronica Nealy-Morris

Copyright © 2018 Veronica Nealy-Morris

ISBN-13: 978-1724816818

ISBN-10: 1724816810

Published by:
Veronica Nealy-Morris

Edited by:

Dr. Ruth L. Baskerville

www.ruthbaskerville.com

Cover Design by:

Rob Williams, Designer

ilovemycover.com

Introduction

When I began writing this book, my title was *ALL JACKED UP!* because that perfectly described my life, from the time I could remember I was alive, until I finally found my purpose for living. God had His hand on me my whole life, guiding and protecting me. However, I was too naïve, too hurt, too selfish and too full of no self-esteem to thank Him, or even notice how much grace was covering me.

My new title came to me when I realized my whole life had been a process of trials and blessings – disproportionately given to me – to shape me into the woman I am today. All believers know that God allows none of us to circumvent or shorten our process because the *Holy Bible* says that our latter years will be better than our former.

My process was complicated, but what brought me through were people God put in my path at precisely the time I needed them. I also read books and listened to spiritual messages, and allowed myself to be open to the human relationships I knew God sent to fortify me. I stopped believing the lie of the enemy and started learning His Word for myself.

I started casting down all imaginations and thoughts that did not line up with GOD'S TRUTH. I daily journaled for twenty years because I didn't have a voice, and once I put my deepest feelings on paper, I grew to understand the benefit of cleansing my body and soul by simply using a pen and paper as a silent therapist. I actually titled it, *"My Dreams Revealed Journal,"* and as I reflect upon the book I've just written,

I pray that my family has found, or will find the kind of inner peace that only comes from accepting the whole truth about our collective past.

Maybe the single-most important thing I started doing was to make daily confessions of who I AM -- (A-Z -- Abundantly Able, Beautifully Blessed, and so forth, all the way to Zealous) -- VERY POWERFUL.

So what advice do I give to those reading my book who see yourselves stuck in any situation from which you feel you can't emerge? Drop the word "shame" from your vocabulary because shame says that the person herself is bad, of no value, or unworthy to exist -- that she is hopelessly defective, unlovable, inferior, and worthless. If I were to review my life backwards, like a movie re-winding to the beginning, I would say that shame followed me until I found the courage, through God, to dismiss the feeling of worthlessness from every aspect of my life.

Sometimes the victimizing acts done to a woman may be so shame-producing that she is still emotionally bound by that shame, even though she mentally understands her worth in God's eyes. That's my story! Ultimately, only God brings full emotional cleansing and freedom. Ask God to do for you what He did for me, and you will experience real joy and peace! Amen!

Veronica Nealy-Morris

Table of Contents

Chapter 1

I'm happy now. I have a daughter who has two kids, so now I'm a grandmother. I'm married too. I have a husband who adores me, and whom I love and adore dearly. But it hadn't always been that way. No, sir, it hadn't always been that way at all. You see I was born in a city called Clewiston, Florida. It's about sixteen miles north of Belle Glade. My little town was called "Harlem" because the people are predominantly African-Americans, and much of what goes on in Clewiston parallels Harlem, New York.

My father, "JD" is deceased but my mother, Veronica is still alive. My dad was considered a handsome man, standing at 6 feet and weighing 210 pounds. He was born in Flatwood, Alabama, the eldest of about fifteen kids. When I was born, I was told that my dad named me "Esther," but my mom chose "Veronica." I don't know what it was about me that even at my birth there was confusion about what to name me. We lived in a single wide trimmed trailer, painted green. It had two bedrooms, and most of the time only one side of the trailer had electricity.

My dad wasn't able to read correctly, since he had only gotten to third grade in school, but he was a good painter, welder and truck driver. He made a lot of money in his lifetime. At one point, he owned a lot of land as well as eighteen-wheelers. My dad was able to sign his name at the local Clewiston bank and get whatever he wanted, but he never invested in his family.

As far as I can remember, my story started when I was five years of age, or at least that was when I became aware that my world started to change. My father was a powerful man, and I was a small five-year-old. I guess he found me to be the weakest of the pack. I had two sisters before me. There were eight of us as kids, and I was the third.

I was my dad's sex toy; he would use me for the fun of it. I was a child who didn't understand what was happening. I thought what he was doing to me was what parents were supposed to do to their kids. Little did I know that this man was evil, and that what he was doing to me was also evil!

I don't think my mom was aware of what was happening. She was twelve years younger than my dad, and when they married, she was only seventeen. My dad was cunning and controlling, and Mom trusted him. I guess she loved him and didn't want to lose him, so she wasn't willing to believe anything terrible about him   [it wasn't that she wouldn't believe me I simply didn't know how to explain what was happening]

My dad would normally sit in the living room at times when it was just he and I at home. I would have to pass by my dad whenever I wanted to go the bathroom. So when I came in from playing outside he would wait until I passed in front of him, and he'd lift my dress and make crude remarks. He would touch my bottom, and sometimes even give it a rub or a slap. I didn't know it for sure at the time, but I felt something was wrong when he did that.

Back then, even if you knew something was wrong you couldn't tell anyone, especially if your father was the one doing the wrong. My mother was only twenty-one when I was born, so I guess my mom wouldn't be the best one to tell about my problems with Dad. Even as a small girl, I knew in my heart that it would be futile to look for help from other adults and I didn't want to dare put my mom in a position of choosing.

Quite a few times I was left with my dad and my mom would take the other kids with her. I guess he had given my mom the impression that I was his favorite. It was a pity my mom didn't know in what way I was. As normal kids would do, I sometimes played outside, but there were times when my dad would call me inside to satisfy his perverse, sexual desires.

I can remember this one evening after my mom had left to pick up my sisters from the daycare. My dad was inside and I was playing outside. When I heard his voice, I cringed inside because I knew coming inside would cause me to be alone with him, and I knew what he wanted to do.

I was hesitant to go into the house, and I even pretended not to hear his voice. But then he pushed his head through the open doorway and shouted. *"Didn't you hear me calling you?"* he asked, obviously pissed. "I'm sorry, what did you want?" I asked, trying not to let my voice tremble. I guess I was hoping he would forget about getting me into the house, but I was wrong. I hung my head and went up the stairs into the trailer.

My sisters were happy. They had the chance to get out of the house and play with other kids. I wasn't allowed to go anywhere, first because I was too young, and second because it seemed as if my dad always wanted me around. Who wouldn't want the opportunity to please the family breadwinner and father figure in the home?

I was in the room I shared with my sisters when they came back. My oldest sister was the one who seemed to take an interest in me. When she came into the room and saw me, she must have figured something was wrong. I was lying on the bed, curled up in a fetal position with my face to the wall. She turned me over onto my back. *"Are you okay, sis?"* she asked. "Yeah, I'm fine." My sister could see that I had been crying. *"Did dad beat you?"* "No," I answered; "I'm fine. How was school?" *"It was okay. I wish you were old enough to come."* I wished for that too.

I could share my little secrets with my eldest sister; as young as she was then, she seemed to understand. I was too ashamed and afraid to tell her about the sexual abuse, and wasn't even sure if she had faced the same thing and never spoke about it either. No, I didn't share that dirty secret, but I did share how the kids at school bullied me and how I hated my dad and wished he were dead. She seemed to understand that I was miserable, and that gave me some small comfort.

During dinner, my mom saw the somber look on my face and wanted to know what was wrong, but even at that tender age I knew I couldn't tell her the truth. I told her that I wasn't feeling well. Our seemingly normal lives continued, as my sisters went back to school while I was left alone with my dad.

I went to grade school when I was six years of age. I wanted it to be a haven because my home wasn't one, but unbeknownst to me, I didn't know one had to be an extrovert to fit in. You see, I was shy -- an introvert. I had low self-esteem. I thought that I was ugly, and what was happening to me at home wasn't helping me to feel much better. So school was anything but a haven for me, and my problems mounted instead of lessening.

I remember the name of my teacher, Miss Black. She was a dark-skinned African- American, about five feet tall with curly medium length hair. She was very passionate about education and I will always remember her as an amazing teacher. It was like she was hard on me because she wanted me to succeed in life, so I worked hard to please her. Miss Black also protected me from the bullies whenever she was around. Her famous words were, *"Never say can't!"*

When Miss Black was not around, the kids in school were cruel and sometimes teased me. I remember the name they used to call me – "black cookie" -- and it was something that made me feel worse about myself. A few of my sisters had brown skin and I was beginning to look at them as being beautiful. I thought that because I was dark I was ugly. So I felt extra badly being called "black cookie." So this was what school was like. The kids were evil; if they thought that you were someone they could pick on, then they would never stop picking on you. My sisters were in higher grades, so just like at home, I was left to fend for myself.

Going home from school in the afternoon wasn't something I looked forward to either. As bad as school was, I felt for certain that there was something worse at home. I didn't know if what was happening to me had ever happened to my older sisters, but at least my eldest sister seemed to understand what I was going through at school, and maybe why I hated my dad. We never got close enough to talk freely about all our secrets.

Home was no haven, and neither was school; my life was hell. There were times when I was at school that I felt as if I didn't want to go home, and times when I was at home that I didn't want to go to school. That was some kind of predicament for a young elementary school child to be in.

I thought this was what my life was meant to be, so I made up my mind to accept what my dad was doing to me. I began to look at it as being normal. Maybe other kids were going through the same thing, and they had learned to cope, so why couldn't I? I guess that was the way my mind decided that I would cope with my situation, accepting life as it was happening to me and reaching out to no adult for help. When my older sister assured me that school couldn't be *that* bad, in my mind I said with sarcasm, "Yeah, right, easy for you to say."

Now church was somewhat of a haven for me. When our mom took us there, at least there was no one to make fun of me. Church was a place where everyone was taught to be kind to each other, and I found that I liked it more when people were kind to me. In this way I could forget my mess at home with my dad, even if it were just for a little while.

And I could dress up too. Now that was something I loved doing. I would wear casual clothes to school, but come Sunday I could dress really fancy for church, and I liked it. I liked it a lot. I could sit in that church and for a while I could feel pretty about myself; there was no one there to judge me or tell me I didn't belong.

As if a pleasant dream had just ended, it was time to go home. Church was over and it was time to face reality again; time to face a home I was beginning to fear. The thing was that Saturdays and Sundays weren't too bad for me because everyone was home and that meant my dad wasn't able to get me to himself. I tried to stay out of my dad's way whenever I was there with my sisters, and I tried to avoid eye contact with him as much as I could. Back then we were taught that we shouldn't look into an adult's face when we were being talked to or when we were talking to them, so nobody suspected anything from my doing that.

The older I got, the worse my problem seemed to get with my dad. Initially, it had started with a touch, but as I got older, it had grown into full-blown rape! I got a few moments' respite when I was sent to live with my great aunt in Tampa, Florida, but this breather was only temporary. When I returned to my home again, my dad picked back up where he had left off.

My dad was very crafty, yet subtle. Whenever he wanted to take advantage of me, he would always find a way. There was an old limousine that was parked in our yard. I was told that it had belonged to a pastor who used to live in the area. If the house were full with kids, my dad would call me and send me with something out to the car.

I can remember one day he gave me some newspaper to take to the car. Then once I was in, he would leave the house and come out after me. On this particular night after my father had done his cruel act and had left me in the car, I was coming out just the way I had always done whenever he was finished with me. However, this time when I looked across to the yard beside us, I found myself looking into the eyes of our next door neighbor. This lady was a "Mother" of her church. The condescending look she gave me indicated to me that she knew what was happening. The words she said to me cut me to my very bones. She was standing on the back step of her trailer, and she said, *"I know what you're doing, you filthy wretch."*

I hung my head and went into the house. I knew that what was happening wasn't my fault, but yes, I did feel filthy. I felt like something that was only good enough for someone to wipe his feet on. I never thought about the fact that this woman of God should have had more discernment and realized that I was the victim and not the participant or the perpetrator. But she, like I suspected everyone else in society, looked with disdain on only me.

I was now ten and old enough to fully understand what was happening to me, and it made me feel dirty and unwanted. It made me feel like a piece of rag that was used to clean up mess on the floor, and yet I still felt I dare not tell anyone about my pain because I knew it would only make things worse. They wouldn't believe me and I would be made to look like a fool and a liar; the latter was something I was soon to become extremely good at.

Despite the fact that I hated school, I chose to let it become my haven. I had a friend I could talk to, even though I dare not tell her what was happening to me at home. I was learning to cope. I guess my friend too was having problems at home. It was during lunch period once when she decided to fill me in on what was happening at her home. Earlier that morning, I noticed an extra sad look on her face. She had had dismal looks prior to this, but since I had grown accustomed to it, I never allowed it to bother me. Today she wanted to talk.

We were seated in the cafeteria having our lunch. She looked at me with this sad look on her face. It was a look I could empathize with. No matter how horrific her news, I was sure I could say, "I've been there, done that." I gave her my full attention.

"My father is abusing me," she began tentatively. I tried to look surprised when I responded. I had begun to believe that I wasn't the only one being abused and her saying this to me was confirming my belief. "Oh my God, that's terrible," I said, trying to look as surprised as I could possibly look. "Did you tell your mom?" *"She*

knows, but she is scared of him because he is abusing her too."

My friend's name was Monica; she was my age, but she was thinner than I was. She was also African-American, but with fair skin. I liked people with fair skin because, in my opinion, it meant they were attractive. "So what are you going to do?" I asked. She shrugged evasively. *"I don't know; I might run away. Would you come with me?"* she asked rather pleadingly.

I looked at her and smiled sheepishly, "No, I'm not being abused; everything is fine at my home," I lied. Then she looked at me and sighed resignedly, *"I wish I were at your home. I wish I had your life."* In my mind I thought if she could only know the truth about my life, she wouldn't want to be in my shoes. I felt sorry for her. For a moment there I forgot my problem because I was now confronted with someone who had a similar situation to deal with. Hers may not have been sexual abuse, but abuse just the same.

Monica and I lived in the same area of in Clewiston -- "Harlem," to be exact -- but on different streets. She knew my dad had money, and everyone in the area thought we were living in paradise. They all knew that we lived in a trailer, but if my dad had wanted to, we could have been living better because he could afford to move his family anywhere in the world if he chose to. Problem was, he never chose to move us anywhere more comfortable or spacious than the single wide, green trailer with too many people sharing too small a space.

Monica and I spoke no more about her problem that day at school, and then the school day ended and we had to go home. It was obvious that Monica wasn't happy going home; the truth was neither was I, but I had learned to mask my emotions. I wasn't going to allow anyone to see that I was unhappy. If my dad's intentions were to break me, I wouldn't allow him to see that he was doing a mighty fine job; inside I was a broken person and I was fighting with who I was. Sometimes I felt like I was nobody, other times I told myself that I was as good as anyone else was. I felt at times that I was worth something, even though those times weren't frequent.

At home, no one took the time to see that we did our homework. My dad wasn't a good reader, and my mom had left school to get married at an early age. They placed little value on education; we went to school simply because it was our obligation to go, but if we didn't turn out to be anything as far as school was concerned, I didn't think it would have mattered to my dad or my mom.

Chapter 2

My "Harlem" had a big park where kids could hang out; they had all kinds of rides and games there. Monica and I hung out there a few times during the weekends, mostly on Saturdays. Sundays were my special days, those days where I could dress up and go to church. Sundays gave me the only feelings of self-worth and importance in my whole life.

Well, on this one occasion when we were playing in the park, Monica's demeanor wasn't as gloomy as it had been on those school days. I asked her how come she looked so happy that particular day and she told me about her mom and dad taking her to the movie theatre uptown the night before. I was excited.

"What movie did you guys see?" I asked. *"It was a comedy."* "Hey, I like comedy, did you laugh a lot?" *"Yeah, but..."* she stopped in mid- sentence. "But what?" I urged her on. She became sad again. *"I have seen this already."* "What?" *"My dad being nice one minute, and being the devil the next."*

"Oh, that," I said sadly as my mind went back to my problems with my dad. At least she got a breather once in awhile, but that wasn't the case with my dad and me. She saw that I had become suddenly sad and she asked, *"Are you all right?"* I forced a smile when I looked at her, and replied, "Yeah, I'm okay." *"You're sure?"* "Yeah, let's go play." I changed the subject and we happily went off to play.

Concerning me, "happy" wasn't a word I used on a regular basis. I wasn't a happy child; as I said before, I sometimes felt as if I were a used piece of cloth. But then I found that playing can make you forget your situation, and I played with Monica that day in the park and felt to some extent as if I belonged. To what I belonged, I didn't have a clue. Still, I think back fondly of all the minutes and hours I was able to genuinely escape from my troubles through the world of children's play.

But just when I let down my guard and heard myself laughing with Monica, it was time for a reality check because it was time to go home. We said our goodbyes and went our separate ways. Prior to leaving, I could see that Monica wasn't too enthusiastic about going home. The fact was that I wasn't either, but I had learned well how to mask my feelings. I told myself that I would never allow anyone to know what was happening to me. In retrospect, maybe that was my childlike way of exerting control over my situation. I could control keeping all the horror to myself!

On the other hand, church gave me enjoyment on many levels. I liked it when I saw the people in church start jumping and going wild. My first instinct was to be afraid, but older people in the church called it "getting into the Spirit." At the time I didn't understand what it was all about. I just knew that I liked being around happy people, and if they were in the spirit, I wanted to be there too.

Monica and I attended the same church and we'd sit beside each other. We would look at each other and smile as we saw what was happening with people who seemed to be out of control. We loved the singing, participated in the offering, and tried to understand the scripture being presented with passion by our pastor. No wonder it is called "sanctuary." It's a refuge from the storm; a shelter; a safe haven; a place of safety; it's where one could forget oneself and focus on the people and on God.

This particular Sunday was different. I could see that something was wrong with Monica and her mother. Her mother had a small baby whose hand she was holding as they walked into church. Every Sunday morning she would be fabulously dressed when she attended church, but this morning she was wearing a pair of sunglasses with her outfit. She was still beautifully dressed, as usual. But was strange that she was wearing an added adornment. She had fair skin like her daughter, and it was obvious that something was wrong. She had bruises on her face, and it seemed she was wearing her glasses to hide a black eye, or black eyes. I guessed she had had some confrontation with her husband. Monica was beside her, but she wasn't too interested in looking at me as they passed me and went to their seats.

Normally she would have sat with her mother, but then she would have left to come sit with me. I could see that this wasn't going to happen this morning. Both of them were apparently embarrassed at whatever happened the night before, or earlier that morning. Now I knew what she was saying when she told me her daddy could be an angel one minute and the devil the next.

That morning, church wasn't as exciting as it had always been to me. I wasn't feeling sorry for myself, but I was definitely feeling sorry for my friend, Monica and her situation. I thought how cruel it was when people who said they loved each other couldn't get along without one beating the other. Usually the dad was the hitter because he was the stronger person. It was strange how when you see other people's problems, yours could disappear for a moment, especially when you care for that person. Apparently her problem wasn't sexual, but it was a problem just the same and deserved as much attention as mine did. Trouble was that neither Monica nor I had the power to change a single thing about our respective situations.

Ours was a community that was close-knit, which meant a lot of people knew about each other's problems. The funny thing about it was that mine stayed inside the house and didn't come outside. What was happening to me was not something that could show up on my face; it was something that stayed in the room where it took place. But both were cases of abuse, and both adults – both men who were violating the love and trust they should have been upholding needed to pay for their crimes!

The next day at school, I saw Monica and we spoke about what had happened before she and her Mom came to church. It was during our lunch period while were together in the cafeteria that we shared whatever we felt comfortable sharing. She looked really sad and I think she had done a lot of crying.

"I knew something was going to happen. My dad was all nice and calm, and then for some reason Mom and I still don't know, he became violent." "Yeah, I know what you mean. So what happened before you guys came to church?" I asked, trying not to sound impatient.

"My dad got drunk before he came home on Saturday night. The moment he stepped into the house, he started arguing with my mom, and the next thing I knew there was a fight." "Can't your mom leave him?" I asked. *"Where can we go? Mom doesn't work; my dad is the only one who works."* "Why didn't your mom call the police?" *"She did it once and things became worse after that."*

Now her situation was what I call being between a rock and a hard place. If she and her mom stayed in the relationship with her dad, they were going to be beaten; and if she or her mom called the cops, it would get worse. Come to think of it, my situation wasn't any better. My dad might not be abusing my mom physically, but he was making my life miserable.

I remember once when I got home, my dad was home by himself reading or looking at these magazines with nude women. On more than one occasions he had taken me and shown me pictures of a few of them. I thought it was disgusting the way he drooled over those naked women. Some things he did to me hurt more than others, and I bet he got those ideas from the magazines he shared me. He clearly had no respect for me being his child and he needing to love and protect me.

Even though neither of my parents placed much value on education, we had money. My dad would stash money away in the house, and he would tell us to get some for him. So every time he asked us to bring him money, we would take some for ourselves. He didn't seem to miss it, so we could spend it as we liked as long as we didn't allow it to get back to him how we were spending it.

I came home one evening from school to see two of my sisters fighting each other. Of course they were grounded. But it gave me a sense of normalcy. After all, all the families I knew at that point in my life had problems with sibling rivalries, so it made me feel that my family was normal, despite the fact that there was something carnal going on between me and my dad in my family.

Well, here is one thing I learned: If you constantly focus on yourself, you are either going to become a narcissist, or you're going to find something detestable about yourself. So I figured I might as well just forget about myself, accept what was happening to me, and just move on. After all, I did have a friend who was going through hell and needed my support.

After a time, things seemed to be going better for Monica. We were back to sitting beside each other in church. We were once again able to sit and look at what was happening there. We knew it was wrong for us to laugh whenever we saw one of the sisters, or for that matter, one of the brothers getting into 'spirit,' but who could stop us from silently giggling when we saw them? All we had to do was to make sure we had a straight face when one of the seniors in there looked at us, and we always did.

After church a couple of Sundays later, Monica and I were able to talk to each other for a little while. She seemed upbeat. I commented on her disposition. "You seem happy. What's going on?" I asked. *"My dad's been away for a while."* "Is he gone for good?" *"No, he has a job working in Georgia, so he only comes in now and then."* I put a smile on my face and said, "Your mom must be happy." *"She is sometimes, but I think she misses him."* I wondered how she could miss a man who beat her and even beat their children, but I kept that question to myself.

And then I thought of how dumb people could be to miss something that had been so cruel to them. Monica must have seen the look on my face, so she asked, "Are you okay?" "Yeah, I'm fine. Let's go join the adults," I said, holding her arm and pulling her with me. *"Do we have to?"* she asked, kind of pulling me back.

I looked at her, "Why, you don't want to go home?" *"I wish I could stay here. It's so peaceful here."* "Me too, but this is church; I don't think it's meant for living here." *"You're right. It's just that when we're here, it seems like everyone cares for each other, and there is no problem. I really don't like conflict and if I had my way, I would surround myself with only happy and peaceful things."* "I know what you mean."

We went to join our separate families and we went our separate ways. When I went home to my family, those who could assist mom in making dinner were eager to help out. I joined them and helped prepare and serve the meal.

The following day when I went to school, Monica had good news for me. She was smiling when we me for lunch that day. *"My mom got a job,"* she said excitedly. "That's good," I said. I was happy for her. I was hoping this meant they no longer had to depend on a father and a husband who had been abusive to both of them. "Does this mean your mom will be leaving your dad?" I asked rather hurriedly. I didn't know why I asked that question, but then I instantly wished I hadn't asked when I saw the look of hurt on her face.

"My mom loves my dad, but it's just that he drinks too much and when he does, he doesn't seem to know what he's doing." And then this thought crossed my mind: Why is it that when people do not know what they are doing, they almost always ended up hurting the one they love? I'm sure that if my dad were to be caught in what he was doing to me, he would probably use that same line, trying to convince everyone around him that he didn't know what he was doing. Oh, yes, and if he were forced to look into a mirror to see himself as the monster I saw whenever he touched me, he would probably mumble something like, *"I'm sorry."*

Monica seemed to notice that I had drifted away again; she called out to me. *"Hey, I was saying something to you, but you weren't listening to me."* "Oh, I'm sorry, I seem to have drifted off for awhile. What were you saying?" *"I was telling you that I love my dad, it's just that he seems to have a problem."* "Well, I guess everyone who has a problem needs help; maybe he needs help." *"Yeah, I guess, but mom asks him all the time to get help, but he seems to think he doesn't have any problem."* I thought to myself, "Yeah, but in the meantime you guys will be the one to feel his wrath."

My dad owned a little store that sold produce, and it seemed to me that it was doing well; he always had money stashed away in the house. I think my dad was cheap; these days they call it frugal, but I think it borders on being cheap. As a matter of fact I think it's just another word that euphemizes the word "cheap." Anyway, my dad could have afforded the best place in Harlem, but he chose to live in a trailer.

Chapter 3

I was very young the first time my parents allowed me to stay with my grandparents, that was about my 3rd year of school; I was very excited. Mom hesitated, and wasn't sure that she wanted me to stay, but dad gave the ok; my aunt practically begged him, and that made me feel so good inside; in my little mind that said that I was special and that she loved me. I can remember having the time of my life.

My Aunt Mary allowed me to hang out with her. Now we didn't go many places; she was still in high school and either couldn't drive, or didn't have her driver's license, but none of that mattered; I just enjoyed being around her. My Aunt was short, about 5'3, but she had a heart like a giant.

Grandma's house was dark green, trimmed in white; it had about 10 rooms, inside of the house was made of cardboard, and the roof was your typical thin roof; there were lots of noises when it rained or occasionally hailed. Oh, how I enjoyed lying in the living room just listening to the rain on the roof. I imagined being a free bird and flying all over the world.

I was glad for this, because it got me away from my dad for a while. I wished I could have stayed there for much longer, but pretty soon it was time for me to go back home, but where I was going didn't feel like home to me; it felt more like I was going to a place of imprisonment. But maybe there was hope. When it came time for me to be picked up, which was the following July 4th, once again Auntie Mary asked if I could stay, and you guessed it, they said yes. But I should have gone home.

The second time I stayed it seemed as if something happened to our relationship, and up until this day I felt as if it were never the same. I knew she still loved me, but I don't think she liked me and trust me anymore. I can't tell you exactly what I did, because I can't remember, but whatever it was it must have been bad, because she avoided me for the rest of the time I was there.

That summer when I was about to go back to Clewiston, my Auntie, whom I had grown to love so much didn't even say goodbye, and that hurt me to my heart. Years later she went off to college, or left Flatwood, Alabama. But I later found out she didn't say goodbye because it was too hard and she didn't want me to see her cry. I wished I had known, or sensed that she never stopped loving me. I was already fragile emotionally, and didn't need the setback that ended up happening because of something I thought that wasn't true at all.

My dad was from Alabama, and every year during the summer we would have a road trip. I know that normally all kids look forward to going on long drives, but for me it wasn't so. My dad never took mom on his trips, so he always had us girls on this long drive alone with him.

On this particular day when we were going on the road trip, I wanted my mom to come along because I knew if she were there, then the things he normally did with me he wouldn't be able to do. But my dad was cunning. He would do something to piss my mom off so she wouldn't want to come along. My mom had obviously gotten so accustomed to not going that it didn't matter to her anymore, so she wouldn't be prepared anyway.

Well, we were on our journey without Mom, as usual, and I was seated in the back of that car. I was terribly anxious because I was anticipating what was going to happen soon. I had become acclimated to the ways of my dad, and I knew by now what to expect from him. So instead of playing and laughing like kids do on drives with their parents, my heart was racing and I felt sick to my stomach. I was a kid, trapped with no means of rescue.

My siblings were happily chattering away, while I was in a world I dared not invite anyone into. I didn't know if they were cognizant of what was happening to me, but they must have thought I was pathetic because I never smiled much when I was around them and I always seemed to be carrying the weight of the world on my shoulders. I wasn't afraid to show my siblings my true side. It was the adults I continually had to try to deceive, because they were the ones who would ask the questions.

After being on our journey for a little while, my dad drove into a gas station. I guess he was low on gas or he was going to buy us something to eat. Anyway, he stopped at one of the pumps as if he was going to get gas. He turned the engine off and left us in the car. After he was gone, one of my sisters told me she had heard something about my friend, Monica. She told me she heard that she and her mother were planning on leaving our Harlem and going back to Georgia where they were originally from. The reason was that her dad had left them and her mom was not able to take care of Monica by herself.

I remember that Monica had told me her dad had gone to Georgia to work, and that he would come back once in a while. But she hadn't told me that her dad had left them for good. Well, my mood changed. It wasn't good from the start so you could imagine what it had become now. I was angry because someone was lying to me and I was hoping it wasn't Monica.

Our dad got gas and bought us things to eat on the way, and we were back on our way again. The journey was long and only my dad was driving, so that meant we would have to stop on the way. We would always stay in two motel rooms: one for dad and the other for us kids. But even before we got to the point of resting somewhere for the night, Dad stopped outside wooded areas to pee. His pattern was to stop the car and go into the woods, and then call me to go along with him. I dare not resist because I didn't know what he would do to me if I resisted him.

I knew that my dad had a gun. I had seen it on numerous occasions, and I was aware that it was real. I didn't trust my dad. As much as I had been around him for the past ten years, I didn't really know his temperament. I remember once he had slapped me for doing something I should not have done, and I resented him for doing that. I've been a little angry and afraid ever since.

There were times when I felt as if I weren't a normal child. After all, what typical child was going through what I was going through? What ordinary child was afraid to hear the voice of her dad? Every time I heard it calling my name, it filled me with anxiety and had my heart palpitating in my chest. I realized I was really scared of my dad, and constantly filled with anxiety.

So there we were, my happy and singing siblings and me, seated in the back seat. I could feel my inside churning because I anticipated more than a single stop for Dad to pee in the woods, and that meant that more than once on a day trip, I would be molested in the woods. Why did my father not sexually abuse all the females? Why did none of my siblings question his asking me to follow him into the woods? Did no one notice that I never sang happy songs or enjoy our trips?

I felt like screaming out loud, but I just knew in my soul that any attempt to resist my father would be futile, and no family member would come to my rescue. I was quiet, not because I wanted to be, but because I realized that if I kept silent, then my siblings wouldn't want to drag me into their idle conversations. I was tired of lying.

Our journey continued until the sun was going down and my heart was starting to be filled with dread. And then I saw from the car window a nice wooded area, and my heart sank. I knew this was going to be the spot, and the speed of the car was slowing to a stop. He drove over onto the side of the road and stopped, putting the car into park. He asked me to accompany him into the woods, and I followed like a dumb animal being led to slaughter. This was the third stop on this journey, and I felt ugly, disgusted and sore, not to mention dirty inside and out.

When I walked out of the woods, I had tears in my eyes. I knew my siblings must have known what we were doing there, but no one asked any questions or offered me silent comfort. My dad got back into the car and I went back to sitting in the back seat.

I knew that what my dad was doing to me was wrong, and I knew that he was aware of that too, but he wasn't stopping it. I was dying inside, but I knew I couldn't tell anyone. My dad had people, who respected him, and those people would make me feel worse than I was feeling now if I ever uttered a word. I sensed that they would look at me as someone evil, intent on ruining my dad. I curled up on that back seat and sobbed softly all the way to our next stop, which was the hotel where we would spend the night before we finally arrived at our destination, which was Flatwood, Alabama.

It was hard pretending in front of my grandma and grandpa that everything was okay, but I pulled it off. When we arrived at our destination, we got our hugs and kisses and each one of us smiled as if everything were fine. Flatwood was a country area and we had lots of places to go and play, which was just what we did. While I was there, nothing untoward happened with me. I guessed it was because my dad had too much respect for his mom, and he wanted her to think he was the best dad he could possibly be. I knew differently though. I knew the son my grandma so highly regarded was nothing more than a pervert who thought it was okay to have an incestuous relationship with one of his daughters.

My grandfather wasn't much better, sad to say. He would slap us on our bottoms in suggestive ways and laugh when we pulled away from him. However, we tried to avoid him as much as we possibly could. Well, while I thought my only problem now was dodging my grandfather, my dad had his way with me after all! He said, innocently, *"Esther, come with me to the store. I want to buy something."*

I knew what he wanted when he said that, but still I couldn't be rude to him, so I went along. On my return my eyes were red from crying, but I dared not let my grandparents know what was happening. In retrospect, I'm amazed that I could compartmentalize my pain and enjoy the many things for kids to do while we were at the grandparents' house. When it was time to go home, it was especially sad for me because I knew what was going to happen at least three times on the way home.

My grandma and grandpa must have thought I was sad because I was leaving them, and I must say that I led them on to think all my anguish was due to leaving them. I let them think I loved being there so much that now that I had to leave, I was very sad. They didn't know that what I was sad about was the fact that I was going to have to re-live the molestation I had endured on the drive coming there. My dad was a monster, and that's the kindest word I can use to describe him!

Chapter 4

The drive back home to Florida was as eventful as it had been going to Alabama, and even though I made my mind accept my father's abuse as a routine part of the trip, I had made up my mind that I wouldn't let him destroy me. I knew that one day I was going to be old enough to fight my way out, but for now all I could do was to let him take advantage of me. I comforted myself by counting the days until my eighteenth birthday. It was a daily count!

We were back home in the trailer. I detested the fact that we lived in a trailer when I knew my dad could have done better. He had money he didn't spend on his family. Where he spent it, I didn't know. All I knew was that if we wanted money from him we had to steal it. There were ten of us in the family: six girls, two boys, and our two parents, so you can imagine how crowded that trailer must have been. Dad didn't try to get us a bigger or more comfortable space. No, all his efforts where we were concerned were about giving mom more kids.

The trailer only had two bedrooms: one was for our parents and the other was for all of us. Can you imagine how crowded our room was? There was a queen size bed in there, but because we jumped so much on that bed, it broke down. Our dad didn't bother to buy another one, so all we did was to put the mattress on the floor and slept on it that way. Besides the small trailer and the one bedroom for eight kids, our roof leaked in various places. I remember us having to put buckets wherever the raindrops would fall.

The night we returned from Alabama, I cried myself to sleep. I felt as if I were alone, being punished for something I didn't know I had done. I wanted to reach out to someone, but whom could I trust? Who could I reach out to? I was beginning to dislike myself. I was beginning to wonder why was I born. My self-esteem went from "low" to "no" quickly, and I was almost invisible to everyone and to myself.

My miserable summer ended and it was back to school again. I was going into a new class and a new grade. I knew I wasn't learning in school the way I should be because sometimes I found it hard to concentrate. You see, I was always anxious and nervous. I was naturally an introvert, and that didn't help me much. I would rather internalize things than to let anyone know anything about me. I knew that was wrong, but that's how I was. I guess that it was because I lacked confidence. I didn't know how to really express myself.

I was almost always late for the bus. I couldn't be there on time, because there were mean kids there who would pick on me, so often times I arrived just when the bus arrived so that no one would pay any attention to me. Too often, I miscalculated the amount of time it would take me to run to the bus, once I saw it coming. I got left and had to either walk or go back home and miss school altogether. I really wished I could get control of ANY part of my life, but was in charge of nothing. The bullies tormented me as often as they wished, and it was a bonus for them when they saw me running after the bus while they were comfortably on board heading to school.

My verbal and written skills matched my timid personality, so I had difficulty with writing essays, especially the ones where I was asked to respond as if I were the character in the story I had just read. I had enough trouble hiding my own story, so it seemed an impossible task for me to put myself into the position of an imaginary character and write about myself.

Well, I did see Monica in school and enquired about what my sister had told me. Monica denied being in any trouble or confusion. That made me feel a little better because it meant I had my only friend back, and she would be around for a while. How long? I didn't know, but I was so glad to have a best friend that I didn't care how long we had together. We had today and maybe this whole school year!

Monica and I were sometimes called twins because we were so close. Some of the other kids would say things like, *"Those are the funniest looking twins -- one big and one tall."* I didn't mind being identified as Monica's twin. I just hated the teasing part. Monica, on the other hand, seemed to take it with a stride like water on a duck's back. Monica was a little chubby, but very neat and always walking with a sense of confidence. I, on the other hand, felt an inner hurt to the core of my heart, but I knew how to put on a happy smile. I *was* the expression, *"Never let 'em see you sweat."*

I looked forward to hanging out with Monica since I didn't have to explain myself to her. It was like she just knew what I needed when I needed it. For example, I knew if she arrived first to the cafeteria or classroom, Monica would save me a seat, and I did the same for her.

Most of our classes were together, but there were two classes where we separated. I did what I needed to do to get by while anticipating hanging out with my friend as soon as that class ended. Monica had more friends than I did. For the most part, people liked her more than me. I felt insecure, though, because I was afraid they would turn her against me. Instead, we remained friends though it all. The ironic thing was that neither one of us had a perfect home life, but we managed to enjoy life as much as possible and maintain a C average. Monica was pretty smart, but I did just enough to get by because it was very hard to focus.

My dad was a farmer; he used to sell melons in Miami, and when he went there he would be gone for days. He would come back sometimes on weekends. When he was gone I was happy; at least then I wouldn't have to think of what he would do to me when he was home. I went to school, but in the back of my mind I was stressing, looking forward to a Friday I didn't want to see if it was a Friday when I knew my dad would be coming home.

I remember having a pillow and a sheet under the trailer because I could literally feel it when my dad was on his way home, and my heart would be filled with fear, and dread. Other kids would be happy to see their dads, but all I was feeling was anxiety whenever time mine was to come home. If I were in the house when he arrived, I would make sure that I went through that back door almost as soon as I heard the front door opened. I would try not to let him see me, because the moment he saw me he would call me and I knew what would happen then.

One weekend was particularly horrifying for me, and for all my siblings as well. It was late at night and we were in our room, when we heard Mom and Dad arguing. My mother was a very subservient woman, and she never argued much with my dad, but this night was different. My dad was trying to talk to her in the room, and I guess she didn't want to talk or stay in the room with him, because she had recently found out what he was doing to me and possibly my other sisters, so it was like she had a breakdown. She burst out of the room and ran into our room. We were silent and stunned because we had no idea what was about to happen. She reached up in the closet and pulled down a .22 pistol. She went out into the hallway, and then we heard some more arguments.

It seemed as if he were trying to wrestle the gun out of Mom's hand, and as they wrestled he fell out the back door. We heard two shots, and we were jumping up and down in the room saying singing, *"Mamma done shoot daddy, yeah and we hope he dies."* One of my brothers went and peeped out the back door, and I heard as daddy shouted, *"Y'all get back in the house."* My brother ran back into the room, looking as scared as ever. And at that time, my heart sank. I knew it must sound cruel, but we were really beginning to hate our dad, and really hoping that he would die.

The cops came. Apparently the neighbors had heard the gunshots and must have thought someone was dead, so they called them. My mom was very remorseful over shooting my dad; despite what she had heard, I knew she loved him, and wouldn't really want to kill him. When the cops came, my dad went out to meet them. Seemed he wasn't badly hurt, just grazed. He was bleeding, but obviously not too bad.

When they asked my dad what had happened, he told them that he was ok, and that it was an accident. They were local, so they knew him. My dad was pretty famous around Clewiston. They told him it was ok, but they made him go to hospital. We were still hoping that he would die, but six hours later our hearts dropped when mama brought him home from the hospital; he was okay.

There was never anything mentioned again about the shooting, nor was there any explanation as to why it had happened. A few days later the parents called us into their room. I was scared because I had heard Mom saying she was going to leave us so many times; sometimes she would say, *"I am going to leave y'all behind with him,"* and other times she would say, *"I'll come back to get y'all when I get situated,"* but she stayed with us until he died. All in all, Mom is a good woman; she was a mother who did what she knew to do. I often reminded myself that she was fairly young when she married my dad.

We all timidly went to the room, and daddy said, *"I told your mama that I was sorry."* Never did we discuss or talk about it again. Now he never owned up to the rape; he just said sorry. Once or twice mom left all of us, but she always came back to him.

It was when I was about twelve years old that I noticed that boys started looking at me, but I was afraid to get too close to anyone of them; I was scared that if I got too close they would realize that I wasn't a virgin at such a tender age. And how would I be able to tell someone that I wasn't a virgin, because my dad had been having an incestuous relationship with me ever since I could remember? I was already ashamed of myself; I felt as if I were already a woman at the age I was.

I was even beginning to think that I was ugly. I looked at kids who had fair skin, and felt a pang of jealousy in my heart every time I saw them. I wanted to be them to the point where I started to use bleach on my skin, hoping that I would become like them.

As a kid growing up, I was never shown what real love was. I can't remember ever getting a hug from my mom or my dad. As far as the latter was concerned, the only kind of touch he would give to me was one that was pointing to sex. My mom on the other hand couldn't do any better; she had gotten involved with my dad when she was a mere child herself; she was only seventeen when they got married. My dad was about twelve years her senior. My mom should have known better; my dad was a cradle robber, so my mom should have suspected that he would not have made a good father to us. When she married him, he was almost old enough to be her father.

During the week, we would go to school, on Saturdays we would get up early in the morning, have ourselves breakfast and we would be off on our own for the rest of the day. We were told that we shouldn't come back until night. I didn't know why this happened, but as I got older I came to my own conclusion about this. I believe this was my mom and my dad's downtime. Remember, there were eight of us in that house constantly running to and fro. I guess they needed their time away from us, not that it made me feel badly. I wanted to be away from home as often as possible.

My siblings and I didn't communicate much, so I was glad I had a friend like Monica. This particular Saturday she was at the park where I ended up. She seemed upbeat; it appeared as if everything was going fine. She greeted me enthusiastically as I approached her, *"Hey, Veronica, guess what happened?"* she said with a smile.

"What, you and your mom going away?" I asked rather coldly. *"What made you asked that?"* she asked, a bit surprised. "Nothing, I'm sorry. What's the news?" *"My dad came home last night."* I became a little concerned because her dad hit her mom, and sometimes he hit Monica too. "Really? Is everything all right?" *"Yeah. He said he is going to stop drinking. He wants us to move back to Georgia."* "Are you going back?" She shrugged, *"I don't know, my mom hasn't decided as yet."* "Do you want to go back to Georgia?" She lowered her eyes. *"No, not really."* "You like it here, don't you?" I was already grieving the loss of my best friend, and she hadn't committed to leaving me. That's how insecure I was all the time.

"Yeah, I have you as a friend, and I have been here almost all my life, so I don't know much about Georgia." "Oh, well, the important thing is that your dad is treating you and your mom all right." We spent most of the time in the park together; however, Monica left before I did. We had to make sure that we left before it was dark; that was the time our parents were expecting us.

There were some strange customs at our home. Regardless of the time we got home in the evening, we had to line up outside. The person who entered the yard first was the one who got first place in line. That person would get in first, have his/her bath, then supper, and then it was time for another one of us to go in. We were hungry, but we had to wait until it was our time to go in.

At our home there was another tradition; no one of us had dinner before our dad, and our dad normally took his time to eat. I didn't know if he were doing it to spite us, but he would take his dear, sweet time to have his dinner. If we were dying for hunger, it was obviously no concern of his. He would have this smirk on his face as he looked at our faces, which indicated how hungry we were. But it was like he was doing this to prove to us he was boss in this house.

Speaking of dinner, my siblings and I could have eaten a better quality of food, but our dad was hoarding up his money, for what, I didn't know. There were times when he would bring in bags of sweet potatoes, peanuts and other stuff from his farm. We would have these things, but pretty soon they would go bad because we couldn't consume them fast enough. We could get things from his farm all right, but when it came to buying things like meat and other things that we needed, he wouldn't spend his money to buy them. So we continued to eat produce until the last of it rotted in the kitchen, all the time wishing for meat.

My dad didn't believe in putting money in the bank, so he would have a lot stashed away at home. He used to keep his money in the wall in the trailer. We knew where it was and we would take money and spend it how we wanted to. Now we wouldn't buy things that would alert him to the fact that we were ripping him off. There were times when we would take a hundred at a time to the store and buy something and left the change with the store attendants. I guess at that time we didn't know the true value of money, but we did spend a lot of his money doing stupid things.

My dad was a gifted man in that he knew how to make money. At one time he had so many business ventures going on, it was amazing, and yet, we didn't benefit in any way from them. Our trailer was in terrible condition. There were electrical problems with that trailer. I remember that anytime rain fell and we touched that trailer, we could feel an electric shock going through our bodies, so we were careful not to touch it when it rained. One side of that trailer had no electricity, so we had cords running all over the place.

My dad had lots of properties, plus he had pickup trucks and eighteen-wheelers. We could have been living like kings and queens in our private Harlem, but if I had to guess the economic status of my family in that little town, I don't think I'd be wrong if we placed ourselves pretty close to the bottom when it came to our living conditions.

I can't remember ever getting anything more than five dollars from my dad at any one time, and we couldn't just get it by asking. It would have to be for some things we needed for school. Of course that wasn't even enough to buy what we needed, so there were things we needed that we had to do without. All of us suffered some degree of embarrassment in school because we lacked some small and some big things everyone else seemed to have.

Chapter 5

During my early teen years, school was a drag. I hated it. Maybe it was because I was an introvert. I had five sisters and two brothers, and yet I found it hard communicating with people as a whole. Why? Maybe it was because at home we weren't really communicating with each other. We were like normal kids in some ways, having the usual sibling rivalries. We fought like ordinary kids, but we just weren't communicating the way we should have been when it came to important matters. There were times when I would stay away from school because the kids were mean to me. I never let my parents know about it, but I also never confided in any of my siblings about the reason I skipped school.

I had a friend in school, but she tricked me into doing something I didn't want to do. There was a white female teacher in our middle school who was a terrible teacher. We thought she was prejudiced too. My friends told me they were going to write a letter and we would sign it and send it to her. I was young and naïve. My friend brought a piece of blank paper to me one day. Her name was Sandra, and I'll always remember the way she showed the white paper to me saying, *"You sign this paper and the rest of us are going to sign it too."*

I didn't think twice; I signed it. I didn't ask why the paper was blank. The next thing I knew I was in trouble. I found out that it was my name alone on a letter that was written and taken to the teacher. There were curse words and all kind of negative things on it. I was taken to the principal's office where I was punished.

I didn't have a lot of friends, so I had been glad that this popular girl, Sandra was my friend. I didn't have to sign that paper, but I wanted her and her friends to be my real friends too. That's how desperate I was for friendship. I wasn't popular in school, and of course there were times when I would rather be anywhere else than at school.

This again shattered my confidence, and I possessed almost no confidence at that time. The punishment didn't bother me nearly as much as the realization that the person I thought was my friend cared nothing for me. She got big laughs at my expense, and since her friends followed her, they, of course, abandoned me without a thought. Here was another example in my young life where no one seemed to care for my feelings. They just stepped all over them. This experience caused me to lose trust in people, and trust was also something I didn't have much of to start with.

As I had said before, my mom was herself a child when she married my dad; she was barely an adolescent. This meant she had dropped out of school when she got involved with him, so there was nothing much she could have taught us because she was still learning about life. Hence, we were left to teach ourselves what we needed to learn. Imagine as a child having the authority to roam free for one whole day without being chaperoned or checked on by an adult! These days, kids relish this kind of freedom, but as I look back on my life, I wish I had had some kind of attention from my parents that showed me they truly cared for me.

Well, despite the incredibly sad childhood I came out of, and despite my low self-esteem and introverted nature, it was my time to start high school. I would be going to a new school, which meant new faces and new surroundings. This meant that my anxiety was about to be heightened. My high school was a bigger school than middle school was, and a bigger school meant there would be more people to encounter, which wouldn't be easy for me.

What made things easy for me was that my dad was on the road most of the times, so I could stay home and not worry about his perverted advancement. Of course that feeling of safety ended most Fridays because Dad was coming home from his farm. I was certain he would be looking for me!

During my several years in Tampa, Florida, I would withdraw myself from school each time I got overwhelmed by the pressures of trying to fit in with the other kids and hide my ugly secret. The first time I forged my great aunt's name and withdrew myself I was a little scared of being caught. But once it worked, I observed this practice every four to six weeks.

I must have wanted an education, though, because I always enrolled in another school. When I showed up with the enrollment papers carrying her signature, I lied and said my great aunt was too sick to enroll me into the new school. It seemed that by the end of six months, I kinda fell in with the less popular kids. In my fragile mind, that just confirmed that I was a "nobody." I see now that all my transferring among high schools was my desperate attempt to be a "somebody."

Because of all my lying and maneuvering to find that perfect high school where I could feel worthy and validated, Monica and I were not together during all of our high school years. It didn't change our friendship, which actually deepened since our elementary school days.

Still, there was a period where we shared the same high school, and while we were at lunch one day in the cafeteria Monica talked about her parents again. They were at it again. Her father wanted them to move to Georgia with him, but her mother wasn't too keen on the idea. Monica was definitely against the idea of moving to another state and living with her father. Monica's mother was beginning to think she couldn't trust him again.

"So what are you going to do if you don't go to Georgia?" I asked. "Isn't he going to stop supporting your mom and you?" *"I don't know. He got mad at my mom and hit her the last time he was home. That's why Mom decided she wasn't going with him anymore; she just doesn't think she can trust him."* "I understand," I said sympathetically. *"So how do you like your new school?"* she asked. "It's big and new, that's about it," I said. I wasn't too enthusiastic in my response. *"In other words, you don't like it here?"* she asked. "You're right. School is not somewhere I like; I wish I were an adult; then I wouldn't have to go to school."

"Sometimes I wish that too, but we are not adults. And sometimes adults wish that they were kids too you know?" "I wonder why. As kids you depend on people too much." *"You shouldn't be worrying; your father is rich."* True, my family was known around Clewiston as having plenty of money, but I only saw what my dad doled out to us when he felt generous. Other than that, I had the little money I stole from the stash he kept hidden all over the house.

I smiled as I thought to myself: "It would be good if some of the effects of the wealth could spill onto us."

Yes, people in the little town thought we were rich, but I'm sure that those who truly knew us knew something was wrong; we weren't getting what we so rightly deserved from our dad. I'm sure people were aware that we could have done better than to be living in a trailer that had the same paint job for years. The roof leaked; it was obvious! It was also old and raggedy, and I wasn't the only child of eight who felt embarrassed coming to and leaving from the place we called "home."

Everyone knew my dad had a business and tractor-trailers. He was good at whatever he put his hands to. Everything he touched flourished, so why weren't we living like the kids who belonged to the richest men in our little Harlem at the time? I did not know. I remember my brother and I fighting over what was left in the bottom of the pot our mom cooked in. I can remember being stabbed while trying to satisfy my hunger. After each meal, one of us could get the pot and scrape out whatever was in the bottom. Well, it was my turn to get the pot and my brother tried to say it was his turn.

The cool thing was that we alternated who gets the pot, and that meant you had the right to the delicious "stuck-on buttered rice. As a bonus you got all the leftover bones with that good marrow inside of them. My brother, Reggie and I were playing "tug-a pot" and I was winning, so he picked up my mom's sewing shears and stabbed me! Thank God it didn't hit a vein, but at that time I was not going let that pot go -- vein or no vein! It was my pot and my bones, and I was used to fighting for what was mine. I believe that particular leftover food was the best I ever tasted, and I probably scraped out every piece of rice before I tended to my wound!

Our community was a close-knit one; everyone knew everyone else's business, and ours was right there in front for all of them to see. I knew we must have been the laughing stock of the whole town; we were dressed no better than the poorest persons, and yet we physically had more valuables than anyone else I knew there. This was one of the main reasons why I used to steal money from dad.

I'm not saying I was right for stealing from him, but think about it; everyone thought that we were rich and could get anything that we wanted, but that was pretty far from the truth. Our dad would give Mom twenty dollars sometimes to buy food for all ten of us. It was absurd, when you think about Dad being so cheap with his immediate family, and meanwhile, there were thousands of dollars hidden away in the house, gathering mildew.

I liked church. I didn't know then whether that meant I liked God or loved God, but I must have felt there was something special about a church because I loved it so much. The environment was one that showed love; it showed me that people cared for each other. I saw people greeting each other with a smile, even if they were just meeting for the first time. And I guess it made me feel there was love out there somewhere, and maybe I could find it too, even if all my love came from outside my home.

There was a period of time where we were staying with our maternal grandmother for a while. Mom had left Jack (that's what we called our dad) several times, but this particular time he didn't want her to leave so he was extra forceful in trying to keep her in the house. Somehow Mom got the keys to the station wagon and we all jumped in with the clothes on our backs. There was no time to get anything to take with us, and we kids didn't know where Mom was going.

We did know, however, that Jack would follow. In a high-speed chase, Jack tried to run us off the road but we made it to Highway 27 and headed to Lake Placid, Florida, where my grandmother lived. My grandmother and Mom must have had some serious conversations about what was going on in Mom's house because one day, my maternal grandmother came down to Clewiston and she and my dad had it out. She called him a nasty son...so...dog, and some words no dictionary could define.

However, two weeks after she returned, we were headed back to Clewiston. I understand now that the reason we all couldn't stay with our grandmother any longer was Mom had a lot of kids and we 'bought ate Grandma and Pa "out of house and home." It was a 3-bedroom small house with three families living there, and even as a child I could sense we were wearing out our welcome.

Grandma and Mom knew something had to be done about what was happening to me. So what little I had was packed up and I was taken to a small roadside storefront, where the folks in my little town caught the *Greyhound* bus going out of town. My heart was in my throat. I was given a one-way ticket to a place I had never been to before, going to be with people I had never even heard of before. I was told they were family and would take good care of me.

On my way to the bus stop, I was seated in the back seat of the car, scared to death. Somewhere earlier in my memory, I had adopted that *"never let 'em see you sweat"* philosophy. Anytime a family member admitted being afraid, Dad made it crystal clear that fear was not tolerated. So I mastered the art of "tear-swallowing" and putting on a happy face.

As we drove to my destination, I could feel the termites of anxiety gnawing at the fiber of my nerve endings because not to respond to an adult when asked a question was strongly frowned upon. We were taught in almost every other Sunday school about the story of Elisha and the two bears found in 2 Kings 2:23-25. It tells how kids who were disobedient to their parents were eaten by bears, and how those kids who were obedient to their parents and grew to become adults had a long life (Ephesians 6:1) Yet for some unknown reasons, not many sermons from Ephesians 6:4 or Colossians 3:21, admonishing parents not to provoke their children, were ever preached.

The ride on the bus to see my great aunts was extremely long, or at least that's what it seemed like at the time. I just wanted to get it over with. The thought of just having five dollars to my name weighed on my mind, so when the bus stopped to pick up the other passengers, or the driver took his break, I stayed on the bus for most of the stops because I was alone, scared and didn't want to spend any money just in case I needed to make a phone call or catch a taxi. Perhaps that was a part of my "survival mode."

The first few hours of the trip I tried to silence the noise in my stomach, but to no avail. So one stop before I reached my destination I gave in, left the bus for few minutes, bought some *David* Sunflower Seeds and rushed back on. All I could think about when I stepped off that bus was getting left behind, a dream I had night after night for many years.

Finally we arrived in this strange new place where the roads were paved with red bricks. The clacking noise alone seemed to set my nerves on edge. The driver made his announcement, thanked us for choosing grey-line *Greyhound*, and off we went.

I had no idea who or what to look for. I may have been given the name of the party that was supposed to pick me up, but my mind was blank. The anxiety was so high, it was amazing I even remembered my name; however, in all that, I forced myself to look happy and put on a half way smile. I mean they did agree to take me, and to a large degree I was grateful for that.

My great aunties were awaiting my arrival. They approached me and one aunt looked at me and said, *"Yeah, that's her; she looks just like Lou."* They were referring to my maternal grandmother. They smiled and I managed to muster up a smile, and off we went. I didn't remember having a lot of luggage, maybe a small bag, because I remember them taking me to the thrift shop to buy clothes. There were three of us because the parents also sent two of my sisters with me.

After they had finished doing what they were doing, they once again looked us over and I heard one of them say, *"I'll take her."* I can't begin to tell you how that made me feel. I was already feeling like a used up, contaminated piece of meat, and now to add injury to insult, I felt like the little sister of "Kunta Kinte" (*Roots, the Movie*). *"I'll take that one,"* another aunt said, as they made it sound as if I were some animal or something besides a human being.

We were now in the car on my way to my new home away from home. The three great aunties continued to talk among themselves, and at some point before we reached our destination, the conversation about the favor they did for their sister, my grandmother, in allowing me to stay with them, came up. They began asking me all kinds of questions about what happened, and why and so forth, and they were very blunt and direct in their questioning, bordering more towards the line of interrogation and accusation than anything else.

Now keep in mind my family, or at least the immediate family, was not what you would call strong communicators. Not a whole lot of talking went on when we were growing up. Children just kind of knew what to do and not to do; we basically knew our place.

My aunts were all smokers, and they were smoking in the car on the way to where we were going. Thick, concentrated cigarette smoke filled my already moist, red, puffy eyes; the hairs in my nostrils were working overtime in an attempt to filter out the nicotine, and plus one can only imagine the CO_2/O_2 percent ratio in my lungs. It was at the least higher than what the AMA (*American Medical Assoc.*) considered dangerous, but at no time did I ever display any signs of negative emotions. If I could just keep my head slightly tilted to one side, then no one would ever know that I was struggling, and hence no one would ask any questions. To indulge in a conversation was difficult enough, let alone share something so personal with these people whom I didn't know. They used words that were totally off limits to me, words and phrases that made a grown man flinch.

I soon discovered that the aunt I was to stay with, whose name Mazie Lee, had no kids of her own and didn't really know how to deal with children, let alone this fragile, scared girl. Now to add fuel to the fire, this aunt, who loved me as best as she could love a stranger, was somewhat rough around the edges.

However, as the months and years passed I realized what a blessing it was to have met her. Initially it felt weird to have heard her say, *"I'll take that one,"* but after her death, I realized it wasn't such a bad thing after all. To be chosen was pretty special, especially with the added fact that I had never felt special as a child.

I was away from my dad for now, and I was feeling better. Aunt Mazie was medium fair-skinned with long, thick jet-black hair, and she was about 5'6" in height and weighed a slim 150 pounds. She had a bustline to match her "big personality." In short, my Aunt Mazie was very attractive in ever since of the word.

Aunt Mazie was also a strong woman; she loved to laugh. She loved people and was very outspoken, but she was also a very kind person. I'm not sure why she never had kids. I don't know if it were by choice, or if she were barren. Back then that was a forbidden topic, but the day I arrived she became a surrogate parent, one I really needed, and today I praise God for her.

She taught me posture and poise. I learned how to communicate, how to "walk" as she called it. Auntie did not tolerate a young lady sliding her feet when walking, or assuming a drooping posture while either walking or sitting. If you dared slouch or slide, you got the famous "head thump;" eventually you would catch on. Oh, let's not forget, *"Ladies, don't spit, curse or swear,"* even though she did all of the above and then some. She also said, *"Nice girls, young ladies do not hang out at night clubs."*

Chapter 6

According to Aunt Mazie, she was the ex-party girl clubber, who often bragged about closing down several night clubs in a single night and having her and someone else's share of men. Did I mention that she was straightforward and called it like it was? Here's an example: she would say to me, *"If you are going to play, make them pay."*

And guess what? The funny thing is that I passed this information and wisdom on to my only child, but of course I encouraged her to always take the straight and narrow, "godly route," because the fact of the matter was that you always reaped more than what you sowed. But if she so happened to disobey me and try the world's way, she would be foolish because she would be taking the path of death.

When I went to live with Aunt Mazie I wasn't twelve as yet, so I was very young when she taught me all these things. But today I can still remember them, and they still make sense. She taught me to be strong, and she made me feel as if I were someone special, maybe even important. She was a strict disciplinarian. Back then I didn't see the sense in her being so firm, but now I can see and I thank God for her. If there was one thing Mom did right, it was to send me to live with this aunt, even though Mom wasn't the one, who came up with the idea.

Crossing my legs whenever I sat down was a strictly enforced rule in Aunt Mazie's house; meanwhile today we are encouraged not to cross the legs, due to its not being conducive to good blood circulation. My aunt was interested in social etiquette, and had she known about the health risk, she probably would have opted to honor protocol and skip what medical science had to offer.

I can go on, and on, but let me just say my aunt was a God-sent blessing in my life. I shutter to think of what I might have become without this positive, forceful intervention in my growing up. I turned a corner in the way I saw my self-image and my future. I truly miss her and hope to see her in glory one day, God willing. I just want to tell her thanks, and to let her know that I now appreciate the woman she was. I would also to let her know how very instrumental she was in my becoming the woman I am today.

I realize today that Aunt Mazie was a God-sent angel, though at the time I was with her, I didn't recognize it. Though I was only twelve or thirteen, she talked to me like I was an adult. I was nervous at first, but I got used to it, because to not talk, or to not respond properly to any adult was an absolute no-no! I can remember her words, *"Walk like you are somebody, hold your head up and shoulders back; don't drag your feet."*

We sat together, we laughed, we ate together and watched TV together. In the midst of what I call fun and peace, she carefully laid down her rules, and she told me not to give her a reason not to trust me. I quickly came to value her enough to never want to disappoint her. I vowed to never give her a reason to distrust me.

At that age, and being somewhere new, I didn't have any friends. My people skills were lacking. Because of what I had been going through with my dad, I was afraid to open up to people; I didn't know whom I could trust. I befriended this woman who couldn't have been more than twenty-five years old, but back then that was considered old. I used to admire her clothes, shoes, and hair; her nails were always looking nice. I would see her in the neighborhood; apparently she lived in close proximity to where I lived. In my mind she was someone I could emulate, and with no other role model in sight, I thought there was no harm in doing so.

About six months passed, and she convinced me to go out with her. I lied to my aunt and told her we were having something pertaining to school and I had to stay late. I believed I said it had to do with the prom or yearbook club. I'll tell you about those two later.

I hid my red and white striped sailor shorts and solid blue sailor blouse. We went to this old man lounge called the BLUE NOTE. The lady at the entrance to the club gave me a long look up and down my body, which made me self-conscious and a little anxious. Then she said, *"Girl, you got a money maker; the men will buy you drinks all night; just get that money."* I smiled nervously at her because, even though I pretended I was older than my age of thirteen, I didn't know what she was talking about.

Picture the youngest man in the club; he was, or at least looked fifty plus years old. The place was so small that everyone seemed to be bouncing off of each other. You see, that was my first time going out to a bar, or to any place away from school for that matter. I didn't know that a bar, or a lounge was one and the same.

Anyway I walked in with my sailor outfit on, including socks and sneakers. I twisted up to the bar,

54

trying to appear grown. Aunt Mazie actually showed me how to knock'em dead with my walk. How at sixty something years old she could move like that, I didn't know. She never told me her real age, but all I knew was she had a birthday every year and for some strange reason, she never got any older.

I took about five steps and was at the counter. I reached to steady this raggedy stool with the yellow stuffing coming out of it, and heard a man say, "Little girl, come here." So I turned, and he said to me, *"You don't belong in a place like this. Go home, and stay away from that tramp lizard who brought you here. I told her to take you home."*

The time was about 10:00 pm on a Friday night. At that moment I felt naked and ashamed because I knew he was right. I didn't like the bar scene the moment we pulled up, but I went along just to go along; heck, I was tired and sleepy before we got to the club. I I had gotten dressed at 6:00 pm, and then hid out in the park waiting for this lady. I didn't know the clubs didn't start jumping until what would have been my bedtime. Shoot, that was the time Auntie told me to be home! But smart me, I had already planned the "flat tire story." I figured that if we get to the club in the early evening, why surely she would wanna leave between 10:00 and11:00 pm. It showed how naïve I was; after all, I was just thirteen!

This grown woman who was fully aware of what happens at bars after dark knew I was just a child. But because I was such an introvert who wanted a friend so badly, and because she paid me attention, I felt as if I had no choice but to accept friendship from wherever I could get it. I wasn't the type of person to go around approaching potential friends; I was too shy for that.

But at the same time it didn't mean I didn't want a friend. We all need companionship in some way, but with me, choosing a friend was tantamount to going to the river to catch fish and choosing the one I wanted to catch. It was that hard! And because I lacked the confidence to pick a friend, I would choose whoever approached me and chose to be my friend. Of course, I figured out this was a big mistake, but that lesson didn't become clear to me until after I was thirteen, in a strange bar, past my bedtime, having violated my aunt's trust in me!

I don't like to play the blame game, but if my parents had done what they should have done, I would not have been in the situation I was presently in. As a matter of fact, I would not have been living with my Auntie in the first place! Now here I was at a club -- me, barely a teenager in a club where I had no right to be. And where was the lady I had come here with? She was nowhere in sight. I couldn't find her. I was really scared. How was I going to get home, since I had no money? It was late. I had never been out this late before. My Aunt Mazie must be going crazy. I knew she was waiting up for me. How was I going to explain to her where I was? I was planning on using the flat tire thing on her, but I knew she would have seen through me if I brought that up at this late hour. Right now I was scared, and my mind was beginning to play tricks on me; all I wanted to do was to get home.

I couldn't find that lady, and I couldn't stay out any longer. I knew by now that my Auntie must be going crazy, because I had never been out this late. I had to catch a cab, since it was about midnight. At that time the place was wall-to-wall with people packed in like sardines. I kept searching, but I still couldn't find my friend inside. I cried. I finally mustered up the courage to call a cab. I had no money, but I got in the cab anyway when it arrived.

I had him let me out two blocks from my house. I pretended to reach in my shoe to get some money, but then took off running as hard and as fast as I possibly could. I was scared, terrified, not of him, but of the trouble I was in. Still I was so glad to be home that I almost didn't care what punishment I would face.

I walked in, unable to even form my lips to tell a lie. Auntie met me at the door and beat me within an inch of my life. I didn't care; I was just glad to be home and to get it over with. Then the next week, Auntie gave me the silent treatment, which hurt worse than the beating. She didn't have to give me the lecture about losing her confidence and trust in me because I chastised myself repeatedly when my promise to never give her reason to distrust me played over and over in my head. At thirteen, I didn't even know what to do with that amount of guilt, so I was miserable every day Aunt Mazie refused to talk to me.

Did I learn my lesson about that "friend?" No. Some time had passed, and she introduced me to someone she called her buddy; he was perhaps a forty-five-year-old man. He seemed nice. Again, I should have been running away from an older person; this man was more than three times my age, but I found myself gravitating towards older men and older people in particular. Why? At the time, I was subconsciously trying to get away from people, who were my age because I felt they wouldn't understand me. I felt they wouldn't be able to empathize with me.

I had a burden that I wanted to unload, but in my mind, kids my age would only turn up their noses at me if they were aware of what I was going through. I knew kids at school were cruel, and they tended to make fun out of things that were detrimental to a person trying to connect with them. I think you don't develop empathy until you're grown, but definitely school-age kids have none! At my age, kids only tended to think about ways of having fun, and it didn't matter to them if in the process of doing so they devastated someone who was a peer. In their not so developed minds, fun was all they were thinking of having. They meant you or me no harm.

Well, according to my so-called woman friend, she wasn't trying to hook us up, but was just introducing me to someone who could be my friend, seeing that I was at this strange place and didn't have any. The guy said he had just moved in not too long ago, and he needed a friend. I thought that was cool! My friend had taken me to meet this guy at his home. He was a huge guy; he weighed around two hundred and fifty pounds and had bulging muscles.

I must say at the time that I felt intimidated by him, but I couldn't let my friend know that. I wanted my friend to think I was older than I was. Thinking back now, I don't know how old my friend thought I was, but she probably assumed I was much older than I really was. It was either that or she was conspiring with that man to have his way with me, and no doubt, she would get some money for offering me up to him. After that Friday night incident, my aunt had told me to stay away from her, and I had promised her I would. You would think that after I felt enormous guilt at betraying Aunt Mazie's trust once, I would never do it again if only to avoid the terrible feeling I experienced the first time. But youth is youth, and young people do more foolish than wise things. I was no exception!

I visited him several times. He lived few apartments over from where I was living with my aunt. Of course I couldn't let her know about this. I am sure she would have freaked out because I wasn't living with her so that she could pimp me out to men. I was there because of what was happening to me at my home.

Even though we hadn't spoken about it, I was almost sure that my aunt knew about it.

One day I was going to visit my friend when I noticed cop cars in the vicinity; there were caution tapes blocking this man's apartment door. Newspapers read the next morning: *"Man rapes and murders a girl last night, age 12, after recently being released from a 20 year prison term for rape."* I thanked God! My heart was racing and my face was red. I wanted to fall to my knees in gratitude to God, but I had a secret, so I had to act as if I were only reading the newspaper. It seems God Almighty had a plan for me because that dead girl could have been me. The man was a pedophile and a felon, and I didn't know.

Apparently this man only liked kids who were around my age. I was beginning to wonder if my friend knew about this. She said she wasn't setting us up, but I'm sure it wasn't by coincident that I was introduced to him. Sure it was possible that he could have seen me, told my friend he liked me, and she was doing him a favor when she introduced us. My God, thinking back now, maybe I was supposed to have been his next victim. I guess even back then God was watching over me. Glory to God for ordering my steps!

I went to three different schools while I was in Tampa, but I didn't like any. I had grown to hate school, because the kids there found me to be "easy picking," and they did pick on me. I was alone, didn't have any friends, and had come from a family of people who weren't communicators. So that didn't help me at all to fit in. Imagine being in an environment where there were so many people, but yet I still felt as if I were the only one in the world.

Being shy didn't help my situation either. If a boy looked at me with a smile on his face, my heart would start beating wildly in my chest, and I wanted to do nothing but bolt. Maybe if it were an adult, who had smiled at me, I would not have felt the way I did when someone my age did. I didn't know how it was possible that I felt more comfortable around adults, even though my two adult "friends" were responsible for making my life miserable.

Anyway, I found myself a friend in a girl who told me her name was Beverly, and she was fourteen years of age. I was twelve, but we were in the same class. I found out that she had had to stay two years in one class. How did that happen? I thought I was pretty dumb, but now it seemed like there was someone dumber than I was. She was a good-looking girl, very shapely, had bowed legs and very short hair. The other girls called her "dumb, bald-headed Beverly." She was a smoker, and looked very mature for her age.

Beverly didn't seem to care about school; all she wanted to do was to hang out with as many guys as she possibly could. The guys called her "easy Beverly." I wondered what that meant. Well, it was good to have a friend; it didn't matter to me what they called her. She wasn't too popular with the girls; she was more so with the guys, who seemed to relish her company.

I started hanging out with her. I was in Tampa, away from Clewiston, my personal "Harlem," and I didn't have any other friends there. She was dating an older guy, but she didn't want me to know she was. He was a handsome guy, and from the moment I saw him, I knew he was up to no good. He looked to be around twenty, much too old for her. He was tall, and not bad looking.

One day after school and before he came to pick her up, she was telling me about him. I blatantly told her I thought he was too old for her. *"I like him; he thinks I'm older than I am."* I could certainly have shared two scary stories about my life when I pretended to be older than I was!

"How old did you tell him you were?" I asked her. *"I told him I'm sixteen."* She was smoking. "And he believes you?" *"Yeah, he is dating me, isn't he?"* She looked away from me long enough to take a long puff of her cigarette, and blew the smoke in the direction away from my face. Maybe she didn't want me to see her eyes, since she may have been sad instead of glad this guy was dating her.

"Are you the only one he is dating?" She shrugged, *"I don't know, and I don't care. He makes me feel good when I'm with him."* Now she shoved the cigarette at me, *"You want a smoke?"* I brushed it out of my face, saying, "I don't smoke." "Have you ever tried it? It's cool." "I'd rather not." Smoking wasn't something I craved in order to fit in, so I had the good sense not to take up that dirty, expensive habit.

"You don't have a boyfriend?" she asked. "No, I'm just twelve." *"I had a boyfriend when I was twelve."* "I bet you told them you were fourteen, or fifteen." *"Guys are easily tricked; they're stupid when it comes to girls; anything you tell them, they believe you."* "Have you always been dating older guys?" *"Yeah, the younger ones are dumber than the older ones."*

I was a little puzzled. "If you think guys are so dumb, why do you date them?" *"Because I don't want to date women."* Under my breath I muttered, "I don't think they want to date you either; they think you're dumb." She must have heard something because she said, *"You're strange; you mumble to yourself too much."*

The car pulled up to us; she threw away the butt of the cigarette, and jumped in. She pushed her head through the window. *"See you in school tomorrow."* I waved to her as the car drove off. We were close to my

Aunt Mazie's house so I walked home. I had no regrets about not jumping in the car with her.

Going home from school to my aunt was a good thing. I had no fear of anything un-toward happening to me. Aunt Mazie talked a lot to me because I was the only one in the house with her. To me, being alone with her was a good thing. This way I could get some attention, and it made me feel special. Back home there were eight of us as kids, so no one was given any particular attention, at least no attention that was positive.

There were times when we would sit and watch television together. I remember one time when she sat me down and spoke about her younger days. Apparently she was quite a woman when she was much younger. She wasn't a bad looking woman at her age, so I imagine she must have been a looker when she was much younger. She loved playing cards and numbers for money; she taught me how to cheat on the game of pity-pat. We played almost weekly with these men, who would come over and visited her. These men loved their beers, so as they got tipsy I would double stack the cards, or look at them and tell her their hands. We would sometimes win fifty dollars and she would give me five out of that.

When I moved in with her, her rule for raising kids was, *"Do as I say, not as I do."* She loved dressing up when she was going out; she wore a beehive type of big hair wig. She had a very attractive, medium-brown skin tone. I would have to address her as "Ma'am." It was "No, Ma'am" and "Yes, Ma'am" whenever I was addressing her.

She would sometimes send me to the local "mom and pop" store once a week to get household supplies, and monthly to cash her Social Security check. I loved it because I got out of the house, and she always gave me soda and chip money. She didn't allow me to go many places, and the ones she allowed me to go to had so many restrictions. I found it was better to stay home than to go to them. She didn't have a car, so we had to ride the bus everywhere. I used to be so embarrassed to have to carry our groceries on the bus, but looking back now, I realize that was my childish pride.

One day while we were seated in the living room watching television, Aunt Mazie was telling me about her days going to clubs. I was inquisitive, and I wanted to know more about her life as a youngster. *"I was quite a catch in my younger days, you know,"* she began. "What did you use to do?" I asked. *"Well, in my days when I was young lady, I could take away any man I wanted to."* "You mean you used to take away other girl's boyfriends?" She gave a slight grin in my direction. *"Most of these men had wandering eyes, so they would look at me, and they would talk to me."*

"So what did you do?" I asked. My inquisitive mind was working overtime, and since I had never had anyone talking to me so candidly, I pushed my luck; I asked questions I never would have asked under normal circumstances. *"I talked back to them,"* she responded. "You must have made a lot of people jealous," I said.

"And what about the clubs?" *"Child, the club was where I used to meet them. I used to be the girl who would close nightclubs. I used to go from one to the other."* "So you would come in late in the mornings?" I had a flashback to my one night coming in at midnight after being in that packed club looking for the older woman who brought me. I quickly focused my attention back to the present conversation, which was getting very interesting. *"Yeah, but remember those were weekends; I couldn't do it during the week, because I had to work."*

My aunt spoke to me like we were two adults, but she sure wasn't allowing me to do what adults do; she forbade me to ever repeat that stunt I had pulled on that night when I so foolishly went out with my so-called friend to a club where I had no right to be at my age. I really enjoyed talking to my aunt that evening. She was funny, loving and kind, something my parents had proven not ever to be. At that time I wished we could have chosen our parents, because I surely would have chosen Aunt Mazie to be my mother. My mom is still around today, and I do love her, but at that particular moment I really did appreciate my aunt, and fantasized about what my childhood would have been like if my aunt were my mother.

I was in school one day when Beverly suggested we leave and go by the mall, which was very close. I had no problem with that; I hated school and would prefer to be anywhere else. It was lunchtime, so we decided to go. Unbeknownst to me, Beverly had made plans to meet another guy who was different from the one she had gone out with when she walked with me close to my home. I knew she was promiscuous, but how licentious she was, I didn't know. Well, I was about to find out.

We were at the mall, and I had had my lunch already so I wasn't hungry. We did window shopping as well as going into stores and looking at things we would one day like to own. In this one particular store, I saw a watch that I liked, and I drew her attention to it. It was in a glass case, but apparently it wasn't locked. It was among some other watches. It was a nice looking, gold colored lady's watch. I pointed to it. "Hey, Beverly, that's a beautiful watch, don't you think?"

She looked at it and agreed, *"I like it."* She looked at the price, which was one hundred dollars. It was a *Seiko* watch. *"I'm going to get it."* Beverly said in a definitive voice. "You can't afford that; it's too expensive." *"What do you think I have so many boyfriends for?"* I had to wrap my head around being a girlfriend for money, but then a promiscuous girl would get money every time she saw her guy or guys.

"I thought you only had one." *"One?"* she laughed, *"Who told you that?"* I shrugged. "No one, I just thought you only had the guy, who picked you up the other evening." Beverly held my hand and we started walking away from the unattended glass case where the watch was. We continued to do our mind shopping, looking at things and wishing we could buy them. At one point Beverly told me she was going to the bathroom and I should wait for her.

After waiting for about fifteen minutes I decided to look for her. I couldn't find her anywhere in the store. When I went outside, I saw her in the distance; she was beckoning for me to come over to her. I walked up to her. "Hey, what happened? I was waiting for you in the store." She looked serious and a little evasive. *"I changed my mind about using the bathroom."* "So why didn't you come back and get me?" *"Because."* "Because?" I asked, waiting for her to continue.

She held my hand. *"Let's go sit down."* So we walked to the food court, and sat down. *"I have something I want to show you,"* she said almost whispering. She went into her pocket and came out with the watch we both liked in the store. I opened my mouth in shock. I couldn't believe what I was seeing. "How did you get that?" *"Didn't you see that the glass case that it was in was opened?"* "I noticed, but..."*Well, I took it."* "But that's stealing!"

She put a finger to her lips for silence because my voice had risen a little when I said what she had done was stealing. Thank God the food court wasn't crowded because someone might have heard me. *"I don't call that stealing,"* she said speaking softly. *"I just saw an opportunity and I took it."* "That's still stealing. What are you going to do with it?" *"I'm going to sell it."* "To whom?" I was debating in my mind whether to run out of the mall and back to school without looking back at this little thief. I didn't. She shrugged, *"I don't know. Anyone who wants to buy it."*

Well, I was beginning to find out that my friend was not only promiscuous, but she was also a thief. While we were talking, out of nowhere this older guy came up and kissed her. I had never seen him before. She introduced us. *"Veronica, this is my boyfriend, Andrew; Andrew, this is my new friend, Veronica."* He pulled up a chair and sat down. The way he stared at me before he said anything scared me. Finally he extended a hand across the table, *"Nice to meet you, Veronica."* I nervously shook his hand.

"Have you got a boyfriend? I could get you one you know," he said. He couldn't have been any younger than twenty. He was tall and lanky and wore braids. He was average looking. "I'm not ready for a boyfriend as yet." *"You don't know what you're missing."* He turned to Beverly and put an arm around her neck. *"Hey, baby, how you been doing?"* She replied, *"Fine."* He looked at the watch she had on the table in front of her. *"What you got there?"* he leaned forward and picked it up. *"Hey, this is a nice watch. Is it for me?"* Beverly grabbed at it, and he moved it out of her way. *"Hey, take it easy,"* he said.

"That's a lady's watch." He had it firmly in his hand now, and she hesitated to reach for it to grab it back. *"Well, it belongs to a lady; I know one I could give*

it to." He pocketed it. *"That's mine!"* Beverly protested. *"I'll decide who will get this watch,"* he said. He looked at me, then leaned close to me and asked, *"What about you, did you pick up anything from the store you went into?"* "No," I said indignantly.

He looked at her. *"Aren't you teaching her the trade?"* "She's new," Beverly replied. *"Well, she can learn, can't she?"* "I guess," she responded with a little uncertainty in her voice. *"Well, it was nice meeting you, Veronica, but we've got to run."* He got to his feet. *"Come on, Beverly, we've got to go."*

Beverly got up. I was looking at her with a questioning look on my face because I had thought we were going to hang out as she previously said. But it looked like she had just needed the company to go to the mall and meet the man she intended to spend the rest of the day with. *"I guess I'll see you in school tomorrow,"* she said.

"I thought that we were hanging out," I said in a voice that was more like a protest. *"We're going to hang out, but we have things to do."* Her boyfriend had walked off a little, and now he stopped impatiently, waiting for her to join him. *"Come on, Beverly, we've got to go,"* he urged. "I guess you had better go," I said with a disappointed look on my face. She must have felt a small bit of guilt because she repeated, *"I'll see you tomorrow though, won't I?"* I replied weakly, "Yeah, I'll see you." She ran off to join her boyfriend.

Despite the fact that I now knew who she was, we started hanging out on a regular basis. Most of the times it was just the two of us, but occasionally we would meet up with another one of her friends. One of them was a girl. She was Angela, a little bit taller than Beverly, and a little bit older. We hung out and I watched them smoking. I wanted to join them. I asked for a cigarette and Beverly lit one up and gave it to me.

I took a drag, and the next thing I knew I was coughing uncontrollably.

They started laughing at me. *"I thought that you were a smoker,"* Angela said. "No, this is my first time." *"Girl, that was the same thing that happened to me the first time I tried,"* Beverly said. "So what did you do?" I asked. *"I kept on practicing,"* she responded. It took me a little while to learn, but then I started smoking as good, or maybe as bad as they were. Later on I quit because I knew it wasn't good to smoke.

This particular day we were hanging out when Angela decided she was going to teach us how to make some extra money. I was glad that these girls were accepting me, despite the fact that they were teaching me a lot of bad things. When I was in Clewiston I had a few people who said they were my friends, but these were the same ones who would make fun of me and get me into trouble. At least these girls weren't just telling me things, they were doing it too, which meant that if one got into trouble, all of us would. Right then I didn't know if that was a good thing, but it felt good to be accepted.

I didn't know exactly what was going to happen; all I knew at that moment was that I was with friends and they were treating me as equal, even though they knew I was younger than they were. We were on our way to the local department store, small compared to big city shopping centers, a hint above a "mom and pop" store. The two of them whispered something between them, after which I could tell something was up by the look on their faces, but I didn't say anything. We walked in, greeted the middle- aged cashier, and then Angela handed the clerk a paper bag which appeared to be full, but I knew it was empty because I had seen her as she pulled the bag out of what looked like thin air, and then fluffed it just minutes before the three of us entered the store. *"Can I leave my bag here? I don't want to be questioned,"* she said to the friendly cashier. The cashier agreed.

When I heard what the money making scheme entailed, I wished I could just turn round and leave, but I didn't want them to think I was a coward. You see, I wanted to fit in so badly, and if it took doing something negative to do so, then I was prepared, or so I thought. I was still as nervous as hell, even though I tried to put on my bravest face ever.

I followed Beverly to the deli, and ordered a $ 2.00 meal. This meal consisted of tater fries. These were the best seasoned, tater fries I had ever tasted. Our plan was to eat the taters while in the store, and then throw the boxes away before we left the store. Presumably, we'd get away without paying for the food. But Angela, who was at least three years older than Beverly, was a "seasoned" thief. Not that Beverly was much different. The saying, *"Show me your company and I'll tell you who you are"* really applied in this situation. These two were longtime friends, and they were self-taught, professional thieves. Now that I was about to join them, I would have to prove to them that I was a thief too, or that I wanted to become one.

We weren't finished yet; we had other things to do in the store. After eating our fries in a surreptitious manner and throwing away the boxes, I was told that we were going to have to take other things with us out of the store. Now I was really sweating; I was really feeling my heart palpitating, as if it wanted to jump out of my chest. I knew stealing was wrong. Yes, I had stolen money from my dad, but that money really belonged to my siblings and me, and if I were even caught doing it, I knew I would not be taken to jail. It was different here. Yet still I was going to stay and do whatever they wanted me to do, all in the name of fitting in. All I needed to do was what they wanted me to do. How hard could that be? They were going to do it too!

We got ourselves shopping carts, and we all took different aisles, but I kind of peeped around to see how and what they were doing. I was just amazed at how many things they were able to hide in their socks, their bras and their oversized underwear. First I couldn't believe that Angela was wearing oversized men's underwear, and second, I couldn't believe how she stuffed those items in so fast, without breaking a sweat. Obviously this was something she was accustomed to doing.

I never did get around to observing Beverly because Angela caught me watching her and gave me the evil eyes, so I quickly got my butt out of her view. A few minutes later Beverly showed up out of nowhere. I was somewhat taken by surprise because she had a strange look on her face, plus she came up behind me, tapped me and said, *"Leave the shopping cart here, let's go."*

We walked towards the door. Now we may have been in that store for at least forty-five minutes, all three of us pushing a cart and filling it with stuff. I guess the whole idea of pushing these carts and filling them with stuff was to give the impression that we were really shopping; we would give the impression that we ultimately left everything we had put in the carts just where they were.

Beverly and I were now outside; we had made it without anyone seeing us. Angela was still in the store. Our school was close by, and we could still make it back in time to catch the bus that was taking us home, but we were waiting on Angela. We waited for about another ten minutes, which to me felt like forever because I was nervous and scared. Neither one of us said a word; maybe she was nervous too. Finally

Angela darted around the corner with the same bag she had given to the cashier upon entering the store. It was full of stolen items. Angela didn't look my way, nor acknowledge that I was there. They "high fived" each other, and she gave Beverly about four items from the bag and she left.

Beverly and I started back to school, and then without a word, she started running so that we could make it back on time. So off I went running alongside her, or at least I tried to. She was fast! She was on the baseball team and was the fastest girl at the school.

We were back at school, and just in the nick of time. We entered our different buses. I rode home nervous, sad and scared. First, it seemed like my friend didn't like me anymore. I figured that Angela must have mentioned to her that I was watching her. Then I felt badly, because Angela did not share, or showed me what they had gotten. You see, I hadn't taken anything! I was so scared that I found myself sweating profusely, hoping and praying we could just get out of the store and not continue with what we had initially started.

I didn't necessarily want anything from the bag because it was late, and plus Aunt Mazie didn't allow me to just bring stuff home without knowing who or where I got it from. I just figured that as my friend she would have stood up for me and would have told Angela that we were good buddies. I was really feeling sad because I figured I had lost a good friend.

A few days later, things were back to normal with Beverly and I. Once again we were two friends laughing and having fun at school. We eventually left the campus again, back to that same store. We went and got our tater wedges and ate them as we walked up and down the aisles. We had our shopping carts in hand, pushing them, pretending we were buying things. She was in one aisle, and I was strolling down the dry cereal aisle. I love dry cereal even now, with or without milk.

It was fun to us to get shopping carts and to pretend we had lots of money to buy whatever we wanted. We were putting into them any and everything we imagined we would buy if we had money while at the same time we were eating the deli cooked tater wedges.

When our carts were full we met up and compared who had the best stuff. We had stuffed the empty deli bag behind the neatly stacked merchandise on the shelf. Just as we had done the first time we had been there, we left the carts with the stuff in them. I should have walked out of the store then, but maybe I wanted to see if I had the stomach for stealing. I went to where the candies were and surreptitiously, but nervously stuffed a bag of *Bubblicious* 10-pk gum in my pants, and something else from the candy family. I walked around that store for a while trying to gather up my nerves.

Finally I walked toward the front and I could have sworn that I heard a man say, *"Grab her when she walks out the door."* Honestly I couldn't tell you if the man had said that for real, or whether it was God who was speaking to me, because I could not shake that voice for a very long time. Months had passed and I could still hear and feel that voice. Looking back, I realize that I wasn't a thief; I wanted to fit in, but maybe stealing wasn't for me. I didn't bother to go out the door. I went back in and removed the stuff out of my pants in a way that the man, or whoever was looking could see that I had put them back. I walked out the store without incident. I never shared this with Beverly or anyone else.

I was scared for a long time. I kept it to myself, but I never went back into that store again. I never left the school grounds again either. As a teenager, I didn't know a lot about God, other than He will get you if you are not good. But I told him no less than a million times I was sorry and that I would not do that again. My friend, Beverly and I drifted apart. I realized that I was never cut out to be a thief, so I could not fit in with thieves. Since Beverly and seeming all her friends had no problem stealing, she and I thought it best that we went our separate ways. No doubt God's hand was in that decision, too, because He was quietly shaping my life.

Chapter 7

While in school, I had never gone to either the junior, or senior prom. One of the reasons was that no one ever asked me. I never used to talk to boys my age, and they never seemed to want to bother with me, except for the few times Pede tried to beat me up. One time I ended up getting a beating for it when I told my dad.

I tried not to think too much about prom because if I had had a boyfriend back then who asked me to go with him to either of my proms, I would have been embarrassed because I would not have had the money to buy the gown or the shoes, or to get my hair done up all fancy. By the time I became a high school student, I was used to doing without whatever wasn't presented to me. Asking for something too often produced a resolute *"No,"* so I stopped asking. I had an uncomfortable, though not outright hostile relationship with my dad, so I knew better than to ask for a prom dress he would never buy me.

Well, to my surprise, Aunt Mazie wanted to know what was happening with my prom. About that time all my friends were getting together and buzzing with excitement about their gowns. My aunt asked me if I were going, too. I guessed I must have looked somewhat piteous to her. We were at home together and were talking about school, but not prom. Truthfully, I had so little to be genuinely excited about, so I kept our conversation to how matters of school. She wanted to know how I was doing in school. Of course I lied to her and told her how great I was doing.

Despite how a few people had made me feel, I knew I wasn't an ugly person; I was filling out my jeans, and I had noticed that a few boys were looking at me sometimes when I passed them. They didn't approach me, but they made me feel that they would want to if I just gave them the chance. I was scared to get too close to any of them, so I kept my distance, thinking it best not to risk forming any ties to a young boy in my school.

My Aunt was a wise woman, so she turned the subject from my studies to the usual teenage topic. She wanted to know if I had a boyfriend. At this point in my life, I had become a really smooth liar, so I could answer anyone with a convincing lie and never have sweat beads appear on my forehead or upper lip. I was a master liar! "Yes, Aunt, I have a boy who likes me," I lied. I was fourteen; it would be strange for me to be that age and not have someone showing an interest. I had my reasons for being distant, but I had also mastered the art of hiding all my true and deep feelings.

Her next question was, *"Has he invited you to the prom?"* I knew I was going to get myself into trouble with my next answer, but what could I do? If a guy was interested in you, and he was going to your school too, he was going to invite you to the prom. So since I had already lied by telling her that I had a boyfriend, I knew I would have to lie again and say that he had invited me. Of course I was convincing, which meant I should have anticipated her next question that caused me to dig a deeper hole than I could ever get out of!

Now she wanted to know what I was going to wear. Well, I didn't have anything to wear, and I knew she was aware of the unhealthy relationship I had with my dad, so in the back of my mind, I wanted to believe that this would end the conversation. I was wrong! She offered to take up one of her dresses for me to wear. I accepted the offer, and as soon as I did that, my mind began racing faster than I could comprehend. What a mess! It was time to think how I was going to pull this one off. How was I going to go to a prom with a boy who didn't invite me? And the adults in my life would never have agreed to let me meet a boy on prom night anywhere except in the living room of my home. I felt my face getting red and hot, but didn't have the nerve to confess even one of the several lies I had just told.

Well, my Aunt Mazie did the measuring and got her dress taken up to fit me. It was a beautiful gown, fuchsia pink with the 1960s flare and sleeves that came to the middle of my elbows. It even had diamond-studded buttons that glittered and followed the zipper from the top to the bottom of my dress. I knew I had a good body; I had curves in all the right places and the dress fit me well. I was proud to wear it, but the question was, where was I going in my new, lovely gown? I couldn't tell whether time stood still or moved at the speed of light, but It was the night of the prom and time for me to go.

My aunt sat anxiously waiting for the doorbell to ring, and I made no comment. It's true that teenage minds are not fully developed because I assumed that I could just leave without being questioned. I gathered my wrap and headed for the front door. Predictably -- or unpredictably -- my Aunt wanted to know why my boyfriend wasn't coming to pick me up. Being the liar that I was, I instantly conjured up a reason for my boyfriend's absence. I told her I would be meeting him at school because he lived nearer to the school than I. So naturally, there was no sense in him coming this side of town for me. Well, my story seemed to work because she let me go.

I took a taxi and went to the school. When I arrived there everything was in full swing. I stayed for a little while, but I felt out of place. I was all alone, too shy to ask anyone for a dance, and too bashful to even accept one dance if he were bold enough to ask me. I wanted to leave, but I knew I couldn't just leave like that. I had to find someone and take a picture with that person, so that I could show my aunt and anyone who asked that I had really gone to the prom, and that I had a boyfriend, too. I searched for someone who I could feel comfortable talking to.

The introvert inside of me wouldn't allow me to approach someone and just ask him to take a picture with me, so with my heart palpitating in my chest, I approached and offered a boy some money to pose with me and take a picture. I was walking around and found the boy I wanted, just as he was exiting the bathroom. He looked at me and asked, *"How much do you have?"* "I can give you thirty dollars," I said, my eyes glancing quickly from his eyes to the floor. *"I'll take fifty."* "Forty!" He thought for a moment, hoping I would give in, and finally said, *"Okay, forty."* I gave him the money, and we found ourselves a photographer.

After taking the picture, I left the dance and took a taxi to the park. It was too early to go back home. If I had gone back home that early, I knew I would have had to answer a lot of questions, and I wasn't up to answering any. I was feeling ashamed and embarrassed, wanting to know why my life was so miserable.

When I was at the prom, I saw girls enjoying themselves with their boyfriends. I knew they weren't prettier or sexier than I was, but then I knew that the secret I had hidden inside of me was more terrible than anything they were hiding. I stayed away from adults and from kids my age, because I didn't want them to know what my dad had done to me. In my not-so-developed mind, I thought that if I had gotten with boys my age, they would have known that I wasn't a virgin. Looking back at that now, I realize how stupid I was. The boys back then wouldn't have known the difference between a girl who wasn't a virgin and one who was.

Anyway, I spent the rest of the time at the park in my prom dress, praying and hoping no one would see me there and tell my Aunt Mazie. I knew the news of me having to pay someone to pose with me at the prom would be all over school the following week, but there was nothing I could do. I was beginning to accept that this was to be my fate. I felt as if I were to be ridiculed and embarrassed for the rest of my life. Maybe I had done something terribly wrong in a past life and was now paying for it. I didn't know, but whatever was happening to me was pretty terrible.

Prom was finally over and becoming a distant memory. For the next few months I lied about the pictures and said that the boy who took me to the prom had kept all the pictures. Auntie was a little upset. The truth was that I got to hold the one picture we took together at the prom. But then he snatched it from me and told me I better not show anyone that we were together or he would beat me up, or rag on me for the rest of my life. He even threatened to tell people I had to pay someone to take a picture with me, so you can imagine how mortified I would be if any of that news surfaced.

I surrendered the picture and never saw it again. A few years later, I did see this guy who took me to the prom, and sadly, he was on drugs. I actually felt badly for him, and wondered since then if he were dead or alive. I had gotten away with a really big lie surrounding my prom, and that was what mattered most at the time. I feel sad now to admit it, but Aunt Mazie left this world without knowing the truth about the prom and so much more!

My aunt was a chain smoker; she had been smoking for over forty years when we met. I remember her using one cigarette to light another one. Three days prior to her death, I went with her to visit the doctor. He told her that her blood pressure and her cholesterol were both high, and he warned her about smoking and told her not to eat pork. That meat was apparently my aunt's favorite. After leaving the doctor's office, she and I went to the grocery store where she bought herself some pork. I reminded her that the doctor said she shouldn't eat it, but my aunt was an obstinate lady who told herself that she wasn't going to allow anyone to tell her what to do She said she wasn't going to allow the doctor to tell her what to eat and what not to eat.

A few days later she cooked that meat and we had a good dinner, but about thirty minutes later, she started complaining of a severe headache. She got up from the table, holding her head. A few seconds later, she fell to the floor. I heard a groan. I was scared. I didn't know what to do. My Aunt Mazie was on the floor and she was barely moving. Everything was happening so fast; one minute she was standing, the next she was on the floor, moaning, and the next there was silence. I franticly called one of my aunts and told her what was wrong. She told me to call "911."

I called and told them that I thought my aunt was dead. I remember how calm I was, and I don't remember crying and I thought something was wrong with me. When I asked the person I was talking to on the phone why I wasn't crying, the person told me that it was okay; what had just happened hadn't really hit me as yet. I'm sure she was right because she took dozens of calls just like mine everyday. Still, I felt a little strange, not wanting to always be a person detached from my emotions.

Yes, my Aunt Mazie was gone, and it seemed like a whirlwind of activities all of a sudden surrounding me. Relatives came from everywhere, and there were loud and subtle arguments about funeral arrangements. Seemed like everyone had an opinion, but it was as if I were not even present in the room where discussions were taking place. That was just as well because I was having a hard time processing the fact that the only person I knew for sure cared about me was gone forever – at least until I saw her again in Heaven.

During Aunt Mazie's funeral I was still perplexed about why I didn't feel anything. Actually, I did feel much, but I wasn't able to articulate it, nor could I cry. I missed her but it wasn't like I thought it would be. I guess I thought I couldn't put one foot in front of the other without knowing she was somewhere nearby, but I was able to do my normal routines in a mechanical way. I remember greeting Aunt Mazie's sisters who had talked so terribly about me in the car when they drove me from my parents' home to Aunt Mazie's home. Either they thought I couldn't hear them or they didn't care if I heard them or not. This was the funeral day, and I was cordial to everyone.

The church was packed, with some guests having to stand in the back. There were a lot of family and close friends at the funeral, and a good number of them stood up to speak on her behalf. I mused to myself how people who have plenty of negative things to say about a person while they are alive find only the good memories to reference at funerals. My Aunt Mazie's was no exception. I was sitting in the front row near the open casket. While everyone was speaking, I was staring at her still face with just a hint of a smile. She looked like her self, with make up done well, and she had on one of her fancy black dresses. Her funeral attire was perfect.

I was suddenly brought back to the moment when the last speaker stopped talking and there was a moment of silence. Everything ended and the whole assembly of friends and relatives moved to the burial site and then back home to the repast. There were tears and laughter, noise and silence. The food was plentiful and tasty. Finally, everyone went home and back to their lives, and I had to process living without Aunt Mazie without the benefit of therapy, which I probably needed.

My Parents did not come to the funeral, most likely due to financial and transportation issues. What I mean is either we had too little money in general, or the money we had went to pay specific bills. Aunt Mazie's funeral was not in my parents' budget! Jack always had Mom on a tight budget that was usually below the standard of living most families enjoyed. When I called to tell the parents Auntie had died, I didn't expect them to come. Mom still had lots of kids to care for and our family really didn't travel much because the cars we drove were always breaking down.

Mom Loved Auntie though, and I know this because once a year I would catch the *Trailway* bus to go home, usually around a holiday, and usually staying a few days before returning to Tampa, Florida. It's amazing that each time I prepared to go home – rather to my parents house – I felt an excitement and anticipation of feeling something good when I got there. I was hyped to go, but once there I remembered why I initially left. The painful reality that I would never feel good about going to the place where my birth parents and siblings lived was almost too much for me to bear. But then again, I had long ago suppressed my true feelings, so I just added this unhappy reminder to the rest of my life's disappointments. Predictably, my dad was at his old games, so once more I was forced to hide or avoid him until I left. Sadly, there were visits where I stayed only a day before leaving because Dad's pursuit of me got so bad.

Weeks went by, during which time I became distinctly aware of the providential hand of God, who intentionally placed me in the home of Mrs. Mazie, my beloved Auntie. Looking back I can still recall the times we would sit and talk for hours, about girls, boys, sex and simple things pertaining to real life. Well, she did most of the talking anyway. I just for the most part sat and listened, feeling very uncomfortable. I felt this way, first because she expected me to talk to her, and second because I felt like the things she talked about were inappropriate for children. Plus it was considered disrespectful in my book to even sit and have a conversation with an adult. My childhood was filled with *"Yes"* or *"No"* spoken via head motions and then you moved on. But with Auntie, disrespect was defined as when a child didn't look eye to eye when an adult spoke or was spoken to, so you can image how I felt. Of course, over the years I grew more comfortable, or at least less inhibited as I sat and spoke with her.

Because my aunt was a chain smoker I didn't think she was a Christian, but most of the times I heard her praying and asking God to heal her body and to protect her from all hurt, harm and danger, both the seen invisible. She also prayed a lot for her favorite "man," Dr. Frederick Elkerenkoether. You might know him by the name "Rev. Ike." Yep, that famous television personality was the man to whom my dear Aunt Mazie prayed for salvation! The way salvation manifested, however, was that Aunt Mazie prayed Rev. Ike would give her the right set of numbers to play when she gambled. I only hope God kept an open mind when listening!

Auntie loved her some Rev. Ike. He would send her numbers for her to play. They had a special relationship that included gambling. Rev. Ike encouraged gambling, though he preached abstinence from the sin of gambling. I wondered if anyone besides me realized that he practiced what he didn't preach! I guess Aunt Mazie used Rev. Ike's numbers to play the lottery or whatever she wanted to play with them. Now as I recall, Dr. Frederic Elkerenkoether rarely, if ever got the numbers right, but he did a fantastic job of encouraging Auntie to never give up, keep on playing the set of numbers and believe in her heart that luck favored her. She, too, could be prosperous like her idol, Rev. Ike, if she simply believed and continued to plant monetary seeds into his Ministry.

Well, my aunt has been gone for a while now, and I still haven't cried. I did love her; I guess I was trying to be tough or it must have been that my emotion was so out of whack that I just couldn't cry back then. Whatever it was I just didn't know; all I know for certain is that I was cut up inside. She was the only true adult friend and mother figure in my life, and she came into my life when I was on the verge of going so deep inside myself that I might never have grown into a "normal" adult. Yes, I did grow into a normal adult, which is God's biggest miracle in my life!

Chapter 8

I had only been with Aunt Mazie for a little less than three years when she died. I was beginning to like it. I had no fear of being with her; she had become a good friend as well as an aunt. Initially, I didn't like it that she was so strict, but I had grown to love and respect her because I knew she had my best interest at heart. At least she wasn't taking advantage of me like my dad was doing. And now I thought I was supposed to go back home to my mom and dad. I wished I didn't have to, but there was nowhere else for me to go, so I had to go back home to them. I dreaded the thought! Mind you, I wasn't upset with the things my Mom had done because as I got older, I understood how she felt trapped in her circumstances. But my Dad was a totally different story. I was repulsed by the sight of him because he never stopped wanting to violate me. And he never seemed to get punished for his sins!

My aunt was the only one who really showed me love. We were able to talk to each other the way people were supposed to. I had no fear of her; I had grown to realize that she was strict with me because she meant well for me. She made me feel special. For once in my life I was in a situation where I could get some attention from someone, attention that wasn't in any way negative. I wish I had had more time to spend with her, but I guess what is to be must be.

Now I was looking to be going back home to a place I had hoped I wouldn't see for a while. If I were back home when I was an adult, then I knew things would be okay. But I was still a child and I was going back to face a man I considered a monster, a man, who was my dad. He was someone who was supposed to be my protector, someone I should be running to, not hiding from. But wait! Maybe I wouldn't have to go back home to Clewiston after all. My Aunt Eatt, one of Aunt Mazie's sisters, was about to save the day.

When my Aunt Eatt heard about her sister's death, she came over. The first thing she asked me for was the check that my Aunt Mazie used to get from social security. She knew I was the one who used to cash it for Auntie, so she was aware that I knew where it was. I gave it to her. She took the check, looked at it, and then looked at me. *"It seems like you're going to have to come and live with me now,"* she said.

I wasn't looking at her facial expression when she said it, nor was I listening to the tone she used. I was happy because at that moment when my aunt died, I felt I would have to go back to Clewiston, and the thought of going back caused me to cringe inside. I knew what my dad had been doing to me, and what he would want to do again once I got there, and it wasn't appealing to me at all. So when my Aunt Eatt said I could go live with her, I was feeling good. However, for some reason, I didn't think she would have been good to me the way Aunt Mazie was. And my feeling turned out to be right.

After I started living with Aunt Eat, I realized the type of person she was. Her real name was Eleanor, whom we called Aunt "Eat." She was a mean, five-footer who was bow-legged. She loved cats and loved

85

to fish. Her skin looked yellow, to the point that she almost looked Chinese. She kept her natural nails long, and sometimes I thought they were actually longer than her cats' claws. Aunt Eat was greedy for money, which I figured out as soon as I realized she was the only one asking for Aunt Mazie's social security check. She was never married and had no children. She started treating me mean from the very first day I went to live with her. After Aunt Mazie died, all Aunt Eatt wanted was that little money Mama sent her every month for my care. She was always vexing and provoking me. It was like she wanted me to fight her, or give her a reason to hit me.

I had three years of a normal life before coming to live with Aunt Eatt, so maybe that was all I was allowed by God. No, that couldn't be true. Still, I was beginning to wonder where my life was going. As soon as it had started to get a little better with Aunt Mazie, death happened, and now I was almost back in the same situation I had been in with my dad. Aunt Eat was a quit a bit shorter than my dad, but as mean. Think about this: she and Aunt Mazie were sisters, but while Aunt Mazie was petite, charming, and good-looking, Aunt Eat was like a monster, both in her appearance and her personality.

She once said that I probably liked what my daddy had done to me. If ever I were going to raise my hand to strike her that would have been the time. She had no idea what my father had done to me, and her words cut me like a knife. I was determined not to show her any sign that I was hurt by anything she said. I made no response to her vicious and inappropriate comment because I knew she was just evil. The word was that she was on probation for twenty or more years for shooting a lady who came to her house to confront her about her sleeping with the woman's husband. She got probation because the lady was on her property and it was considered self-defense. Now that was not something we talked about. Heck, we hardly ever talked about anything at all; she was just a mean old lady. I had no proof that what was being said about her was true, but I can tell you that she had to get permission to leave town, and she paid a fee every month, and she had a probation officer, so maybe she was angry about the whole situation, who knows?

I stayed with Aunt Eatt just three months, which was just long enough for me to finish out the school year. I had about three months left back in grade eight and I wanted to finish it. At times she would try to provoke me into a negative conversation. I think I was afraid of this woman who was smaller than my dad, and I dare say meaner. Maybe she wasn't sexually assaulting me, but she was downright cruel to me. School remained a haven for me, even though I never liked school because of the mean treatment I got from children there. I was never mean to anyone, so why were so many kids and adults so mean to me? I used to ask God that question.

I didn't have to do anything wrong for my Aunt to get mad at me. I remember a few times when she held me up against a wall in the house and dared me to hit her. This woman wanted badly to hurt someone physically, and I wasn't about to give her the chance to do that to me. I was taught to respect those who were older than I, and I wasn't about to break that rule by being rude to her and giving her a chance to hit me. This woman was a monster whose hands were so rough that she could do serious damage to me if she hit me. All I wanted her to do was to let me go, so I always behaved myself, and she always dropped her fighting pose and let me go.

Aunt Eatt lived in a one-bedroom house, and of course it only had one bathroom. It was a very small house, made of wood, with a front porch and a living room. She would go out of her way to hide from me whenever she was about to change her clothes. Of course some of my clothes were in that little room, and the rest were in the family room where I slept on this narrow couch. If I needed to change, that's where I would have to change. There was no privacy. Imagine how uncomfortable I was when I needed to change. She was always at home because she was retired and she never worked, so we were always in each other's way. If I noticed she wasn't in the house, I would always try to have my bath quickly and changed back into something fast before she got back into the house.

When I used to live with Aunt Mazie, I had my own room. Her house was a two- bedroom wooden house, and I had my privacy. I could sleep in my own bed, not some cramped up couch like I was sleeping on now. Trust me, I didn't say anything to my aunt unless it was imperative that I did so. I didn't want her to misconstrue anything I told her. I just knew she was evil, and was very much capable of doing anything to me and getting away with it. After all, where was I going? She knew she had the upper hand.

Aunt Eatt didn't want me to go anywhere, so I would always be at the house if I weren't in school. One day she was about to change her clothes when she said to me, *"Don't look at me; I'll knock you out if you ever try me with that female disease."* Apparently someone had told my Aunt that back in Clewiston they used to call me "Billy Jean." I guess in her mind she was thinking I was someone like Billy Jean King, the tennis player, who was a lesbian. I guess she had never heard Michael Jackson's song where he talked about Billy Jean being his girl. And I think someone should have told her that she wasn't an attractive woman in the first place. Back then if I had had homosexual tendencies, I wouldn't have wanted anything to do with this unattractive, unfeminine aunt. Of course I made no reply to her general accusation, which we both knew was false.

Aunt Eleanor vexed me day and night. She hounded me for money. I had a little job, and she would meet me at the door to get my *Burger King* check. Sometimes I would pretend to be sick, and I would tell her that I needed special things like OJ, or medication, and I would tell her that the extra money was what I needed to buy these stuffs with. I made about eighty dollars a week, and she would take about fifty. I was not allowed to cash my check before she saw it. Can you imagine how terrible this woman was? I was told she received Money from my mom for keeping me, and yet what little money I was making from work I had to share with her too. It was all so unfair!

Once out of the clear blue she just started with this mess about the female disease. She actually accused m of being a lesbian. I was so tired and fed up with the whole situation that I murmured angrily under my breath, "If I did like ladies I would not look at a jail bird, or an old biddy like you." I didn't say it with the intention for her to hear it, but somehow she heard me and then she started getting hysterical and started calling all her sisters, telling them lies about me. No one had ever asked me to tell my side of any story, and this situation was no exception. No one cared what I thought or what was true about me. At this point in my life, I didn't care what anyone else thought of me, so it didn't matter if all my aunts thought I was a lesbian.

Things eventually settled down, but I had already asked the neighbors if I could spend the next four weeks with them until the end of school. They were a little reluctant at first, but then they agreed for fifty dollars a month. I was happy to pay that. It was better to do that than to live another day in hell and be forced to pay the devil to stay in that hot place! I didn't want to go home, so I stayed with these kind neighbors for the next four weeks. It was hard because I knew that they were tired of this extra body in their house using up their stuff, so eventually I went back to Aunt Eatt's house.

While living with Aunt Eatt, I tried my best not to be rude to her, but it was hard. When I used to live with Aunt Mazie, she never attended church, but she would make sure that I did. In church I learned that God didn't like kids who were disobedient to their parents, nor did He like ones who were rude to their elders. I guess knowing that helped me in some ways to cope with the way my Aunt Eatt was treating me. It's amazing how two people who were fully related to each other could be so different. To me Aunt Mazie was so gentle and kind, and yet her sister was so mean and terrible.

The next time I took a trip to my parents' home, I convinced myself that if he tried to touch me inappropriately, I would stand up and confront him. I had known that what my dad was doing to me was wrong, and I decided now that it had to stop. The first time I stood up to my dad was a scary experience. I knew I was about to be beaten down, but at this moment that was more appealing to me than for me to allow him to have his way with me again. I was thirteen years old now, and I wasn't really a small person. I had a pretty developed body; no wonder my friend in Tampa had thought I was older than I really was. But I knew I couldn't physically handle my dad because he was a big man.

I remember him calling me one day when I was there, playing outside. I knew what he wanted, and I decided I wasn't going to give in to him. He got me into the house and slapped me around, but I decided I was not going to take my clothes off for him. We had a fight, but in the end, he was the one who lost because I had made up my mind that he was not going to touch me in that way anymore. I actually felt empowered after that, and I didn't realize it at the time, but my standing up to him probably caused him to think twice about touching me again. It didn't mean he wouldn't try it again, but it definitely meant he would think long and hard about the potential consequences of his having his way with his child.

My dad was beginning to openly dislike me. He couldn't get what he wanted, so he became a pest and made my life a living hell. I remember coming home from school one day and my dad asked me if any of the boys out there were bothering me. I felt good because he had never asked me that before, so I thought this was his way of trying to show me that he cared. The fact of the matter was that there were boys out there who would bully us, and we never had anyone to protect us. Now I thought my dad was going to defend us, but that wasn't his intention.

When my dad asked if any boys out there were messing with me, what he actually meant was if I were allowing any of the boys to have sex with me. At the time, I didn't know that was what he meant. I said, "Yes," and my dad gave me a beating. Needless to say, that didn't cause me to love him or respect him, and it certainly didn't give me the comfort of knowing my dad had my back against bullies outside. If it did anything, it caused me to hate him even more than I already did.

I remember well how I used to gather my clothes and my two favorite hair bows and socks. As a child I loved bows and socks, which seems kind of silly looking back at it now. But back then, socks made me feel like I was dressed up, even if they had a hole in the bottom or if they were dirty. I figured with so many siblings in the house, that if I didn't hang onto my stuff somebody else would get them.

Now the bows made me feel like I had long, "good hair," and when I added those bows and socks, man I felt like a million dollars. Even if my dress or shoes weren't all that, just give me some bows, split my little pony tails in half, put every bow I had in my hair, and I was a fashion statement, ready for the world! Usually there were twenty bows in a package, and then I had found more on the ground. So my hair did shake when I swung it dramatically from side to side. I felt so pretty.

Hair bows were my substitute for affection, I think, because I obsessed over them. Brush, brush and into my hair all of them went; it didn't matter what color I had on or what color the bows were, I put those babies on right away and it seemed to put a boost in my step. As I bounced, you guessed it, my hair bounced; I felt like I was on top of the world. Even though I had those bows on the very ends of my hair and they often times hit me in the eyes as I bounced, that didn't matter; I still loved my bows. Yep, in retrospect, they were my "security blanket." They kept me feeling a little bit positive about myself, and perhaps these silly bows kept me from sinking into a depression from which I would not have emerged.

Looking back, I realize that, as a child I had this need to be seen. Maybe my need to wear too many bows and fold my socks a certain way had something to do with it. I was starved for attention, and I found creative ways to be noticed all the time. I was looking to fill the void in my heart with praise from strangers. It's sad to say, but this need followed me throughout all of my teenage years and a large part of my younger adult years. Even when I reached my early thirties, I had this need to be seen. I craved adoration from those around me, and consequently my insatiable desire for attention caused me to do a lot of stupid things. I must have gotten enough attention to keep me "performing" before any audience that would receive me. But praise God, He saw me through it all, and never stopped loving me. I didn't know it when I did all the wrong things to get attention, but I always had God's attention because He had a master plan for my life and was going to seen reveal to me my destiny.

Another thing I can remember like it was yesterday is that, as a child I was always looking down when I walked. It didn't matter if I were on my way to church, or during school, I focused my eyes on the ground looking for bows and pencils. Now it wasn't abnormal to find a couple of little pencils and about three nice cute hair bows. I just couldn't figure out for the life of me why someone would lose these great bows and not search all over for them. Truthfully, I was looking down to avoid making eye contact with anyone who might ridicule me or hurt my feelings. If no one noticed me or engaged in conversation with me, then there was no risk of physical or emotional harm coming my way.

I continued to find my main solace in church, despite hearing the negative things God didn't like about children. I knew instinctively that I was a good child and a good person, so I never doubted that God loved me. I learned much about Him in church, and I discussed Sunday lessons and sermons with my siblings when we were together. My siblings and I were very excited about Sundays, and especially excited when we had a visiting minister or a singing group 'cause that meant we were going to be in church for a long time, and there were going to be a lot of people for whom I could show off. I wasn't fresh or anything, but I could make people look at me when I sang loudest or stood up quickest during *Bible* readings.

We had visiting choirs and guest ministers, but most times the music came from just our church choir, and, boy, could they sing! Back then they called it a "singing" when practically a whole service was spent with the congregation listening to one choir after another. I remember that more than once, five blind boys would come, and I always had a good time. Now I cannot remember much of the preaching, mind you, but, man, do I remember the music, the singing, and the shouting. I cannot forget the man we called "ST. James. That man sure could play that *Hammond* organ!

There was this old lady who always seemed to get into the spirit. That was considered a good thing, but the way it manifested was for people to feel so close to God that they couldn't control what their bodies were doing. They had temporarily left their bodies and joined Christ until the spirit released them, or left them alone. We knew in just a few minutes this woman was about to "catch the spirit," because, whenever she held up her right hand and those two fingers started to shake, you could tell the spirit was about to hit her, and off she went running around the church, followed by others who, I guess caught her spirit. Once they started, the church went wild, and the singers sang long and loud.

Sometimes we sang the same song for what seemed like hours;. As long as they were jumping, I was jumping up and down too, and singing at the top of my lungs, hair with bows shaking all over the place. By the time I left church I had shaken until I couldn't shake anymore, and my clothes were soaked with sweat. When we were leaving church, I always remember the adults saying, *"Boy, did we have church."*

Oh, yes, I, too, thought, "Boy did we have church," until I got older and wiser about the meaning of being in God's house. I never remember the *Bible* being opened, or a Word being taught, but, man, did we have church! Even so, I thank God for my Pentecostal roots and my Christian foundation. If I don't remember one thing, I do remember that hell is hot and that you've got to live holy. I was never taught about the grace, mercy and love of God until I became an adult. Then I could say to myself, "Boy, did I find the Word of God!"

I really did love church growing up, so I guess that's why I love it now. I remember driving uptown, or sitting on the bus going or returning from school, when I could see the 18-wheelers parked out on the field. I could see men putting stakes in the ground, and then putting up a banner that read *"RIVIVAL 5 NIGHTS ONLY, Reverend So and So; come get your miracle 5 nights only."* Then other times I would hear someone say, *"Did you know the prophet will be in town next week?"*

I started planning how to get to those inspirational revivals. I was excited, anxiously waiting for 6pm to come because that's when I would be heading to the revival. But first I wanted to make sure my mother was going to let me go. So of course I did everything I was supposed to do, and then some, and I stayed out of my mother's way too, 'cause I wanted her to let me go. I didn't want to aggravate her. Soon revival nights, when we asked to go, she said yes and allowed us to go.

On this particular revival night, I was so glad. I got my socks/bows and about a dollar. You see, you wanted to have money to go by the local store and buy hot sausage before church. Like all kids, we made our mother think the money she gave us was for offerings, but we knew that wasn't what it was for. Now we had everything that was needed; it was going to be a good night.

It was 6:45 pm when we were walking down Front Street. I got my candy and junk food and was on my way to church. I was glad when they said let us go into the house of the Lord's, or better yet, the prophet is in town. Ok, we made it to church without getting jumped. Kids jumped us all the time. They would threaten to beat us up, and oftentimes take our candies. But all in all, it was worth the gamble even though for most of my childhood I had to lookout for these bullies. Lord, we could never just go to the store or walk to or from school without somebody trying to beat us up.

Hearing the word "Holy Ghost" stirred up a bitter taste in my mouth and a negative vision in my head. I never shared with anyone why "Holy Ghost" was so offensive to me, but it was because my neighbor, who used to watch my Dad rape me in his car day after day, year after year, called me nasty every time I exited the car in tears. She used to point her finger at me in disgust, as if I had power over the situation. She couldn't have been that stupid or willfully ignorant! This same neighbor often held Bible study at her home, and all she talked about was how strong the Holy Ghost was in her life and how people needed to live holy lives. I figured that if she represented the "Holy Ghost," I wanted nothing to do with it. The Holy Ghost, not I, was nasty!

I will never forget this one night when the preacher said that the Spirit was high and a lady went up for prayer. She was from one of the poorest families in my hometown. I think this lady suffered with mental issues, since, as long as she lived she struggled in some area or another. She was very nice and friendly, but it seemed like she loved her kids to a fault. Of course there was no dad around for these five or six kids, so I guess she did her best. The house they lived in was filthy nasty; clothes were strewn everywhere; the windows were out, no central air, always a house full of nasty, sticky little babies.

One day while I was supposed to be at the tent revival, I stopped by this particular house. I don't remember why, because we were not friends. I skipped church to visit at their house. I remember eating rice and lots of butter; the mom was there, but she never asked us what we were doing. She just kind of went with the flow. The kids did and went anywhere they desired. She's deceased now, but like I said earlier, she really did struggle with emotional, and mental issues. In my mind, she was another example of someone relying on the Holy Ghost to change her life. Well, the Holy Ghost never changed anything in her life that I could see.

But she was a really nice lady, and the story goes that she was an absolutely beautiful woman who had had a fabulous body when she was young. She was married to a very mean and abusive man, and she stayed in the marriage for too long. He beat her so badly that she lost both her inner and outer beauty, and she was never the same since. Her husband died in his early 30's, while she recently died. Maybe the Holy Ghost did something for her after all, because she lived much longer than her mean husband.

While I continued to have emotional turmoil regarding my dad, my immediate problem was with school. I hadn't fit in when I was in elementary school, and I didn't fit in while I was in middle or high school. I didn't have any friends, and thanks to my people skill, or lack thereof, I was finding it harder and harder to make even one friend. Ever since I was a small child, I felt like "Rudolph, the red-nosed Reindeer." I can remember even back in elementary school that I never got picked during "Duck, duck Goose" games, and never was I the first, second or even the eighth person to be chosen by those appointed captains and co-captains. I didn't know why, but I can only imagine that they saw me as I saw myself -- a nobody!

Most of the time, I was reluctantly selected because of one or two reasons: the other person left was fat; or I was the only one left to pick. Imagine how that made me feel when I would play with those kids who didn't want me around but had no choice. If I made a mistake, the looks I would get from my teammates would be enough to make me want to hide myself away from them.

In my class I was probably the oldest student. I felt embarrassed just attending my classes. Many a times I hid away from classes because I felt as if I didn't belong there. You see, my self-esteem was so low that I didn't think I belonged in class with those ordinary students. At that point in my life I was well aware that my father had caused me to feel so unworthy, and the very thought of it made me miserable and sick to my stomach.

My period started when I was fourteen years of age, and when it started I felt as if I were being punished by God for the things that had been happening to me over the years. Somehow in my little mind I felt as if I were responsible for the things that my father had been doing to me. I didn't tell my mom or anyone what just happened to me because I thought I knew what it was, and I was afraid that by saying it to anyone, I would confirm my suspicion about God's wrath. So I thought I would leave things as they were. I had no real understanding of menstruation, but I knew I needed to use socks, rags and toilet paper to stop blood from coming through my clothes.

Finally, I asked a couple of girls at school what they did about our "problem," and I learned about sanitary napkins. We called them "pads," and I didn't wear them until I was seventeen. I remember feeling too embarrassed to buy them, but I was more afraid of tampons because the girls said if you're not a virgin when you insert one of those things, it will get lost and you'll die. My sisters and I didn't communicate, so I relied on what I learned at school, which became my only truth.

During the whole time that I thought God only sat in judgment and punished sinners, I didn't know He wouldn't punish an innocent child. I certainly didn't know He was merciful and kind. I had been going to church and enjoying church, but I was going there, not to learn about God, but to escape from my troubles and enjoy myself. I couldn't tell you what the pastor preached about, once I left church, but I could tell you that I enjoyed the singing and the shouting, and I liked it when I saw people getting into the spirit and doing all kinds of things. Clearly I was enjoying the lesser part of church, and completely missing the main part, which was hearing the Word of God and applying it to my life when I left church. What did I know as a child? God revealed the truth to me in His time.

At thirteen or fourteen, I didn't know what God would do, and what He wouldn't do. I just knew I didn't feel as if I were someone He wanted in His organization. I knew God loves cleanliness, but I figured that I was dirty. I felt dirty because my dad had made me feel unclean. But was it my fault? I somehow thought it was. I mean I couldn't do anything to stop my dad, who started violating me before I even knew myself. I was only about five when he started touching me, and I didn't know it was wrong at that time. I was just a baby! I didn't know the difference between right and wrong, or what constituted a father's love for his child. Ironically, the person who should have been teaching me right from wrong was the person who was doing me wrong. And because he did this for over a decade of my young life, the scars were so deep that even God had a difficult time bringing me to a place where I felt blameless.

Chapter 9

After living through what a bunch of mean girls had done to me while I was in middle school, I had decided to stay to myself in high school, thinking I didn't need any friends if the only ones approaching me were insincere. Clewiston is such a small city that there is only one high school there, so everyone, who leave out of middle school was going to end up here in Clewiston high, which meant the same people, who used to tease me in middle school were the people I met again while I was in Clewiston high; it seemed like there was going to be no escape for me.

Imagine not being able to get away from your past when it comes to going to school. The same people who knew about me in middle school were here, so I couldn't pretend to be who I was not, just so I could maybe get along with someone else. In this town, everyone knew everyone, so if you were a good girl while you were in middle school, your reputation would follow you to high school, and the same thing would happen if you were a bad girl. Me, I didn't even know what category I fell into; the kids in middle school didn't give me a chance to prove who I was, and now I was in high school.

It wasn't like I was unfamiliar with high schools, and what they were about. I had been to two different ones while I was in Tampa, so in a sense I was more familiar with high schools than my so-called friends, who were in middle school with me. I hated it because it appeared as if my life were going to get worse. Kids were older and bolder now; things they wouldn't do in middle school, they would do in high school, and I didn't think I was paranoid to believe my life would be filled with deception and humiliation until graduation day.

As an adult I came to realize that kids on a whole could be very terrible to each other. When they pick on you, it doesn't necessarily mean that they hate you. It just means they find you to be an easy picking. Back then I didn't know that, so they had the power to make me feel as if I were something repulsive to look at. And I had low self-esteem before I entered school, so kids who picked on me easily achieved their goal of making me miserable.

Well, there was one bright spot in high school. My friend Monica was here with me and I was thankful for that. She and her mom had not left for Atlanta after all, but had instead stayed in Harlem. Her dad had decided to leave them alone. She told me she hadn't heard from him in quite awhile. She didn't seem too sad bringing me up to speed about the relationship her dad had with her mom and her. I'm sure they felt a great weight lifted off of them. I never volunteered how horrible my young life had been, so I couldn't now share the fact that my terrible weight was still heavy around my neck. Sure I stood up to my dad, but I had no permanent solution, like him leaving the way Monica's dad did.

I was still having problems with my dad; I hadn't given him the chance to take advantage of me the way he used to when I first returned from my Aunt Eatt, and he was really mad about that. He kept telling me how rude it was for a child to be disobedient to her parents. I guess he had never read in the *Bible* where it tells the father that he shouldn't provoke his children to wrath, lest they be discouraged. I don't know if my dad were doing the things to my sisters that he was doing to me, but I knew he was a terrible father to all of us. I remember once when our next-door neighbor gave one of my sisters a machete to chop him. That was a pretty bold thing to do, and yet my sister took the weapon. She never cut him, of course. We all just put up with our father's consistent verbal abuse and neglect of our needs.

I was unable to halt the progression of my feelings for my dad, moving from disgust and anger to contempt and outright loathing. Everything was all about him. I think he was a sex addict who was never diagnosed and who never got treatment. I don't know if he had ever cheated on Mom outside of the house, but I wouldn't put it past him. With that insatiable appetite he had for sex, anything was possible.

In school I used to hear other girls say to their friends, *"Darn, you are lucky. I started my period at ten years old."* At that time I was twelve and didn't really know why they followed that comment with, *"You can still have fun and not worry about a baby."* I didn't have my period yet, and didn't know what they were talking about. I was too naïve to realize that nearly every girl in school was sexually active before their menstruation cycles began. Getting their period only meant they had to be more careful, since none wanted to get pregnant.

The fact that I didn't know where Mom's babies were coming from was something that gripped my heart with fear. I would watch Mama, scanning her with my eyes when she wasn't looking, 'cause you as a child never looked your parents in their eye. That was "being grown," which resulted in a whooping. I would ponder in my mind things like: I don't see any cuts, so maybe she has it on the part of her arm that is covered up, or maybe she has the cut on her stomach because that was always covered up too, and I couldn't see it so I didn't know if it could be there, or maybe she had it on her legs.

You see, I was concerned about my mama, because I was thinking that daddy was cutting her every now and again, 'cause I didn't see the blood soaked rags all the time; maybe once a month. I wasn't able to connect menstruation, the stopping of menstruation, and having babies. Because of that, when I did see blood stained rags in the trash, I figured another woman in the home, including Mama, had her period. When I didn't see the rags and Mama's stomach got really big, I wondered if my mean father was hurting her. I had no adult to help me sort all t his out, so I was left to my imagination. Even though I was a full teen, I was a child in so many ways!

Suddenly, the talk from the girls at school, about being lucky if you hadn't started your menstrual cycle, became clear to me. Young teens were having sex at an alarming rate, and not having to worry about becoming pregnant was a "lucky" break. Now that I fully understood this idea, I was repulsed. Here I was fighting off my father when he couldn't keep his hands or other body parts away from me, and my classmates were luring boys and men straight to their vaginas!

This brought back the memories of when I was about six or seven years old. My Aunt Joy was still living at home in Alabama, and she begged my daddy to let me stay the summer. She really liked me. I was a little scared to stay, but she promised me lots of fun and sugar cookies. Now who would turn that down? I was happy because I felt I was special because Aunt Joy requested to have me stay with her for three whole months. She was practically out of high school, so I expected to learn everything about being a happy young woman from Aunt Joy! She was my grandparents' child who lived with them, and I always enjoyed being around my grandparents. So I had a double blessing being in Alabama that summer.

I think I knew it was wrong, but I snooped around at my Aunt Joy's room, and in my snooping I found what I thought to be cute little baby *Pampers.* They had no pins to attach to the baby, but they ha an adhesive strip going down the middle, which I thought was weird since there were no babies here. I was young enough to think maybe she bought them for me, so I used one or two inside my panties.

Once I conquered the "diapers," I crawled around on the floor, making little baby noises, and then I became bored. So I went out to play with the baby chicks, and watched granddaddy "slop" the pigs. On a farm, when you fed pigs, you called it "slopping" them because they ate anything. Hence, "slop." I loved to see those pigs eat. They made everything sound good.

Every other day I would play baby, putting on one of those weird diapers. No big deal, right? Yeah, until one day when Aunt Joy was rushing to catch the yellow bus just three houses down. From our house, you could see it coming down the orange clay dirt road. Suddenly, I heard this loud scream. *"Who's been messing with my pads? I hate it here; as soon as I finish school I will be leaving."* Maybe because she was really almost out of high school, she always seemed frustrated with something about her environment and she often made outburst about "getting the hell away from Flatwood, ALAMBAMA!

When Aunt Joy stopped yelling in a disgusted voice, I felt a knot in my stomach. As she stormed out asking me if I had been messing with her stuff, I guess by the look on my face she knew it was me. But then she said, *"I ought to beat your ugly, black behind!"* And from that point on, I felt she never really liked me. What she said in anger was her true feelings about me. We never said too much to each other after that, and it's been thirty-five years since that dreadful one-sided conversation. I had the maturity of a first-grader, but I clearly understood that she considered me dark and ugly, and worthy of a beating for doing something she had to know I didn't understand.

I knew I was dark, but to use the term "ugly" with it was something that really ripped through me. As young as I was then, I knew that the term was something that was negative, demeaning, and condescending. Right then it made me feel unloved, dejected, and really, really hurt. Those were emotions I would experience for a long time, on top of the confused emotions I carried after being sexually abused by my father.

Looking back on that summer, I think I played at being a baby because that was my way of coping with my father's repeated sexual abuse. Being a baby denoted innocence and simplicity. I probably needed therapy from a psychiatrist, but since that would never have been part of my young life, my mind found a way to deal with everything.

The other thoughtful observation I made in retrospect about that summer was that I believe Aunt Joy was so frustrated because we lived far from the shopping plaza, and she knew the next time she could purchase pads would be at the first of the month when Grandma go her SS check and we all loaded in and on the back of my uncle's pickup and headed miles up the road to do our shopping for a whole month. It was a long ride there and back and we made a full day out of it. Grandma purchased all her supplies she needed until the next shopping trip, so I'm guessing Aunt Joy knew she had to wait until the next trip for more pads. I'm also guessing her period didn't wait for her to replenish her pads.

It seemed like Aunt Joy was eager to leave the house and the small town, and as soon as she graduated high school, she did just that. As for me, it felt good to be a baby sometimes, as an escape from the real world around me. Now keep in mind that I honestly didn't know what feminine pads were back then, so it was natural for me to mistake them for baby diapers. And also, I had no idea of the cost of pads, or budgets, or having to wait for monthly visits to the store to make purchases as important as sanitary pads. I had no understanding of why my Aunt Joy turned on me like she did. Truthfully, even though I get it now that I'm grown, I still feel she went too far in hurting me so deeply by attaching my dark skin to being ugly.

It took me awhile to connect sanitary pads, rather the absence of these pads, with conceiving and having a baby. And it took me a very long time to grasp the concept of how babies were conceived and delivered. All I could remember was Mama getting fat in her stomach, and sometimes my Aunt Theresa would come stay with us for a few days. Daddy never really liked her to come, probably because her presence cramped his sexual activities. Nevertheless, when Aunt Theresa came, we were glad. I loved her so much, but I never told her that as a child. I thought she was the prettiest lady in the world. She was "bright skinned," with pretty, thick hair, and big brown eyes with long lashes. She seemed to always have a nice, fast car. I remember that Mark 7! She smiled a lot and always seemed to be happy.

I wanted to have her kind of happiness when I grew up, but I also wanted her confidence and beauty. "Bright skinned" seemed to always be attached to what was universally accepted as beauty. Well, I wasn't bright skinned, which added to my perception that I wasn't a pretty girl. I used to admire a lot of women who had light complexions, also known as being "bright skinned." I wanted to be like them. It may have been twisted logic, but in my young mind, I think I felt that if only I were not dark-skinned, I would not be abused at home, taunted at school, and generally miserable most of my waking hours. I was in love with my Aunt Theresa.

You would think I learned my lesson about snooping around other people's things, but there was a time when I would go through my mom's dresser drawers, and then I would sneak and read her *TRUE DETECTIVE* magazines. I didn't understand everything, but I did know that my mom's magazine was for adult readers. Looking back, I think I just wanted to know my mom. I wanted to read what she read. It was like I was always searching for something. I now know I had a hole in my heart, and I just wanted to fill it with something -- anything would do. We were a family of non-communicators; as strange as it was, my mom didn't seem to know much about me, nor did I know much about her. She didn't do much talking, and since I thought I had little to say, I talked even less than my mom.

I don't know why, but I also had this strange habit of going through the trash; it was like I was always looking for something. For example, I remember finding a perfectly good half-eaten sandwich, something Daddy would have tossed in the trash after he came home from a watermelon run. I wanted to find it before the others did. Now I can't tell you that the others looked through trash, or sought to find food that had been tossed in the garbage. But I can say that for me, I just wanted to be the one to find the food, so I could hide and eat it without sharing.

I know, you must be wondering why was I going through the trash when my dad had so much money. If our dad were treating us the way he should, I don't think I would have had to do that. I guess he was just a "dead beat dad." Back then the term wasn't used as frequently as it is now, but I guess that was what he was. I can empathize with a man who doesn't take care of his kids because he doesn't have the resources to do so. But I cannot understand someone who has money, but refuses to treat his family the way he knows he should.

I was now sixteen, and had even found myself a boyfriend. He was older than I was and we had been talking for a while. I met him when I was almost thirteen. At that time I used to go to and from my Aunt Mazie's place in Tampa. Here is how it happened. I was on my way to the store on foot. A boy others called "John" was out at the park, with the hood and trunk of his *Grand Torino* opened. A bunch of different guys of different ages were with him. They whispered among themselves and sort of bet no one could talk to me because I didn't give guys a chance. I heard someone in the group say, *"She must think she is so cute."*

Michael Jackson's "Billy Jean" was a popular song at the time. I heard another guy said, *"She ain't going to talk to you, that's Billy Jean."* I saw when he smiled at that comment, and from that moment I knew I wanted to talk to him. I was too shy at the time, so I kept walking, regretting in my mind that I didn't at least say, "Hello." I returned to my Aunt Mazie's home, and didn't return to that neighborhood until the next summer. I thought about John from time to time, hoping to meet him when I came home again.

That next summer I saw John again. I actually went to look for him to see if he was still interested. I had never had a boyfriend and I wanted one. I was excited to know that someone liked me, but I needed to know the truth, and there he was out in the park. It was like a party there. There was lots of loud music, and guys were fooling around with their car stereos and making lots of noise. He saw me, and I could see a smile on his face. He shouted out to me, *"Hey, I see you're back in town."*

My heart was in my throat. I had never had a guy speak to me the way he was speaking to me at that moment. It seemed a little playful, but also sensual. I said, "Yes, so what is it to you?" If I sounded rude, I never really meant it that way. It was just that I didn't know how to really communicate well with people, especially boys. I knew he was older than I was, but how much older, I didn't know. He was about five-feet, eight. He parted his hair down the middle and wore braids. That, plus the fact that he was very skinny made me think of *Snoop Dog.* His complexion was one shade lighter than mine. Even though his teeth protruded a bit and he had hairy nostrils, I thought he was a hunk!

I stayed in the park, pretending to be watching the guys, but I wanted him to come over and talk to me. I didn't have to wait long before he made his way over to me. *"Hello, how are you?"* "I'm okay," I responded stoically. I didn't want him to know how excited I was that he was actually talking to me. Meanwhile I could hardly contain myself. Finally it looked like I was going to have a boyfriend. Most girls my age were already having intimate relationships. The guys in the park thought I was being proud, but they wouldn't understand that pride wasn't the reason I wasn't with anyone at the moment. It was low self-esteem. I didn't feel as if I were good enough for anyone. What my dad had done to me made me feel unworthy, as if I were incapable of being loved. In my mind I didn't think anyone would want to love someone whose dad had used that person and made her feel like trash.

"My name is John, what's yours?" he asked. "Veronica," I responded. I knew where this was leading, and it was the place I wanted it to go. I was longing for someone to love me because I had felt as if I would never find love, at least the kind of love to which I would gladly surrender my heart. *"How come I have never seen you before?"* he asked. "I stay in most of the time; I don't have anything on the street." *"Well, you have me now."*

"Are you trying to tell me that you live on the street?" I asked, with a chuckle. *"No, you know what I mean."* I looked at his car; the music was playing loudly in it. "You like loud music, don't you?" *"Yeah, all my friends do. You wanna go get something to eat? Not now though, later. I still have something to do with my car."* "Sure." I wasn't even sure I was hungry, but the invitation made me want to devour anything at any place where he wanted to take me. *"You wanna meet me later?"* "Where?" He flashed a smile of white teeth. *"Meet me back out here in a few hours, OK?"* "Sure."

He was nice and cordial. I was feeling very excited as I walked away, but I didn't let him see how excited I was. When I got home I put on my clothes about three hours early and left the house. I sat out on the bleachers in the ballpark because I figured no guy would come to my house. I sat out there until I saw him coming. As usual the music in his car was blaring. I didn't want him to know that I couldn't take any company home. Anyway, I got into his car and we went uptown; we were going to get some *Dixie Fried Chicken.*

I was in his car, and this was definitely somewhere I wanted to be. For the first time in my life I was close to someone I wanted to be with. I was nervous, filled with great anticipation, already thinking of having a relationship with this guy. I knew he must have felt the same way about me. After all, he had invited me out, and he had kept his promise and come back and picked me up. Now here I was in his car.

On our way uptown, we talked; he wanted to know why he hadn't seen me before now. "I guess I like staying in my house; there are too many things going on the street that I don't like," I said. It seemed like he had forgotten about seeing me last summer when I was visiting from Tampa. I didn't remind him about that. *"So I guess you're one of those good girls?"* "Yeah, you like good girls, don't you?" *"Yeah."*

"Why were those guys calling me "Billy Jean?" I heard them you know." He looked at me and smiled. *"They were just saying that you were a cute girl, but you think you're better than everyone else."* It made me feel good to hear someone saying that I was cute. "Well, I don't think I'm better than anybody else; it's just that I'm not as brave as those other girls are." *"What other girls?"* "The ones who have boyfriends." He looked at me, *"Are you saying you don't have any?"* "If I had one, I don't think I would be in the car with you." He had a look on his face that made me wonder if he were puzzled about something. *"You have never had one?"* "No."

He looked at me as if he couldn't believe me. *"Serious, you have never had a boyfriend?"* he asked as if he were finding it hard to believe. "No, really I have never had one." But then I felt like adding, "But don't think you're going to be having a virgin; I'm far from being one." Of course I would never speak that out loud. A sudden sadness came over me and I turned my attention to looking outside the window. A tear trickled down my cheek as I tried to imagine what my dad could have been thinking when he was using me, his daughter, for his own sexual pleasure. Well, I had to be a big girl right now, since I couldn't let John see me crying. I used the back of my hand to dry my tear. He saw me and asked, *"Are you okay?"* I looked at him and forced a smile, "I'm okay." *"You're sure?"* I didn't know how to receive genuine concern for me – just me. "Yeah, I'm fine; don't worry about me."

I got myself a four-piece chicken with fries and coleslaw. I didn't eat that much, but I was thinking about my mom. I wanted to take some for her. I wanted her to be proud of me. I wanted her to know that I was thinking about her. You see, I did love my mom, and I knew she loved me too, but sometimes I wonder if she were just too naïve to have known what was happening. I mean it was happening right in front of her face, so how could she not have seen it? I didn't know anything back then about adults who are in denial about situations too painful for them to address, but that was probably what was happening to my mom. She felt helpless to do anything to save me from my father and her husband. I found myself feeling sympathy for her.

John and I talked for hours abut a lot of things. It was easy to talk to him. I felt like he didn't make fun or seem aggravated about anything I said. It felt like finally someone was actually listening to me when I had something to say. I found myself freely sharing information about my life that I hadn't shared with anyone else on earth. John encouraged me to talk, saying this was the only way he would get to know me.

We eventually arrived at the movies and I ordered everything I could think of. John never said a word about the cost or the amount of food I was consuming. He tried once or twice to steal a kiss, but I turned him down by turning my head away from his lips. I really wanted to kiss him but not with popcorn breath. So he asked if it was OK for him to put his arms around me and hold me. To that, I said, "Yes," and having his arms surrounding me made me feel safe. I had a real boyfriend who enjoyed my company, liked the food and the movies we saw, and provided me a meal to take home – the chicken I never intended to finish eating myself.

After the movies, John drove me home, and just as I was getting out of his car he stole a kiss. This time I didn't push him away. His long, stiff, skinny tongue forced itself to the back of my throat, followed by a full mouth of spittle. I maintained my composure, but that was not what I had imagined kissing John would be like. I exited the car as he told me he really wanted to see me the next day. I agreed, and then quickly crossed the field to my home. I couldn't let John see my home because my parents didn't know I was dating. I felt so good bringing a good portion of chicken home, which my siblings and my mom devoured quickly.

John and I hung out every chance e got, which was about three or four days a week. I really liked him, and I appreciated the fact that he was nice and very generous. After we spent hours together talking, I would leave feeling like I couldn't wait until we were together talking again. We both knew that once school started, we'd be tied up with schoolwork and have to hang out on the weekends.

Sure enough, it was back to school again; the weekend was over and it was time to face this place called school, a place I had come to hate. As I had mentioned before, I didn't have a lot of friends here. I wasn't talking to Sandra while she was here, and Monica was a bit mad with me for not communicating with her while I was in Tampa. I don't know what was happening, but boys were paying a lot of attention to me now. I knew I was filling out my jeans and I felt in myself that I was looking good, despite the terrible comment my Aunt Joy said in anger when she threatened to "beat my black behind."

I was trying to keep my head up and always show a positive personality. The incestuous, nonconsensual relationship that I had had with my dad had ended. I knew it was to his chagrin, but it was to my delight. I was feeling good; I had found myself a boyfriend and for once in my life things seemed to be looking up for me.

I was going to my class one day when this boy held my hand. I didn't know who he was, and so I roughly pulled my hand away from him. He looked at me angrily and said, *"You think you are better than everybody else, don't you? But don't worry; I know your secret."* He then turned and walked away. I was scared. I didn't know what he was talking about. I was hoping it wasn't this secret that I had been trying to hide from everyone. As I watched him walking away, I could feel my heart sinking. Had someone been talking? But who could it be? I never told anyone what my dad had done to me, so how could he have known?

When I went to my class I was extremely sad. Monica saw it and asked me about it over lunch. When I saw her approaching me, I was a bit surprised; we haven't spoken in a while. We were in the cafeteria. She pulled a chair and sat in front of me. *"Are you okay?"* she asked. I forced a smile, "Yeah, why did you ask?" *"I noticed you were pretty sad in class this morning."* She was right, but I wasn't about to break down emotionally and share my life. "You know how much I hate school; I wish I didn't have to come," I lied. In a sense it wasn't completely a lie. I did hate school, but that wasn't why I was so sad that morning. I would never tell her truth.

She may have changed the subject to give me insight about our relationship becoming more distant. *"Well, it seems sometime like you're not even coming, one minute you're here, the next you're gone."* I got her point right away. Who wants a best friend like that? "If you're talking about Tampa, I won't be going back there anymore; my Aunt, whom I used to stay with, is dead." *"I'm sorry to hear that"* Monica said with real sympathy in her voice. "It's okay. So how are things with you?" *"Not bad. My mom is still working; dad has turned his back on us. We're used to it by now."* "I'm sorry." "That's okay, it was for the better. My mom has learned to be independent; she knows now that she can do without him, which is something I've know since I was able to understand what a controlling man was."

I looked at her; she was looking as attractive as ever, and she would be one about whom you could say, *"You don't look like what you been through."* Actually, that would fit me, too! Monica noticed my appearance about the same time I noticed hers. *"You're looking okay. I guess you're taking everything in strides. You seem to be coping with school even though you said you hate it."* "Yeah, I'm coping. I wish I didn't have to come back here." *"Well, since you're here you might as well make the best of it."*

I wasn't aware of exactly how old John was, but neither was he cognizant of how old I was. I had lied to him about my age. I knew if I told him I was sixteen, he wouldn't have wanted to talk to me, and I couldn't afford to lose his friendship. I didn't mind that he was older than I because I didn't think I could ever feel comfortable with someone my age. John had told me that he was twenty, and he looked young enough to be, so I didn't bother to question him.

116

Now I was trying to forget about John in school today. I wanted to know what he knew. What my dad had done to me wasn't something I wanted to be made public. I wanted to leave it behind, just the way I had left him behind. I was still living in his house, or trailer rather, but it was like we weren't having a relationship. I had made up my mind that I didn't want anything to do with him ever again, and I was serious. My dad had mentally maimed me; there were times when I felt as if I were dead inside, times when I felt as if my life was over. I was only sixteen and yet I had such a terrible secret that I needed to hide from the world.

Well, I had to say thanks to Sandra's mother. She and I were just talking at school about Monica. Her place wasn't the best, but at least I could go there to get away from my dad. The crowd there wasn't an alluring one, but I wasn't being forced to participate in something I didn't want to take part in. Here I had my free will to guide me. If I did something, it was what I wanted to do and not what anyone forced me to do.

her place wasn't the best, but at least I could go there to get away from my dad. The crowd there wasn't an alluring one, but I wasn't being forced to participate in something I didn't want to take part in. Here I had my free will to guide me. If I did something, it was what I wanted to do and not what anyone forced me to do.

Sandra, too, had a boyfriend. He was older than she, and was abusive. I went to her home one evening because I didn't see her in school and wanted to know why. When I got there, the usual crowd was there, but I didn't see her. She would normally be outside with them on the porch, but she wasn't there. When I asked one of them where she was, he told me she was inside. I made my way inside. The house was messy, with the usual clothes strewn all over the living room. The couches were raggedy and old. In the kitchen there were always dishes that needed washing.

The door to Sandra's was open. When I went in, I saw clothes lying on the floor; the room was in a mess. She was lying on the bed with her face turned to the wall. She was still in her nightclothes. "Hey, Sandra, are you okay?" I asked. *"I'm all right,"* she said, but I knew something was wrong. "He beat you again, didn't he?" I asked. She rolled over onto her back. I could see she was crying. Her face was swollen. I was shocked at what I saw. "My God, did Gary do that to you?" *"Yes."*

"Why don't you leave the guy?" *"And do what? He gives me things."* "So what? Are you going to let him kill you just because he gives you things?" *"You don't understand,"* she said. "No, I don't, so tell me. Why are you sticking around this guy when all he does is beat you up?" *"He didn't mean to do it and he said he was sorry."* "This is not the first time, Sandra." She had a pitiful look n her face like she didn't want to hear any more truth from me. *"He said he won't do it again."* "Leave him." She looked down towards the floor, helpless. *"It's not as easy as you think to leave someone."* "So you're going to stay around and let him kill you?" *"He is not going to kill me."* I could tell from her weak insistence that he wouldn't kill her that she wasn't sure if he would or wouldn't attempt to kill her.

"Have you seen your face?" *"No."* Sandra was fair-skinned so you could readily see that her face was red as well as swollen. "Well, maybe you shouldn't, but it looks terrible." *"Why do you think I didn't go to school today?"* "What did your mom say about this?" *"Nothing."* "Your mom didn't encourage you to go to the police?"

She looked at me as if I were crazy. *"No, mom doesn't want him to get arrested."* That made no sense to me at first. "Why?" She was about to answer when I held up a hand. "Oh, don't worry, I know, he gives her things too, right?" "*Look, you can say what you want to say; your father is rich; you don't need anything.*" I didn't know whether to laugh or cry out loud at her last statement. Of course everyone assumed my dad was rich, based on what they saw on the outside. They had no idea how cheap he was when it came to giving his kids or wife anything more than the bare minimum. "You're right; my father is rich," I said with sarcasm. I wanted to add, but I didn't bother. "So I imagine you won't be in school tomorrow?" "*Would you want me to go to school with my face looking like this?*" she asked with an incredulous look on her face. "I guess not."

I didn't like the crowd that hung out in front of Sandra's house, but I didn't have anywhere else to go. I wanted to get away from my dad, so going anywhere from my house was better than staying there. I left Sandra in the room and went outside for a little while. There were about four boys and a couple of girls out there, and they were talking and making fun of each other. They were obviously under the influence.

Sandra's boyfriend wasn't out there; usually he was one of them in the crowd, but I guess he was hiding out after what he had done to her. This wasn't the first time he had beaten Sandra. He was pretty jealous and if he saw her looking at someone he would get jealous and start beating her up; he was just crazy and possessive. But he was always giving her money, especially after beating her up, which was his way to show he was sorry.

I was beginning to wonder if that was what John would do to me if he thought I was interested in someone else. He was pretty nice to me, but isn't that what they always do at the beginning of the relationship? They are always nice to you. I guess it's just to draw you in, and once they have you, they don't want you to look at anyone else. Sandra's boyfriend was very nice initially, but look what he was doing to her now! He was really hurting her. I was hoping she would get out before it was too late.

It was getting late and I was supposed to meet John tonight out by the park where we had met the first time. The guys who were at the front weren't paying any attention to me, so I sneaked off. When I arrived at the park he was already there and he was alone. I opened the door of the car and got in beside him. He leaned over and kissed me quickly on the cheek. I looked on him and smiled, "You're bold, aren't you?" I asked with a nervous smile. *"Well, I like you."* "Only like?" *"We've just met."* John wasn't about to be shamed into saying he loved me until he was ready. So I said, "Actually we met last year." *"Yeah, but I think you were living in Tampa then."*

I looked at him, "How did you know that? Were you checking up on me?" *"Not really, but if I like someone I try to find out who they are."* "Where is your girlfriend?" He gave a slight smile and responded, *"I don't have one."* "Are you trying to tell me that a nice looking guy like you don't have a girlfriend?" *"Well, I used to have one, but she left me."* "Was it she who left you, or was it you who left her?" He shrugged, *"What does it matter? We're not together now."* "Are you sure?" He looked at me and smiled, *"What, you don't trust me?"*

"Anytime a person is getting into a new relationship, they have got to be careful." I felt my natural desire to establish distance between us rising inside of me, but I fought that feeling because I really wanted to get closer to John. *"You don't have to be afraid of me; I won't hurt you."* My mind went back to Sandra, and what I saw on her face that evening. I'm sure her boyfriend had told her he wouldn't hurt her, but look what was happening now?

I was afraid of being hurt, and I mean physically hurt. Because of what my dad had done to me, sometimes I felt as if I had no feeling inside. I like this guy, but it was like I was forcing myself to love him. I could not afford to be abused again, so I was approaching this relationship cautiously.

When I went home that night it was my mom who opened the door for me. It wasn't all that late, but I could hear my dad arguing with my mom just before she opened the door for me. If it were left up to him, I know he would not have opened the door. It was a Thursday night. I was going to school the next morning, but I still didn't have to get up too early.

I passed my dad at the entrance to his bedroom as I made my way to the room my siblings and I shared. As mom closed the front door and went up to her room, I heard as he said, *"I don't know why you keep opening the door for her. Why don't you let her stay outside? That's where she belongs."* I could almost feel his eyes cutting into my back; I knew he was staring at me in a condescending manner.

He pulled back in as my mom approached him. My mom went in and closed the door of the bedroom and I didn't hear anything else. My mom was very meek and subservient, except for the time when she had shot my dad. She had never done anything to disobey him, but I knew my mom loved me, and I knew now that she was aware of what my dad had done to me. That's why she was not angry when I would come in at that time. Unbeknownst to him she had earlier told me that she would prefer to see me away from him than to see me continuing to argue with him. I had made up my mind that I was not going to allow him to continue to use me, and I was sure that was why he was showing so much hatred towards me.

Chapter 10

It was Tuesday morning. I hadn't gone to school the day before. I was supposed to, but I didn't; I just wasn't up to facing those kids who were a constant bother to me. Anyway, I came to school Tuesday, and was having lunch in the cafeteria when Monica joined me. She had a mischievous smile on her face as she pulled up a chair and sat. *"Hey, you weren't in school yesterday, why?"* she asked. "I just didn't feel like coming; the kids are getting to me." *"Are you going to let them stop you from learning?"* She had a good point, but I had a good response. "They are not going to stop me."

Monica changed the subject. *"Hey, are you going to the prom this year?"* The remembrance of that awful night I went to the prom and had to pay a boy to be with me came rushing to the front of my mind. I had no intentions of telling Monica or anyone about that! "No, I don't think so." *"Have you ever been to a prom before?"* "Yeah, when I was in Tampa." I tried to make my voice sound casual, as if going to a prom was no big deal. *"Did you go with a boy?"* "Yeah," I lied. I didn't want Monica to think I couldn't get a boyfriend, and what's more, I could use this as the reason for not calling her while I was in Tampa.

"Oh, so that's why you didn't call me when you were there," she said. The way she said it was like she had caught me in a lie. *"You had a boyfriend!"* "Yeah." She smiled at me. *"Was he cute?"* she asked excitedly. "Yeah, he was." *"Are you still talking to him now?"* "Yeah, we talk now and again." Monica looked hard at me, as if she was feeling frustrated for having to pull every bit of information out of me. She asked questions meant to bring forth lots of words and some excitement, but I stuck to few word answers, and I couldn't muster enough false excitement about boyfriends and proms to be credible. I stayed in my "safe territory."

"So you're not serious about him?" "No, I'm still in school; I don't want to get serious with any guy." I was lying, but my answer made sense. I liked John and I wanted to have a relationship with him, but I didn't want Monica to know how serious I was about him.

"I heard about your friend, Sandra. Wasn't she loving some guy who started out treating her like a real girlfriend?" "Yeah, but sometimes really pretty and fair-skinned girls attract guys who want to be around them all the time. They get jealous for the wrong reasons, and they start pushing their girl around. Before you know it, that mean side in them comes out and they are doing what this one did to Sandra. I went to see her; she was beaten badly." *"Why won't she leave that guy?"* I thought about my own terrible home life. Why had my Mom never left my terrible Dad? Maybe you get so used to abuse that you think it's all you are worth receiving. "You know she made excuses for him, even suggesting that she did something to cause him to beat her. Now that's just wrong!"

Truth was, I had the same questions about Sandra as Monica did. "I asked her why she really stayed with this angry man, and she said he gives her a lot of things." *"What did her mom say?"* I chuckled. "Her mom is afraid of losing the money too." *"Are you serious?"* "Yeah. Her mom is not working, so I guess she is thankful for whatever money she can get from him." Monica almost stood up from her seat in the cafeteria because she was feeling anger and disgust. *"So she is going to allow him to kill her daughter because of that?"* "Let's hope not," I said in a matter-of-fact tone. I had been through worse trauma, but Monica just didn't know about it.

When I visited Sandra at her home that evening she was looking better; the swelling on her face had gone down a little, and her face was beginning to look normal again. "Why didn't you go to school today?" I asked. *"I'm still feeling like crap, and my face doesn't look the way it should,"* she responded. *"Did you hear anything about this at school today?"* "No." She looked seriously at me, and then blurted out, *"Don't lie to me, Veronica."* "Well, only one person asked me about it," I said as if I were being forced into a confession. She guessed whom I was talking about. *"Your friend, Monica?"* "Yeah." *"What did she want to know?"* Sandra didn't want to draw any more attention than was absolutely necessary. "Actually she was the one telling me about it." *"You didn't say anything to her?"* "I only told her I saw you." *"And I can imagine the graphic way in which you told her."* Sandra had a helpless look on her bruised face now. "Yeah, a little." Sandra shifted in her bed, trying to find a more comfortable position. I didn't ask to see what the rest of her body looked like.

After an uncomfortable pause of quiet between us, Sandra asked, *"Hey, when are you guys going to be moving out of that trailer?"* "You had better ask my dad." *"He can afford a better trailer, can't he?"* "My dad is mean; people who are working for him are living better than we are." *"That's terrible,"* she said showing genuine concern for me. "You're telling me!"

That evening when I went home, I was confronted by my dad. He wanted to know where I was coming from. I hadn't gone straight home from school because I stopped by Sandra's to talk to her and I stayed much longer there than I was supposed to. I didn't care anyway; I wished I didn't have to go home at all. I hated coming home so I'd do anything to avoid coming straight home. If I could have done better, maybe I would not have come home at all.

My dad confronted me at the entrance of the house, just before I climbed the steps going into the trailer. I hadn't answered him when he spoke to me the first time. I was about to go up the stairs when he grabbed my hand. *"I'm talking to you,"* he said. I pulled my arm roughly away from him. I turned and glared at him. "I don't have to talk to you," I said angrily. I had found my voice and he should have noticed that fact before now. *"As long as you're under my roof, you're going to respect me,"* he said sternly, trying to regain control of the conversation. I could see that he was angry, but I didn't care.

I chuckled, pointing my finger up towards heaven. "You really call this a roof?" I asked. "This place is a mess. You can do better, but all you want to do is to please yourself." I had lost all fear of this man, so I felt comfortable saying everything that had been on my mind since I was a child. I turned and walked up the stairs, opened the door, and went into the house. Since lately we had been having a lot of arguments, I wasn't afraid to let him know how I was feeling about him. He knew what he had done to me. Sometimes I felt as if I was nobody, and that was all because of the things he did to me. At this time I didn't have it in me to forgive him; all I could feel for him was hatred. The very sight of him was enough to turn my stomach.

I couldn't get my mind off what that boy had said to me in school that day. He claimed to know my "secret," and I decided I was going to confront him the following day. I wanted to know what he knew. I would surely go crazy if the whole school were made aware of what my dad did to me. As it was, the kids were already terrible to me, and they didn't know that about me. What would they do if they knew? I had to find out how much of the truth he knew.

I found out who he was -- Andrew White, footballer, who played for the Clewiston Tigers. I also gained the knowledge that he was pretty popular. With him being so popular, I knew that was going to make it harder for me to approach him. Luckily I saw him by himself in the cafeteria when I went for lunch the following day, so I boldly approached him, pulled up a chair and sat uninvited in front of him. He smiled at me.

"To what do I owe this honor? Yesterday when I touched you, you roughly pulled away from me. What can I do for you today?" he asked. I looked brazenly into his face, and asked, "What do you know about me?" He was taken aback by my audacity. *"What do you mean?"* he asked. "You said you know my secret. What do you know about me?" He chuckled, *"Is that what is bothering you?"* "It's not bothering me; I just want to know what you know about me."

"Look, everyone has secrets they don't want anyone to know. I just said that because I wanted you to think about it, and in doing so you might want to come back and talk to me, just like what you're doing now." I could tell if he was being condescending towards me, or if he genuinely cared about me. I took him at his word, though, quietly sighing to myself because I was confident that he didn't know my dirty secret.

"So in other words, all you did was to trick me into talking to you?" *"Yeah, and it worked. I've been looking at you for a while now, but you just would never look at me."* My female guard was up now. "Why are you looking at me?" *"You're an attractive girl, very shapely, looks very nice."* I never thought I would have heard that from anyone; after all, I had always felt as if I were ugly. I mean, I knew I was filling out my jeans, and it seemed to be what guys liked, but I didn't think there was a guy in school who thought I was cute.

I was happy that that was all. Now that I knew he didn't know anything about me, I could move on and stop my worrying. I pushed out my chair and told him I had to go. He held onto my hand. *"Why do you have to go so soon?"* he asked. "I have something I have to do." I gently pulled my hand away from him and got to my feet. "See you." I left and walked out.

As I walked away I could feel my heart as it slowed its beating because while talking to him it was beating so fast that I felt as if I were about to faint. I had never been so audacious in my life. I mean, anyone who saw me talking to him may have thought that was the way I was -- bold, without inhibition and unafraid. But they wouldn't like to know what it had taken out of me to just sit in front of him and talk the way I did. I was still an introvert, even though I badly wanted to get out of being one, but I found out it wasn't going to be as easy as I wanted it to be.

Anyway, I was happy he knew nothing about me, and that was the way I wanted it to stay. I didn't want anyone to know about the terrible secret that wasn't my fault. It wasn't because I wanted it to happen, it just happened because the person who was supposed to have known better was taking advantage of an innocent child – his own flesh and blood, no less!

A few adults knew my secret, but they were keeping it amongst themselves; at least that was what it seemed like, and that was okay because I didn't have to have a confrontation with anyone of them, and the ones who knew it, were relatives. My dad was still a respectable person in Harlem, and that fact alone made me know that no one knew about his disrespectable self who shouldn't know.

Things were going well with John and me, and he was very good to me. Even though he knew my dad had money, he actually gave me what he could. He never asked me for anything, not even for sex, but he showed me that he was interested in a relationship. I was glad he wasn't pressuring me for sex because even though I loved the intimacy we shared I was really fearing the day when he would want to have sex with me.

Once I began spending much of my time with John, Monica wasn't seeing me in the park on Saturdays, as she used to do. I was spending as much time as I possibly could with John. I hadn't told him my real age. I actually told him I was eighteen. I didn't know it then, but I was to later find out that he not only had another woman, but he also had two kids and was much older than being twenty, like he told me.

Things were still not going right with my dad and me, and I could see the stress it was putting on my mom. I was alone at home with her one day. I wasn't feeling well and was lying on the bed in my room. She came in there and sat on the edge of the bed. *"How are you feeling?"* she asked in a tender, motherly tone. She used the back of her hand to put on my forehead to see if I still had the fever I had been complaining of earlier. *"You still have the fever. Did you take any of the pills I bought for you?"*

"Yeah." I was lying on my back. Mom may have been a little nervous because she knew just by looking into my eyes that she had failed to protect me from my father, her husband! *"You know you're going to have to talk to your dad, don't you?"* she said. "Mom, I'm not going to talk to him!" *"He is your dad, and you guys can't keep arguing like that."* I began to display the same boldness I had around my dad now. "I wish I didn't have to see him." *"You're under his roof."* "His roof?" I asked with sarcasm. "Mom, you really call this a home? This man has so much money, and look where we're living." *"He is doing his best."* "Mom, he is not doing his best; we're nothing to him. Look how crowded this place is, and how small."

Mom refused to engage further in that conversation, so she brought me back to what she wanted me to know. *"You're dodging the subject; I'm talking about you talking to your dad."* "Mom, I cannot forgive him; I don't know if later on that will be possible, but it's not possible now." *"You hate him that much?"* I almost lashed out at her at that very moment. Of course I hated him as much as she thought, and more! I took a deep breath to gain my composure, and then said in a slightly raised voice, "My dad screwed up my life, Mom; most girls choose the man she wants to take her virginity, so why couldn't I have been given that chance?"

Mom was weak and tired. I could sense she was having a hard time processing all of this, and so was I. I didn't want to make her life any more miserable than it was already, but deep inside, I wanted her to understand what I was feeling for so many years. I couldn't bring myself to push my mother against the wall with guilt, so, just as I had done all my life, I suppressed feelings and focused on loving her because I couldn't bear to hate both my parents. She said meekly "He said he was sorry." "Yeah, but even after that, MOM he still continued and YOU did nothing about it. You never came to rescue your little girl, and now we both have to live with this guilt and shame because I'm scarred for life." Wow, everything in me intended not to hurt her so deeply, and here I was driving a knife right through her heart. Was my need to finally release all my anger stronger than my common-sense knowledge that my mother never had strong character. She was no match for my father.

I quickly shut my mouth, fought back tears, and embraced my mother, who was heading to the kitchen for tissues. Oh, no. I had brought her to deep tears, and I knew how to shut my mouth. I was totally ashamed and deeply sorry for forcing Mom into this whole conversation.

I lowered my voice and got control of my tone. In a much softer voice that was void of finger pointing, I said, "There are times when I wish I didn't have to come back to this place." *"This is the only home you've got."* "Don't remind me," I responded sarcastically. I thought to myself, "What's wrong with you? You just told yourself you would lose the sarcasm, and here you dragged it right out in the open! Stop it!" I wasn't giving my mom a tiny space to keep her dignity, and I tried hard to care about that. But I was very bitter, and there was no hiding that.

"I thought that when I was taking you to church it was teaching you something." I realized she was talking about forgiveness, but how could she understand so little about how I felt and how my life was changed forever when I was a small child? "Mom, I can't, I can't forgive him," I said. There were tears in my eyes. "You don't know how I've been feeling over these years. There are times when I feel worthless, when I feel like I'm a nobody, and it's all because of him."

I think Mom was really moved by my words and my tears. But all she could think to remedy the situation was church teaching. *"Honey, the best form of revenge is forgiveness."* "I don't understand, Mom." Now I was thoroughly confused. *"A lot of times when people do things to you, they want to break you, but if you can forgive them it means you're not broken; it means that you're stronger than they think you are."* "You think that's what dad wanted to do to me?" *"I don't know."* She got to her feet, rubbing her hands nervously. *"Get some sleep."* She left the room without showing me any parting affection.

My mom had never hugged me, no matter what the situation was. It was as if she were afraid to get too close. Actually, her sitting there on the edge of the bed and touching me was the closest she had ever been to me. What she said to me about the best revenge being forgiveness wasn't something strange coming from my mom. She had always been vague when it came to talking to us. She would say something and leave you hanging, wondering what she meant.

I was feeling better a few nights later, and I went to see John. Our meeting spot was the place we had met the first time in the park. He had never invited me to his house, and I was beginning to wonder if it was because I had never invited him to mine. I wasn't thinking he was hiding any secrets from me. If there was anyone who was hiding a secret, that would be me. I had something I didn't want him, or anyone else to know.

For the few days I was home feeling poorly, John hadn't called me to come visit him. I just went to the park hoping to see him because I hadn't seen him in a while and this was the only place I was expecting him to be. He was there when I arrived, and he had a worried look on his face. As usual, when I got into the car beside him he gave me a quick peck on the cheek. But this time I was a bit disappointed. After all, he hadn't seen me in two days, and all he gave me was a quick peck on the cheek. Come to think of it, I didn't know what I was anticipating.

"How have you been?" he asked. "Okay." *"Okay? I've been waiting for you for the past two days."* He just cleared up the matter of my feeling badly because he didn't try to find me earlier. "I was sick; I had the fever." *"I was worried; I thought that maybe you had found someone else and had decided to kick me to the curb."* I smiled, "I wouldn't do something like that." *"Are you sure?"* "Yeah, I'm sure." He had a genuine look of concern on his face. *"So how are you feeling now?"* "I'm better."

"I'm glad. So what do you want to do?" "Maybe go uptown." *"Anywhere in particular?"* "When we get up there I'll see and decide what I want to do from there." Whenever I was with him, he was always giving me the option to do what I wanted to do, which was one of the things I liked about him.

It was funny how we never talked about ways of contacting each other when we were away from each other. He knew where I lived, and I'm sure he was aware of who I was. Everyone in that little town knew my dad and I imagined they also knew his kids. I was afraid to ask John for his phone number because I didn't want him to ask me for mine. In those days, there was no cell phone, so one had to either call one's home, or call one at a phone booth. But the latter was rare; I have never known of anyone who would call anyone at a phone booth.

We had stopped at a little place where they sold ice cream. I was seated on the bench while John went and bought us some ice cream. My mind was far away when he came back and handed me one of the cones.

"Penny for your thoughts," he said as he too, took a seat in front of me. I forced a smile, "Is that all they are worth?" *"No, maybe that's all I've got."* We both laughed. That was another of the things I liked about him; he was always making me laugh whenever I was feeling down. He looked seriously at me and asked, *"What's really on your mind?"*

"Someone said something to me, and it has me thinking." *"Well, it's good to think. You want to share with me what you're thinking about?"* "Maybe another time." I wanted to know more about him, but then I was afraid to ask, because I didn't want him to ask me too much about myself. You see, I had become good at lying, but it wasn't something I enjoyed doing. I did it because I thought I had so much to hide. I didn't want sympathy from anyone, and at the same time I didn't want anyone to look condescendingly at me because of what I had been through with my dad.

I tried to brighten up. I looked at him with a smile on my face. "The name 'Billy Jean,' you know it almost got me into trouble," I said. He looked at me with a perplexed look on his face. "How come?" "I was living with my Aunt in Tampa, and she thought they were referring to Billy Jean King, the tennis player." *"So what? She thought you were gay?"* "Yeah, exactly; she thought I was gay." *"So I imagine she wanted you to stay far away from her."* "You're right again." He looked me up and down in a cute and sexy way, and then said, *"That woman must be crazy or something."*

"Well, she was crazy all right; she made my life miserable." *"Is that the reason why you haven't gone back?"* "No, originally I was staying with another Aunt who died, and then I started living with her." *"So she was pretty mean to you?"* "Mean is not the word I would use! She was downright terrible." *"Well, I'm glad you're out of that."* He looked straight into my face. I blushed and turned away my face. *"Has anyone ever told you that you're cute?"*

I wanted to laugh. All my life I had thought I was ugly, and now here was someone telling me that he thought that I was cute. I didn't know what to think. I looked at him. "Maybe you need glasses," I said. *"You don't think you're cute?"* "I don't know. I look in the mirror, and all I see is this dark person looking back at me." *"And what do you think?"* I shrugged, "I don't know." He held my face in such a way that I had to stare into his face. *"Let me tell you something; you're a beautiful girl, so don't let anyone tell you different."*

Well, if his plans were to build up my self-esteem, he lifted it a little right there because I did feel pretty good with that comment. But then the thought of what my dad had done came back to me, and that lift I just got went flying out of my mind. This was one of the reasons why I found it so hard to forgive my dad. One minute I would feel good about myself, but then somewhere deep in the back of my mind this image of him and what he did to me would rear its head, and I would be back to feeling as if I were a nobody.

Chapter 11

When I got home that night, my dad wasn't home. I was glad because I was tired of the confrontations we had been having lately. If it was fun to him, it was excruciating for me. I was really sad whenever I had to go back to the trailer. There were too many sad memories there for me, and I wished I could just go somewhere else and never return. I was having such a fun time this evening, and then suddenly my mind went back to what my dad had done to me, and I was loathing him all over again. I was sad, really sad! John realized something was wrong, so he was the one who suggested that I go home when I did.

There were good times in my life, but they were few. One was when my maternal grandmother from Lake Placid, Florida would visit us. She loved to smile and we would always eat *KFC*; the coleslaw and biscuits were my favorite. I remember reaching down into the bucket, feeling for the breast, which was the largest piece of the chicken, and eating it with all the original fries I could get my little hands on. Those were the days.

And then there was Mrs. Gloria Riley, my mom's best friend. I loved to watch her walk. She was tall, what we called "hippy," and had big curvy legs and a small waist. She spoke proper English with a strong Jamaican accent.

When she walked, she moved so gracefully and seemingly without effort. I will never forget the weekend we got the news that she and her son had been missing for a few days; it was the weekend one of my sisters or I was supposed to have stayed the night with her. You see, every other weekend, one of my three other sisters or I would stay a night with her. She had one son and he was in college, so most of the times she was alone, and she hated being home alone. Looking back I think maybe she was afraid. I loved staying the night because we had our own bedroom. At home there were eight of us, including my two brothers who were sleeping on one mattress, which was on the floor due to the fact that the foot and head were all broken. Of course we were the ones who did that! As kids we were constantly jumping on the bed, and predictably, one day it broke down. Dad never even bothered to get it fixed because it was going to cost money, money he so hated spending on his kids.

At Mrs. Riley's home we got to fill the bathtub with hot water. At home we heated a pot of water on the stove when we wanted hot water, so it was nice to run a tub full of hot water. And whichever one of us spent the night had several choices of food for breakfast the following morning. I always chose *Corn Flakes* and pancakes and I ate until I was stuffed. Well, that weekend neither of us stayed the night. I think we had gotten Mama mad and we were not allowed to stay. All I knew was that the following overnight stay would have been mine, and I was excited. But Mom was so pissed that she said no one was going, so no one went.

Later that week Mrs. Riley and her son's bodies were discovered in their house beneath the bed. We were told that someone had broken into the house while they were asleep, and literally chopped them up into pieces and stuffed them under the mattress. We cried for weeks over her death. I cried mostly because she died and now I wouldn't be able to stay the night at her place anymore. In retrospect, I feel selfish for having my primary reason for sadness over such a gruesome act the fact that I no longer had my weekend getaway with all the food and hot water I desired. But I was a kid, and kids think of the "here and now" and "what's in it for me" mindset. So I forgave myself.

Come to think of it, it seemed like even then unbeknownst to me God was watching over me because she died on the night I was supposed to have been there, and I'm sure that the killer would not have spared me if I were there during his rampage. Well, that tragic event seemed to fall into the story of my life, where even in the midst of my happiness, there was a sudden disaster. It seemed as if happiness was never going to be mine. I was too young to appreciate God's favor on my life, so all I saw were my natural surroundings, which seemed to go often from happy to sad and stop somewhere in the middle. My life was a regular roller coaster ride, over which I had no control.

I didn't go to school on the Monday after I heard about the death of Mrs. Riley and her sons. I didn't feel up to it, but when I went to school on Tuesday, I saw Monica, who said she had news for me. But as usual, she felt she had to scold me before giving it to me. We met in the cafeteria where we could talk to each other without any interruption from the class or the teacher. I was seated at a table when she drew up a chair and sat in front of me.

"So you skipped school again yesterday?" she began. *"Why?"* "I didn't feel like coming," was all I said in response. I not only didn't feel like coming to school yesterday, but I also didn't feel like sharing the sad

news today either. Sometimes Monica was so judgmental, without leaving room for a plausible explanation for anything she didn't understand. Still, she was my best friend, so my saying little right at this moment kept our friendship alive and in a good place.

"One of these days you're going to be sorry. You can't keep skipping school like that. It's no good." "Well, I can't go back and correct what I did yesterday, so we've got to move on," I said in a slightly elevated pitch to let her know this conversation needed to change fast. She sighed resignedly before she answered, *"Someone was asking for you yesterday."* "Who was that?" *"Andrew."* "Andrew?" I asked, feeling a bit perplexed. I had completely forgotten about Andrew, the footballer, who had tricked me into talking to him by telling me he knew my secrets. That name brought back a not-so-pleasant memory I never shared with Monica or anyone else. "Who is Andrew?" I pretended not to know him, or even to have heard of him.

"You don't know Andrew, the footballer?" "Oh, him?" I asked, as I pretended that recognition of the name came rushing back at me. "Why was he asking for me?" *"That's what I want to ask you."* Monica leaned in as she whispered that last sentence. She looked like she wanted to giggle, but I wasn't feeling her humor. "I don't know." *"Have you guys ever spoken to each other before?"* "I spoke to him once, no, twice actually." *"So how come you didn't tell me?"* There goes that premature judgment again! "Well, maybe because I didn't consider it important." *"Veronica, the guy is very popular; a lot of these girls are going nuts over him."*

"Are you one of them?" I was deflecting attention from me to her, and she didn't even know how clever I was being. *"No."* "Why not? You're a good looking girl yourself." *"I'm not ready for dating as yet."* "Are you going to wait until you're old and gray?" *"Veronica, I'm still young; I'm just sixteen."* "At this rate, before you know it you'll be twenty and still have no one." She looked serious all of a sudden, and I hid my concern, waiting for her next words. *"It's not going to happen."* I looked at her. I had a sheepish grin on my face. "Are you trying to tell me that you're afraid of men?" *"I'm NOT afraid of men. Why should I be?"* "Because I have never seen you talking to a guy." *"It will happen."* She looked into her plate of uneaten food and there was a long pause with neither of us saying anything. "Well, when it happens, make sure I'm the first one you inform."

I was going back to class later that day when I bumped into Andrew in the hallway. I was walking along with Monica, and we were talking and I wasn't paying attention to where I was going. So when he stepped into my path I bumped into him. When I saw who it was, I stepped back and looked up into his face. "What was that for?" I asked. Meanwhile, Monica had continued walking to her class, so Andrew and I were alone in the hallway.

"I was looking for you yesterday; where were you?" he asked presumptuously. "I didn't know I was supposed to report to you when I'm about to do anything," I responded. I knew that my response was as presumptuous as his was, but I didn't care; he had no right to be questioning me the way he was doing. *"I didn't say you were supposed to,"* he said. This time his retort was not as confident as it was the first time. "Well, then you won't mind if I don't answer that question, now will you?" *"Hey, I like you, that's why I'm interested in you. You don't have to be so rude."*

I could see that his confidence was diminishing, and when a boy's confidence leaves, he usually follows and never returns. No way did I want that to happen, even though I was seeing John at the time. "I'm sorry," I said. I was beginning to feel sorry for him. "Look, I have a boyfriend, and I'm not interested in anyone else." Monica had reached the entrance to our classroom and was standing there, waiting for me. I looked past Andrew just enough to see Monica looking impatient, since I had told her I barely knew Andrew and she told me she wasn't ready for a boyfriend.

Andrew asked if my boyfriend was a student at our school, and I said, "No, he's not! Excuse me," I said as I stepped around him and went to join Monica. I could feel his eyes piercing a hole in my back as I walked up to her. "Is he walking away?" I asked Monica, who was looking in his direction. *"Yeah, he is walking away. He looks hurt."* "I didn't mean to be rude to him; it just happened." I took a couple of deep breaths trying to calm my heart. Monica looked strangely at me. *"Are you all right?"* she asked. "Yeah." I took another deep breath and felt my heartbeats slowing. "Now I'm fine. Let's go." We went and join our classmates.

I was still an introvert. I didn't mean to hurt Andrew, but my reaction to a boy my age, or anyone at my school was like a defense mechanism. I was scared of getting involved with anyone my age for fear of them finding out that I was not a virgin when the time came for that kind of intimacy, so I figured that if I were rude to them, then they would have to leave me alone. In my little mind at the time I thought I was doing the right thing. I didn't hate Andrew; I'm sure under normal circumstances I would have been delighted to have someone like him as my boyfriend, but unfortunately my circumstances were far from being normal.

Sandra and her boyfriend were at it again, but this time she ended up in the hospital and had a miscarriage. A miscarriage? I didn't even know Sandra was pregnant! When I went to visit her, she was in a bad condition; her face was swollen, and I was told she had a few ribs broken. It seemed as if her boyfriend was out to ensure that she never lived to repeat whatever she had done to get him so mad in the first place. She was embarrassed, when she saw me as I entered the room she was in. She was hooked up to a heart monitor which continuously took her blood pressure; she was also being fed intravenously.

"Hi," I said. I was looking sympathetically at her. She turned away her face. *"I know what you're going to say,"* she said. "I'm not going to say anything; you have to know what you want out of life." *"And about the baby..."* "... Oh, yeah, how come you never told me you were pregnant?" *"I wasn't even certain myself."* "What happened?" *"I was just talking to one of my schoolmates at the corner store when he came up and saw me. When the guy saw him coming he walked off. I guess that gave him the impression that I was cheating, or something."* "So what did he do?" Sandra gave out a slight moan as she tried to position her body to be more comfortable.

"It's obvious, isn't it?" "Yeah, but I want the detail." *"All I know is that I ended up here. They said someone had to stop him from kicking me while I was on the ground."* If this had been the first time, or if this beating didn't involve a dead fetus, I might have looked inside myself for tender words of comfort. But for me, this was tantamount to "the last straw." It wasn't my life, but I was fed up on Sandra's behalf. So without much tact or diplomacy, I said, "Sandra, you need to leave this guy; no money that he is giving you is worth your life." *"I know. The thing is that he is okay when everything is going good."* "Yeah, but he turns into a monster for the simplest of things. Where is he now?" *"I heard they have him in jail."* "Are you going to press charges?" She shook her head from side to side. *"I*

don't know. I love him." "The question is, does he love you?" *"I think he does,"* she responded weakly. I couldn't tell if the weak response was due to her injuries, or her doubting in her own mind whether someone who had to be stopped from kicking her while she as on the ground, bleeding and unconscious, could really love anyone besides himself.

I chuckled, "If this is love, I wouldn't like to know what hate is." I was trying to bring the conversation to a more general topic because what we were saying back and forth was too intense for her medical condition. She looked at me in a different way from any look she had ever given me before. Then she said, *"You're young; you don't know what love is."* I knew exactly what she meant, but tried to ignore it. "Sandra, you're not older than I am." *"I'm not talking about your age; I'm talking about experience."* Well, she was right there. Sandra had been having boyfriends since she was twelve; this was my first try with John, and I was hoping it would work out. I kissed her forehead, being careful not to press myself anywhere on her hurt body. I promised to come again, and left. As I walked away, some involuntary tears fell from my eyes. My condition was terrible, to be sure, but her helpless love to an ungrateful monster might have been worse. Who knows?

The two things we never had in our house while I was kid was hot water, and a telephone, so when Monica told me that her mom had gotten the latter, I was a bit jealous. My dad could have afforded anything he wanted, but for some reason he made sure that we never had the best of what we could have had. We lived in probably one of the worst trailers in Clewiston. I could have invited people to my home, but it was not somewhere I was proud of. Monica was pretty excited about the phone that her mother had recently acquired,

142

and who could blame her? I wished then that I could have had a phone too.

We were at school when she told me about it. She wanted to give me her phone number, but to tell you the truth I wasn't too keen on taking it. Maybe it was because I was kind of envious of her. *"Now we can talk on the phone when we're home."* Sure, that's what normal kids do, talk on the phone. But my life wasn't normal, remember? I replied calmly, "Well, our phone is in Mom and Dad's room, and we're not allowed in there." I had lied. *"My Mom has the phone in her room too, but I am allowed to use it."* "Good for you. I wish it was so at my house; we're not allowed to go into our parents' room at all." *"Well, you can call me from a phone booth."* She kept trying to give me ways to call, but I continued to reject them all. I shouldn't have been so selfish and envious, but I was. That's the reality of it.

"I don't like using phone booths; there are always too many people waiting to use them." *"Well, maybe one day you can sneak into your mom's room and call me from there."* "Maybe." Monica knew it was time to change the subject. So she said, *"I saw Andrew yesterday."* "He didn't ask for me, did he?" *"No."* I felt badly all over again for the way I treated him when we met in the school hallway. "I didn't mean to hurt him; I just don't want to date anyone from my school." *"What do you have against the kids in the school?"* "Nothing, I…just don't want to date anyone of them." We went into lunch in silence.

I saw Andrew as he entered the cafeteria. He smiled rather nervously at me and walked up to the counter. "Don't look now, but he just walked in." Monica looked over her shoulder; she saw him. She had her hand on the table and I slapped it. She pulled it away quickly and looked questioningly at me. "I thought I told you not to look," I said. *"If you didn't want me to look, why did you tell me he just walked into the cafeteria?"* "Actually, I did want you to look, but not right now. Not when he can see you deliberately looking at him, because then he'll know that we are talking about him."

Andrew left the cafeteria; he apparently didn't get what he wanted. He looked sadly at me before he left. *"I think you should go talk to him,"* Monica said. "Trust me; he is better off without me." *"You're beginning to sound like an adult."* And I was beginning to feel like one too.

Later that night when I met up with John I asked him if he had a phone at home. If he should ask me if I had one, I could give him the same excuse I had given to Monica -- the one about the phone being in my parents' room and none of the kids were allowed to go in there, ever. I figured that that could work with anyone. He had a sheepish grin on his face when he answered me. *"I had one, but it got cut off,"* he said. "Why?" *"I didn't pay my bill."* "Are you sure?" He just looked at me. Didn't I hear what he just said? *"What do you mean if I'm sure?"* "Maybe you don't want me to call your house because your woman might answer."

"Look, I told you I had a woman once, but we broke up." "Has she ever bothered you?" He looked strangely at me; we were sitting in his car as usual, and we were in the park. *"What do you mean?"* he asked. "You have some of these crazy women out there who think that once they have a man, he belongs to them forever." *"Well, thank God my ex doesn't think like that."* I had to push harder to be sure he was telling the whole truth. "When was the last time you saw her?" *"It's been a while."* "Did you have any kids with her?" *"No."* "Did you use condoms whenever you were having sex with her?" *"Hey, where are we going with this conversation?"* I had to admit to myself that I was getting more

personal than I had a right to, at that point in our relationship. I needed to back off a bit.

I shrugged innocently. "I don't know; I just figured I need to know something more about you. I'm sure you know about me." Hopefully not everything, I thought to myself. *"What do you think I know about you?"* How stupid could I have been to open a door I never wanted anyone to talk through, especially me! Too late! My heart was racing in my chest in anticipation of his answer. I was being bold, and to tell you the truth, I didn't know why I went there; I didn't know why I said he must know about me. I guess I wanted to know what he had heard, just like I needed to know what Andrew had heard about me.

I proceeded slowly, volunteering the obvious. "I know that you know my father, because everyone in Clewiston does." *"Yeah, I know your father."* "What do you know about him?" *"I know that he has money, and that quite a few people work for him."* "Is that all?" He looked at me a bit puzzled. *"Is there more that I should know?"* "No, I was just wondering what you have heard." *"Are you okay?"* he asked. I looked at him, "Yeah, I'm okay. Why did you ask?" He shrugged, *"I don't know. It's just that the last time we were together, you started looking sad and sick; I was wondering if there was something you wanted to tell me."* "No, there is nothing; everything is fine." *"You're sure?"* "Yeah, I'm sure." I made sure to say that last sentence with the kind of emphasis that tells the listener there is no more to be said on the subject.

He put an arm around me and drew me closer to him, *"That's good; I don't want you to be sad. And I want you to know that you can tell me anything at all and I will never judge you or look at you in any way different."* I should have been feeling happy at what he just said, but instead my heart started racing with dread; had he heard something he was not telling me? Why was my mind going places that made me paranoid about my past? I couldn't control it with Monica, Sandra, Andrew, and now the man I hoped to form a permanent relationship with someday – John. Was I so messed up that I would move into adulthood destroying everything in my life that presented itself as potentially happy or good for me? I didn't want that, and I wish now that I had had the intimate relationship with God when I was a teen. God would not have let me keep feelings of inadequacy, paranoia, defensiveness, and misery because God chose me with a special calling on my life since "before I was in my mother's womb." I took a deep breath, vowing to control my mind!!

Chapter 12

Sandra was out of the hospital and was back to being herself again, and guess what? She was back with her boyfriend! I had met Gary, her boyfriend, on a few occasions and for the life of me, I couldn't see what she saw in him. He was about six foot, two inches tall, weighed about two hundred and fifty pounds, and had a paunch. Can you believe it? He had a big tummy, plus he had bulbous eyes. I didn't like him at all. True, I would have found fault with him for beating up on my defenseless friend. But he was not attractive, all by himself!

Anyway, I could see why *she* liked him. He worked at one of the sugar companies in Clewiston, and I heard they were well paid. No wonder she didn't want to lose the money he was giving her. I heard he was very generous too, when it came to giving. He not only gave her money, but he also gave her mother money, which explains why her mother didn't insist that she kick him out of both their lives.

When I went to visit her that evening, the usual crowd was there -- her boyfriend wasn't there, though. The thing about it was that he worked a lot, and hardly had time to hang out with Sandra. She was very upbeat when I saw her. All of them were in the house and some were snorting cocaine, while others were smoking marijuana. None of these people had any shame about what they were doing, and made no attempt to hide it from me. Quite the opposite! They probably didn't care if I got high or drunk and fell out, along with everyone else in the house. To me, all of it was a waste of some otherwise good minds.

I do remember one occasion where I had tried smoking marijuana too, but it didn't work out. This was how it happened. I had gone to Sandra's house to visit, and the situation was just as I described above. I saw them smoking, and I wanted to try it too. I had heard so much about marijuana, and I wanted to know what it felt like to smoke it. So I asked one of Sandra's female friends to wrap a joint for me. She wrapped one, but she put some coke (cocaine) into it too. I took one draw and thought I was going to die; I was coughing up my whole life. Since that day I never tried it again.

It was hard not to smell the marijuana on your clothes whenever you left Sandra's house. So whenever the situation in her home was like this, I would call Sandra outside and we would talk. This particular evening when she came out and closed the door behind her, I could tell she was high. *"Hey, my friend, how you doing?"* she asked, at the same time hugging me. "I'm okay," I said, at the same time trying to break the embrace. Whenever she was in that state of mind and hugging me, her hug was always too tight and I had to break it in order to breathe properly.

She pulled away from me, asking, *"How was school?"* "It's okay. When are you coming back?" She looked like she was thinking hard about how to answer this simple question. *"I don't know. I don't like school."* "Welcome to the club, but you still need to go; you're not an adult." My tone may have been a little sarcastic. *"So how come I feel like one?"* Sandra snapped right back at me. "Well, I guess it's because you're doing what adults are doing." *"What do you mean?"* She looked genuinely puzzled by my statement. So I clarified myself. "You're smoking marijuana." She looked like she was getting offended because I was judging her lifestyle. *"You tried it once."* "Yeah, but I gave it up; it wasn't for me." *"Yeah, because you weren't adult enough."*

Now it was my turn to look puzzled, or even to get a little sassy. "What does that mean?" *"Never mind. How is John?"* Sandra didn't want a confrontation, and to tell you the truth, neither did I. We both changed the subject. "He is okay." *"Have you guys done it as yet?"* She was looking directly into my eyes as she asked this question. I pretended not to understand what she meant. "Done what?" *"You know what I mean."* "We haven't done anything." She believed me. *"You're serious about him, aren't you?"* "I guess." I was very serious about him, but didn't choose to reveal that to Sandra that night. *"Well, pretty soon you're going to have to do it."* I felt defensive, thinking that just because Sandra was having sex, drinking and smoking and skipping school, it didn't have to mean I was having sex with John!

"He is not pressuring me; he knows I have to go to school." *"Do you know he has another girlfriend?"* I proceeded with caution. "He told me he had one." *"What did he say happened to her?"* Where was she going with this line of talk? "He said they broke up." I made my voice sound convincing, although at that moment, I was not convinced. I was lying to myself, like so many young women in love.

"Do you know that he lives with his mom when he is in Harlem?" "He is only in Harlem," I said, thinking she had made a mistake in her facts now. I was wrong. *"No, sometimes he is in Belle Glade."* I really didn't know this, and I didn't like the fact that Sandra did know

it. Still, I needed to ask the next question. "What is he doing in Belle Glade?" "That's where his girlfriend came from. You didn't know that?" "I didn't ask him. And he said that he doesn't have a girlfriend." She had touched a nerve, and now I was ready for verbal combat. I forced myself to maintain my composure. *"They all said that when they want to get into your pants."*

"I like him, and I don't think he is a cheat." *"If you're not having sex with him, where do you think he is getting it from?"* That was a question to which I needed an answer, but I dare not ask it for fear that he might want to turn around and demand it from me. I was not at all ready to give in; as things were I was dreading the very day when I would have to concede to his request for sex. I was afraid that it might feel the same way it felt when my dad was doing it to me. I was anxious to leave Sandra, her home, and her probing conversation that made me second-guess John. I made up a lame excuse to leave right away, promising to return soon. I had no intentions of coming back there.

The next day at school, Monica was talking about going to the prom; she was talking about the dress her mother had bought for her. She was obviously delighted with it. *"Why don't you ask your mother to buy one for you so both of us could go together?"* "I don't like proms," I lied. *"How do you know you don't like proms?"* That was actually a reasonable question, coming from one who correctly assumed I had no experience with proms before right now.

"I told you that I went to one when I was in Tampa, didn't I?" *"Yeah, but you didn't tell me whether you liked it or not."* I was comparing this conversation in my mind with the one I had just had with Sandra. Why did my female friends feel the need to bait me, or pull me into conversations I didn't want to speak about? I wanted to shut her up, so I said, "Well, now I'm telling you."

"You want to tell me why?" Monica was my best friend, and she wasn't letting me off the hook so easily. She wanted to know some juicy details about my prom experience. I shrugged, "I don't know, it's just that too many people were there." As usual we were in the cafeteria, having our lunches. "Veronica, that's a dumb excuse; I didn't know you were afraid of people." Monica was quick on her feet, and I had no comeback right away. "I didn't say I was afraid of people; I just don't like crowd."

"So you're definitely not going to the prom?" "Definitely!" *"So I guess I'll have to go alone."* "You can always ask your mom to go along as your chaperone." I regretted saying that last sentence the moment it left my lips. Monica seemed oblivious to my weak attempt at sarcasm. *"Oh, come on, who wants to go to their prom with their mom as their chaperone?"* "So how are you going to go?" Monica thought for a moment, and then said, *"I guess I'll have to find someone to take me."* "Good luck." Yep, good luck with that! Our conversation ended – for the moment! It was time for me to go home.

I always hated it when I had to confront my dad, but home was where I lived and where I had to go whatever time I had finished dealing with my boyfriend and my other friends. As I walked home that night, all I could think about was the repulsive sight that he had become to me. I no longer felt anything for him but hatred and contempt, and I was hoping that I didn't have to face him. I know it was his home, not mine, but I didn't care. I only went there because I didn't have a choice.

As luck would have it, he was the first one I saw before I went into the trailer. He was at the front door, seated on the stairs. When I saw him I turned and went to the back. The door was unlocked and I entered through it. He didn't say anything to me when he saw me; he just looked at me with that piteous look on his face. I felt sorry for him sometimes, but I wasn't about to talk to him. I wasn't about to make him feel as if I had forgiven him, because I hadn't.

I met my mom in the house. *"Have you seen your dad?"* she asked me. "I saw him," I answered. *"You haven't spoken to him, have you?"* "No, he was sitting on the steps at the front, so I just walked through the back door." *"You guys have got to start talking to each other."* She left me and went back into her room. It occurred to me that my mother would never understand the depths of my pain after being robbed of my innocence, my childhood, and whatever part of my adulthood directly brought me back to the disgusting parts of my childhood. Her comment was meant to pull at my heartstrings, I know, but it took all I could do not to feel the same level of contempt for her. God knows I wanted my heart to soften and be forgiving before I died and had to stand before Him, but that day seemed an infinite distance away, so I could hate awhile longer.

Besides my ongoing saga when having to be in my home, what Sandra said about John having sex with another woman was playing on my mind, so I decided I was going to ask him about it the next time got together. Now I didn't want the whole of Clewiston to know I was dating John because I didn't want it to get back to my parents. Therefore, we always met discreetly. He would be in the park with his car. The music would be turned down, so in that way we wouldn't draw too much attention to ourselves. After meeting there we would then leave and go wherever we wanted to go.

As I sat in the trailer I called home that night, I thought of how cruel our situation really was. We were actually in a two-bedroom trailer and eight of us were living in one room. I wanted to get out of this situation; I was sixteen, but I felt as if I were not aging fast enough. I wanted to be at an age where I could take care of myself and didn't have to depend on my dad because he wasn't really doing a good job taking care of us. If my dad were poor, then I could have understood what was happening, but he was not. My dad had vehicles that he loaned out to one of the sugar companies in Clewiston, but all the money he got from that venture, as well as others, were doing nothing to help us. The sad thing was that my mom wasn't the type of person, who would demand that my dad do better; she was someone, who was content with just being his wife.

As a young child I thought I had a tapeworm in my stomach because I was always hungry. I told you how sometimes I would go through my kitchen trash to find perfectly good, half-eaten food that mostly my father discarded. But there were also times when I would go through my neighbor's trash to get something to eat. She always had lots of food and oftentimes she would throw out food products that were outdated, but looked perfect to me. They were cakes, cookies and pastries. So I would ramble throughout her trash and eat the food. At other times I would go this neighbor's house. His name was Mr. Woodard and he had a blind man living with him, so there was always someone home. I would go to his house every week and steal food, and today I am convinced he knew that somebody was stealing food, but it's like he made the food and drink available. Today I'm old enough to realize that he probably knew I was the thief, but instead of turning me in to my parents or the police, he set food in places where it was easy for me to think I was clever in taking it.

Looking back now I realized that I didn't have a worm in my stomach as I had thought then, but the fact was that my dad wasn't providing enough for us to eat. All my dad was doing was storing up his money. I didn't know if he were planning on taking it with him when it was his time to leave the earth, but he just wasn't spending it on us. I couldn't have been the only child of eight who was always hungry, but the subject never came up among the siblings. Maybe all eight of us found our secret places to find extra food. Wouldn't that be a laugh if the news came out today?

Every time I thought about these things, I found myself with more reasons for hating my dad. He had not only destroyed my innocence, he had also shattered my integrity. Now because of him I had to be living and hiding the real me. How could I forgive someone like this person, who was constantly in my face, pretending to be the father he was not? I couldn't forgive my father, not then anyway, because at that time if I said to my mother that I had forgiven him, I would only be lying, and it would make me a hypocrite. In my mind, and as long as I was able to see him, he would always be the evil he had come to represent in my life.

I wanted to find out more from John about himself. What Sandra had said to me was really bothering me. I had seen a couple of kids approaching him a few times when we were at the park, but I hadn't asked him about them. I didn't think they were his, or maybe I was hoping they weren't his. For some reason I wanted to think he didn't have any kids, or anyone else, but me. You see, I was thinking that one day I would have a man whose only love was me. I was thinking that we would have a family, and I would be the mother of all his kids. In my mind, I was hoping that this wasn't going to change, but I was a bit leery.

That evening when we met, he knew something was wrong. I was a bit quiet, and whenever time he noticed me like that he knew I had something up my sleeves. We were on our way uptown when I turned to him and asked, "John, have you got a girlfriend you're having sex with?" He was a bit surprised. He glanced at me, before saying in a slightly high pitch voice, *"What kind of a question is that?"* "It's just a question. How long have we been dating?" He didn't have to think about the answer before speaking. *"A few months now."* "Well, I'm glad that you're patient, but you've never approached me for sex, so I was thinking that you're getting it from somewhere." *"Look, I'm trying to be a good guy; I want you to know that I respect you, and that I want a real relationship with you, something that can turn into a real future."*

I was happy to hear that, but at the same time I wanted to know the whole truth, especially if a part was hidden. I knew that he was older than I was. He had told me he was twenty, but I knew he was older than that. Most men his age were either married or had kids, and I really wanted to know the truth. "Okay," I said. "I want to know the truth. Have you got any kids?" *"I have got two kids."* My ego was bruised because Sandra knew something I didn't, and if she knew, others did too. Why was I the last to learn of this news? "So how come you didn't tell me?" *"Because you didn't ask."* "If you really want us to be together, you would have told me everything," I responded rather irritably. *"Okay, I'm sorry."*

We both drove in silence for about a minute. Clearly he was finished with the conversation unless I had another direct question. I did. "Who is the mother of the kids?" *"My ex."* "Where is she from?" *"She is from*

155

Belle Glade." Hmmm....that's exactly what Sandra had told me. "Where is she now?" *"She is living at my mom's home."* "But isn't that the home you go to every night?" *"Yeah."* "So are you guys still having a relationship?" Men are natural liars, starting with my father. There was no way in my young mind that I could believe that this man whom I was falling in love with had an ex-girlfriend and kids, lived with my mother, and wasn't still sleeping with that woman. Now I positioned my body to look right at him as we continued driving.

"No, we're no longer having sex or any real relationship." "How can I be certain?" *"If I was having a relationship with her, would I be here with you now?"* "I don't know; men are cunning, they can do anything they want to do, and give a different impression to their woman or women." He sounded annoyed in a controlled way. *"So you think I'm cheating?"* "I don't know what to think." I was more than a little hurt. I liked him and all of a sudden that dream I had had of being the only mother of his kids were shattered.

For the rest of the drive uptown I was quiet. My mind was faraway, wondering why my life was the way it was. It seemed like nothing would ever go right for me. Maybe for me there was to be disappointment for the rest of my life. I was miserable again, and the happiness I always felt while we were together had begun to fade. The question was, "Do I want to pursue that happiness, or consider this news a warning to run the other way?" I didn't have the answer. Wasn't there a song that said, *"Love hurts?"*

When I was born, one of my parents gave me one name, and the other gave me another, and it wasn't as if they were saying one was for my first name and the other was for the middle. No, they both gave me first names. It seemed like even then things weren't going right for me; even at my very birth, things were wrong. Well, I guess this must have set the trend for the rest of my life because nothing appeared to be going right for me, even at this very moment. I was really disappointed because John was the first man who I had willingly surrendered myself to. I knew I was not the first woman for him because he had made that clear, but I was hoping that I would be the first woman to have a child for him. Now that would never happen since he just admitted to me that he already fathered two kids with another woman. My focus at that sad point was not on the fact that the other woman who fathered his two kids was his legal wife. What was swirling around in my head was all about me – only me!

We were almost to our destination, but there was that short pause that seemed infinitely long, where we exchanged no words. When we arrived uptown John wanted to know if I had anywhere particular in mind that I wanted to go. I told him that anywhere he wanted to go was alright with me. John drove up to the lake and parked. There weren't a lot of cars there; the few that were there were parked at a distance from each other. He sat very close to me, placing his hands carefully around my shoulders so that they didn't come anywhere near my breasts. He knew that this was the time for a tender touch, not a sensual one.

"Look, I'm sorry; I thought that you knew about my two kids," he began. I looked angrily at him, but I wasn't angry enough to push his hand away from resting on my shoulder. "How could I have known about your two kids? You didn't tell me anything about them." *"While we were at the park, you have seen these two kids coming over to me, haven't you?"* "Yes, but since you didn't tell me that you had kids, I was thinking they were maybe one of your relatives' kids." *"They are my kids."* "Well, thanks for telling me now," I responded with sarcasm. *"I'm sorry."* He sounded really sorry for

hurting me, and I had to look away from his eyes or I might fall into his arms and forget the whole matter.

"Maybe the next thing you're going to tell me is that you're still along with their mother." *"Now believe me when I say that it's not so."* "Where is she?" He gently turned my face back towards him, and he looked into my eyes. *"The truth?"* I looked at him, responding, "Of course I want the truth." "She lives at my mom's home." "What is she doing there?" *"Well, she used to live with her dad, but he died, and she lost the home that they had, so my mom took her in."* That was a plausible story. But my nature had become suspicious since I was about five years old, so I challenged him. "You sure you weren't the one, who took her in?" *"What does it matter who took her in? I'm not with her anymore, that's what's important!"* I could tell he wanted to be agitated with my probing, but he knew he had messed up, so I had free reign to grill him until I decided to stop.

"Okay, why aren't you with her anymore?" *"She is too jealous, and we used to argue for the simplest of things."* Wait! Did he just say they broke up because of her jealousy? Was I being jealous right now, or was my heart really breaking? No time to reflect on my motives because I intended to keep the focus on John. "Are you sure you weren't the problem?" *"I'm sure I wasn't the problem."* He was looking at me with that irresistible smile of his. I turned away from his face for the second time because I knew I was a sucker for that winning smile. I didn't want him to see that he was getting me weak from just looking at his smile.

"Have you guys ever tried to work it out?" *"Yeah, a couple of times, but we always end up at each other's throat."* "Have you ever hit her?" *"No."* "You're sure?" I asked looking at him. *"Yeah, I'm sure."* "Ever been tempted?" *"Look, I've never hit her, and I'm never going*

158

to hit you either." "Very clever, John," I said to myself. He had just turned the conversation back to me, or him and me. "You'd better not, 'cause I'm not going to lay down and take a hit from any man, no matter how big he is." *"I knew you were a fighter from the moment I saw you,"* he said with a smile. "So are you trying to tell me that you like a woman who likes to fight?" I asked looking at him with a smile of my own. *"No, you know what I mean."*

I turned my face away and looked through the car windows, "What are their names?" I asked, suddenly changing the subject. *"Who?"* "The kids." *"Oh, one is John Jr., and the other is Carl. John is older than Carl."* "I thought so." I was smiling again. In my heart I had forgiven him because I was beginning to realize that I did love him. It wasn't the end of the world if I weren't the only one to have a child for him. Talking about a child, it takes sex to procreate; would I be ready when that time came? That was all that was in my mind, and it was making me anxious with anticipation. What will sex be like if and when I decided to surrender my body to him? Would I be reminded of the times when my dad took me against my will? Will I feel as dirty during and after the process? I hope not, I sincerely hope not.

159

Chapter 13

Well, Sandra did tell me about his girlfriend, which turned out to be his ex, but she never told me anything about his kids. Obviously she didn't know about them because I was sure she would have told me. I felt a little smug pleasure in learning something that Sandra didn't know, since she prided herself on sharing something with me that she knew would make me feel badly. For the briefest moment, it didn't matter that this was news I didn't want to hear. It only mattered that *Sandra* didn't know everything about everything!

John and I ended the evening on a positive note. We kissed. His kiss was pretty gentle and I found that I loved the way he kissed. I hadn't taken the time to really notice that I loved him kissing me, and now I think my heart was beginning to soften about what he had not told me before. He wanted it to go further and maybe I would have gone along with him, but I restrained myself. I didn't think I was ready to go there yet. What's more my heart was racing too much, just as it always did whenever the thought of sex came up in my mind. It hadn't come up in an "out loud" conversation yet, and I was glad for that because it meant I didn't need to respond "out loud" with a negative answer.

I hoped I would get over that need to pull back soon because I could feel myself enjoying sex with the right person. Sadly, all the sex I had to that point was forced and definitely not enjoyable. How would I ever get those nasty memories out of my head so I could enjoy a meaningful relationship with the guy I wanted to spend the rest of my life with? Once more, my mind went to my disgust for my father, who started the whole ugly thing!

I saw Sandra one evening and asked her if she were going to the prom. She said, *"No."* "Why?" I asked her. *"My boyfriend is not going to go with me, and he is not going to allow me to go with anyone else. What about you?"* I was quick to respond to that question. "I'm not going." *"Why not?"* "I don't have anyone to take me." I knew the next sentence out of her mouth would be the one she uttered. *"John can take you."* "I don't want everyone to know that we're dating." *"Where do you think you are? Everyone knows you're dating him."* I didn't want to believe her, after the lengths John and I had gone to be discreet about our relationship. We always met at the public park, and then drove someone else to eat or talk. Hey, Sandra didn't know about John's kids, so maybe she was wrong about this, too. Maybe!

"How do you know that?" *"Veronica, this is Harlem; everyone knows everyone else's business."* She had a good point. Harlem was a very nosy place, with too many people living in too small a space for privacy, secrecy and discretion. Damn! "So all these times when I'm trying to hide while I was going to him didn't make any sense?" *"No, they didn't. Now are you going to ask him?"* "No." *"Veronica, I know you have never been to a prom, but if he loves you he will take you."* "I don't want to ask him." I really did want to ask him, but I had my pride, you know. *"Why, are you too* shy to?" "No." *"You want me to ask him for you?"* Sandra had gone too far now. Of course I didn't want her to ask my boyfriend anything on my behalf. How lame would that be?

"No, your boyfriend might think you want to get into something with him, and you know how he is." *"But I think you should ask him."* I wanted to shut her up. "Okay, I will. So how have things been going?" I was a master at smoothly changing the subject, and she fell for it again. *"Things have been going good."* "So how comes I'm not seeing you in school?" I was actually concerned about this because I knew that without an education, Sandra would always be trapped into relationships with no good men like the one she had. She chuckled, *"Maybe because he doesn't want me to go to school. I don't know what to do anymore, Veronica."* Had she no backbone? Why would she say such a thing, as if she had no choice in the matter of her own education? I would never let a man do that to me!

I knew the issue was not that she had no backbone. It was that she was afraid he would beat her and not stop until he killed her. "You're scared of him, aren't you?" *"Wouldn't you be?"* "Yeah. So why don't you leave him?" *"It's easier said than done."* "What do you think he would do if you decide to leave him?" She shrugged. *"I don't want to know. He told me already that if I ever leave him, he is going to kill me."* Well, finally she actually said what I was thinking for months. I was afraid for her.

I shuddered at the thought that this man was capable of killing my friend, and he would have no remorse if he took that action. This man could be serious in making good on his threat. After all, on quite a few occasions he had beaten her so badly that she could have died. I knew she was scared, but there was

162

nothing I could do to help her. I didn't respond immediately to what she had said, but the way I was looking at her, she must have known that all I felt for her was pity.

"Why are you looking at me like that?" she asked, finally breaking the eerie silence, which had suddenly shrouded us. She already knew the answer. We both did. "I guess I must have been shocked to have heard what you had just said." Now that she spoke about his threat, she felt comfortable enough to tell me this man didn't just threaten her once and never again bring up the subject of killing her. "He had said that quite a few times." "Seems to me as if he had proven it quite a few times too." "I'm still alive."

"Yeah, but each time you barely made it. Maybe one day he is going to hurt you so bad that you won't be able to come out of it alive." I think I may have said too much, or reminded her of something she said to herself in the middle of the night. "Yeah, I have thought about that, but what can I do?" Wow, a revelation came to me just then. I was helpless and felt worthless because I had no one to fight for me. I had no advocate, not even in my mother, who should have protected her child to the point of her own death. Here was Sandra, feeling just as helpless and worthless because she had no one to fight for her. She had no advocate, and she was alone. No wonder she kept saying she didn't know what else to do. She really didn't!

"The last time he hurt you, you should have pressed charges and then let him rot in jail." "He wouldn't have been in there forever, and when he came back out I would have been dead for sure. Don't you think I thought of pressing charges every time I checked my body and saw all the bruises? Being beaten up still beat being dead!" "Girl, I don't know what you're going to do. I wish I could help you, but I can't." In my mind I was thinking that I needed help myself.

I pretended as if going to the prom didn't matter to me, but it did. I had one experience going to the prom and that was the time I had to pay a boy to take a picture with me. It was a disaster, and I knew if I went again, especially with John, I would erase that awful memory and replace it with a wonderful memory. I resented the girls I knew were going. They were always so neatly dressed, and I liked dressing up. I told myself I would push the prom thing out of my head, and then I told Sandra that I would talk to her later, and left.

I really felt sorry for Sandra. She wasn't a bad looking girl, and I knew she could have done better than Gary, but he had money, and he was generous with it. She was from a very poor family. Her father had left her mom when she was fairly young. Her mother had gotten involved with other men, but most of them turned out to be abusive, so I guess she gave up on them. Right now she was alone. She wasn't working and whatever assistance she got from the government wasn't enough. So this money her daughter was getting from Gary helped with what she was getting from the government, and she didn't want to lose it. I tried to wrap my head around Sandra's Mom's logic, but right now she was in danger of losing her daughter. Then she wouldn't have Gary's money and she wouldn't have her precious child either. Didn't she see that?

I remember asking Sandra on one occasion how they met, and she told me. This was how it went down. She was at the corner store buying something for her mom. She didn't have enough money to pay for what she wanted, so when the cashier told her what it cost and she was pretending to search her pocket to find money she knew she didn't have, he came forward and offered to pay. She accepted his offer, and then they started to talk.

That evening she went home with a hundred dollars from him. I think what really caught her fancy was when he was taking out his wallet to give her the hundred dollars and she couldn't help but notice the amount of money he had on him. The wallet was well buffed, and he brazenly allowed her to see that he had much more than that hundred. After that they started dating and of course he started giving her more. He was really generous with his cash, and even though he was quite a few years older than her, it didn't make a difference to her because she could get anything she wanted from him.

Now I could see that she was really regretting her decision to start a relationship with him. He was not a confident person and he didn't really believe she loved him, so she had to be constantly proving that she did. The thing is that she really didn't. I'm sure Sandra would have preferred someone else closer to her age. I am talking about this guy making a better partner for her mother than he made for her in terms of age. He was closer to her mother's age than he was to hers.

Well, it was time for another day at school. At our regular meeting spot, Monica was telling me that Andrew was asking for me. To tell you the truth, I thought he had given up on me after I brushed him off in a very unpleasant way that bruised his ego, to be sure. Andrew was a member of the *Clewiston Tigers* football team. He was a handsome guy chased by quite a few girls. Why was he so interested in me? Why couldn't I be interested in him right back? Why did I seek the comfort of an older man when a boy my age was right in my school and wanted a relationship with me?

"What did you tell him?" I asked her. *"I told him I would tell you that he was asking for you."* I was happy that someone my age was showing interest in me. There were times when I had thought that I was so disgustingly ugly that no one would want to talk to me, but now I have a boyfriend who professed to loving me, and another guy, who was chasing after me. Then suddenly it hit me. Maybe this was all about conquest. Maybe he had hit first base with all those other girls, and now he was looking at one who was seemingly out of his reach. I knew about these guys. They would at times make bets with each other to see who could score with a girl. Perhaps his plans were to see how far he could go with me. If so, I did the right thing by shutting him down at "first base."

Despite what had happened between my dad and me, I was starting to feel a little bit of confidence within myself. I was beginning to feel as if I were somebody. There were people out there who were seeing me, and liking what they were seeing. Even if it were just the outward appearance that they were seeing, it was doing something to my ego. It was making me feel really good.

But I was being wary of these guys, though. If there was one thing that I wasn't going to do, it was to allow myself to be used again. One man had done it to me already, the one man who should have been teaching me to be aware of guys like Andrew, who I knew had an ulterior motive.

"Where were you yesterday?" Monica asked, bringing me back to reality. "What did you say?" I asked. *"I asked where were you yesterday?"* "Home." I lied. There were times when I didn't feel like going to school, and I would just go by the library and hang out. Yesterday was one of those days. I was dying for the day to come when I didn't have to go to school. Of all

the places that I knew, school was the least joyful of them all.

"You're going to regret it you know." "Regret what?" *"Those days you're missing from school."* I truly doubted that Monica was right in cautioning me against skipping school again. "Why?" *"Because you need an education to survive."* "I've seen a lot of people without education who are surviving." Monica was quick, and she wasn't going to let me off the hook that easily. "But surviving how?" Who cared how they were making it when the point was that they were making it. "They are surviving, that's all that matters." I had kept too many dark secrets from Monica over the years for me to start revealing things now. I was about to change the subject, as I was most famous at doing. But Monica beat me to it.

"I would like to one day live in a big house." "Well, you can." It was easy for me to picture her in a big house because she was motivated in school, which means she was destined to go far. *"But I will need money to buy it."* "All you need to do is work to get it." *"I don't want to do just any work."* "What are you planning on doing when you leave school?" I really wanted to know the answer to that question. *"I want to go to college."* "What are you going to do there?" *"I'm going to become a doctor. And then me and my mom are going to go live in Palm Beach."* I knew that place had a high cost of living. "It's an expensive place." *"I know, that's why I want to become a doctor before I go there."*

Well, I wished Monica all the luck in the world. She had always been an ambitious person. I wished that I were as ambitious as she was, but all I wanted to do was to get away from Clewiston and from Harlem in particular. I wanted to get away from my dad. I wanted to forget what he had done to me, but how could I forget something when it was always staring me in the face? Each time I left somewhere to go home, my nightmare resurfaced because it was right there at home awaiting me. Every time I stepped through that door and I saw my dad, my nightmare was there, staring me straight in the face.

I wanted to see John. I wanted to ask him if he would take me to the prom. I guess I wanted to know if he truly loved me. When I met John that night I asked him if he wanted to go to the prom with me. We were beside the lake. Before he answered me, I knew his answer would have been no; I could see it on his face.

"Look, I know we've been dating for a while now, but I don't really want the whole of Harlem to know about us, not yet anyway." I looked at him as if he were crazy, "John, if one person knows that we are dating in Harlem, everyone knows, so that's really a stupid excuse." *"Prom takes a lot of money. You would need a new dress, new shoes and everything."* Well, I couldn't really argue with that. You couldn't wear just anything to a prom; everyone who was going made sure that whatever outfit they wore was brand new. Prom was where everyone got to show off and who would like to go there looking like the dress they were wearing was picked up off the street?

I for one liked to look real good. I loved dressing up because I thought it made me look good. I knew I was filling out my jeans and my dresses. Maybe that was why guys were now paying so much attention to me. And lately I had been hearing the word 'cute' in reference to me. Was I really cute? I was told that words could build as well as destroy you, and now I was seeing it because the more I heard these positive comments, the better I was feeling about myself.

John was pretty kind to me. I knew he had his kids to take care of so I wasn't going to pressure him. He looked at me with this sheepish grin on his face that

I had become accustomed to. I knew he had something up his sleeves. "Would you like to come to my house to visit me this weekend?" he asked.

I knew he lived with his mom, and I knew she was always there, so I wanted to know where she was going to be. "What about your mom?" I asked, "Won't she be there?" *"No, she'll be visiting some relatives in Miami."* "How long will she be gone for?"

"The whole day." That answered a very important question for me. "What time do you want me to come?" *"About twelve."* "What are you going to if I come to see you?" I knew he wouldn't take advantage of me unless I wanted him to, but I wanted to hear his response anyway. *"Nothing you wouldn't want to do."* "You sure?" *"Of course I'm sure. I wouldn't force you into anything you don't want to do." Either John was saying all the right things, or I was feeling so relaxed in his company that I believed everything he was telling me.*

"Sounds like a good idea. Can you cook?" *"Yeah, I can help myself."* "Meaning you can't!" I had struck a nerve. John answered, *" I can too!"* I was feeling playful. "No, you can't." *"I said I can cook and I can."* He thought that saying something with emphasis ended the conversation. He didn't know me as well as he thought. "What can you cook?" *"Anything you want me to cook."* "We'll see how good you are when I come." He smiled, *"You're coming?"* he asked a bit leery. "Yeah, I'm coming," I said, and then I looked at him seriously. "But you had better behave yourself."

A few days later we were at John's house. When he opened the door, he was dressed only in a pair of shorts, and was bare at the top. John was skinny; he didn't have a six-pack, but he looked good to me. The house was a two bedroom. Apparently there was one for his mother, and one for the mother of his kids and the kids. Now the question was where did he sleep?

Almost as if he read my mind, he gave me the grand tour of where he slept, which to my surprise was not a real bedroom but more like the laundry room or the hallway to the back entrance of the house. There were a few plastic carts on which was a pile of clothes neatly folded. Also, there were cardboard boxes marked with what was being stored in them, and a twin size bed with a blanket and pillow draped over it.

I innocently said. "John, you don't have a real bedroom," and he responded by saying something like, *"I don't need a real bedroom to make you feel like a woman."* I felt my heart melting further into my chest. I wanted to come again and spend more quality time with him. I knew it was just a matter of time before I would let myself go all the way. But for this moment in time, I quickly moved to the other parts of the house, checking out the décor. It wasn't a remarkable place. However, it looked better than the trailer we lived in. The living room was furnished with the famous plaid 3-piece sofa, chair and loveseat. Everyone had one of those from the overpriced *Badcock Furniture* store, which was the only furniture store there at the time.

Then I noticed on the coffee table a large picture of a very attractive woman, two small kids and John! I heard John snicker and then say, *"Don't overreact. That's an old picture of my kids' Mama that she gave to my mom a long time ago, and I can't control what my mom put in her house."* I felt like he wasn't 100% truthful but I played along with it. We ended up back in his sleeping room, and after much conversation about everything, and a few kisses in between, the conversation turned to the picture of those two kids and their mother. John promised to arrange for me to meet the kids soon.

When I first learned about John's two kids, I was angry and hurt. But the more I felt like giving my heart to him, the more I opened myself to accepting the kids as a reality in all our lives. John kept his word and brought the kids to the park a couple of days later. I had seen them and had come to accept that they are his, but the one person I hadn't met was their mother. She was conveniently absent from the "party."

John had told me they weren't talking, but I wanted to have the opportunity of meeting her because a woman knows what another woman is thinking. If I saw her, I guessed I would be able to read her heart if not her mind. I'd know how she felt about John, despite what he was telling me about his lack of feelings for her. My problem of not being able to meet her was soon to be remedied. And the way I met her was something I wasn't proud of. I mean when I met her I wasn't bold enough to stand up to her, and it was all because of John.

I remember this night. We had gone to our favorite spot uptown and we had had a good time. Everything seemed to be going well. On our way into Harlem we saw a car parked on the roadside. It had its hood up and its hazard lights flashing. I knew that this meant that this car was not going anywhere anytime soon. When John saw the car he pulled over. There was a lady by the car, someone I had never seen before. She was an older woman, not bad looking, average build, about five feet, two inches tall.

I had this thing in me where I was taught that when an adult was about to enter a vehicle, and if I were riding shotgun, then I should give the seat up to the adult. Without being asked, I unbuckled my seatbelt and went into the back seat. The lady entered the car in an authoritative way. It was as if she were anticipating that I would have moved to the back so that she could sit in the front. We started to move. I should have known that something was amiss by the way she looked at him.

Then I heard her said, *"John, do you think I'm a fool?"* "It's not what you think," he responded. Then he glanced back at me and said, *"Veronica, tell her that you're just my friend."* Without thinking, I said, "Yes, we're just friends." I didn't think she bought it, but she never said anything more to him or to me. I couldn't believe I just folded like that. I didn't tell the truth, didn't make a scene, didn't ask John to stop the car so I could walk the twenty miles home. I lied to make this woman feel better and to keep John from disliking me. What a chump I was!

When I went home that night I was angry with myself. I had been made a fool of. I knew that that was the woman who had those kids for John, and who obviously he was still having an affair with. He had lied to me because he had convinced me that they were no longer together. I also knew that she was living at his mother's home, and that was where he was living too. I could have easily said to John the same words the woman said: "John, do you think I'm a fool?" How daft could one be? I was in love with John, and I was willing to believe everything he said. I was even willing to deny my place next to him by agreeing that we were just friends.

On the other hand, what kind of a woman was she? John could stay with me as long as he wanted to, and apparently when he went home to her there was no problem, so he could continue to do it over and over again. I was sure that if they were arguing, he would not have continued to see me. So the fact that he picked her up by the side of the road and allowed her to intimidate him about me should have been my cue to leave him. What can I say about love? Nothing!

I was hurt. At that moment I felt as if I never wanted to see him again. For some reason, the woman who was John's ex- didn't appear to be this cantankerous woman that John had told me about. Even though I knew she hadn't accepted what we had told her, she didn't argue. The way he had previously described her, if she were that kind of person, I knew she would have blown up in that car, but she didn't. She was as calm as ever for the rest of the time we were there.

When I realized who she was, I was very uncomfortable sitting in the back of that car, and I was happy when I was finally dropped off. I wanted to stay away from John after that, but I was miserable not being in his company. I couldn't sleep, and I couldn't eat. I realized that I was punishing myself, so I decided that I needed to see him so he could tell me what was going on. In the very far corner of my mind, I knew I could discern truth from a lie. But my heart was telling my mind that John had a plausible explanation for everything he did, and telling me to agree with him that we were friends, thus making his ex-girlfriend feel better, was the right thing to do. Yep, it was the right thing to do. Right?

Chapter 14

I hadn't spoken to John in a week, so I asked one of his friends to tell him that I wanted to see him on a particular afternoon. When we met, he wasn't looking as happy as he had always been. I guess my being away from him was affecting him the same way it was affecting me.

For a moment we sat in the car without saying anything to each other. Then he spoke to me. *"I'm sorry,"* he began. I interrupted whatever he was planning to say next. "I thought you said that both of you were no longer together." *"We're not together,"* he said looking far off instead of looking me in the eyes.

"So what was that? Why did you tell me to tell her that I was just your friend?" True, I didn't have the courage to take a stand for myself when he asked me in front of his ex- to say I was just a friend. But it bothered me every moment since I sheepishly agreed with that lie, and it was time to pass some of the pain on to John. *"She lived at my mom's home; I told you that, didn't I?"* "Yes, you did, but what does that have to do with anything?" *"Well, I live there too."*

I knew he was trying to appeal to my sense of avoiding confusion, but I wasn't in a sympathetic mood. "So what are you saying?" *"Nothing."*

"Come on, John, are you trying to tell me that because she lives at your home, you two have to be into something?" *"No, but think about it this way. You and I are having a relationship, but we're not having sex."* "I thought that you were waiting until the time is right." *"When is the time going to be right?"* He had a point there. Why invite a problem between him and the ex-, while they were both living under the same roof, if his relationship with me wasn't sexual.

I shrugged "I don't know," I responded rather irritably. *"See, you don't even know yourself. What am I supposed to do in the meantime?"* I looked seriously at him, "Are you trying to tell me that you can't live without sex... even for a little while?" *"No, I'm not trying to tell you that. I know that you're hurt, but it's no good making decisions when you're hurt."*

I was really feeling irritable now. I hated being deceived and I was certainly beginning to feel that I had been misled. I was falling in love with John and didn't want to end the relationship, but I didn't want to continue with something I thought wasn't going anywhere. I looked at him. I wanted to hear this out of his mouth, so I asked, "So where is this going, John?" *"What do you mean?"* "I'm talking about *our* relationship -- where is it going?"

"I'm telling you the truth when I said that Joan and I are finished." "Is that her name?" *"Yeah, her name is Joan Anderson."* "How long were you guys together before you broke up?" *"Actually we broke up last year; we were together for five years."* "She looks like a nice lady." I had to admit that, based on her behavior when we three were in the car together. *"She has her ways, but we're not suited for each other."*

I really wanted to see his facial expression when he answered my next question, "Are we suited for each other, John?" *"It hasn't been easy for me, you know.*

These last days have been rough." "Why?" I already knew the answer, because they were rough for me, too. *"Because I miss you."* "I miss you too," I said softly. *"There were few nights when I just couldn't sleep."* "Me, too. Does that mean you love me?" *"You know I love you,"* he said. He leaned over and put an arm around my shoulders and drew me closer to him. At that moment he could have been lying, but I didn't care. I just knew then that it felt good to hear someone saying that he loved me.

All my life I had felt unloved and now I had someone saying he loved me. I cuddled up to him. I had told John that I had never had a boyfriend, but that was stupid of me. I should have told him I had a boyfriend, so he wouldn't be surprised when he found out I wasn't a virgin. That was one of the things I was scared of. How was I going to explain to him why I wasn't a virgin?

John definitely tried to make up with me by asking me to come to his home once more, because his mom and everyone else in the household would be away. I went. So there we were kidding around on the couch, kissing and cuddling. I loved kissing, and I figured that would hold him off for the night. I still wasn't ready to give in to him as yet. I wanted him badly, but I was still scared of committing the act itself while I felt only pleasure instead of disgust. Then there was the reality that I wasn't a virgin.

Suddenly we heard his mom talking outside and then we heard the key in the door. We jumped off the couch. *"Damn, that's mom,"* said John. That was obvious to me! My heart was in my throat, and I started crying, while instinctively buttoning my blouse. He put a finger to his lips, softly saying, *"Be quiet."*

She opened the door. When she saw me, she looked me up and down and asked, *"Who the hell is* she?" I could tell John was as scared as I was. He looked at his mom, *"Mom, she just had to use the bathroom,"* he lied. I was very scared of this little lady because I could see she was very angry. She was stocky, short, around five feet, but had a very stern look on her face. I was trembling as I looked into her face, hoping that John would just hurry up and get the screen door open so I could get out. I didn't want to pass her on my way out, but she was standing in the path of the front door.

As soon as John got the back door opened I was out. I was scared and was running as if for my life. I didn't see the clothesline and ran right into it. It caught my throat and threw me down on the ground. I was so scared that all I could think about was that the lady was attacking me. I got up quickly and started running again. I finally made my way out of the complex. Close to my home, I stopped, brushed myself off, dried my tears, swallowed my pride and walked boldly home.

That night I cried hard and long. I couldn't sleep. I was wondering what I had gotten myself into. I had heard rumors that it wasn't good to date a man who was still living with his mother. John was old enough to find somewhere of his own; he was working. All I was thinking about was the humiliation I had just gone through. I knew it would be all over Clewiston the next day.

The following day a friend of John's saw me and told me that John and his mother had a falling out because of me. He told me that John was planning on leaving Clewiston for good. I didn't want him to leave. So I asked his friend to tell him to contact me. Once again we met at our regular spot. It was night. He looked angry. We were seated in his car.

"Are you okay?" he asked. "Yeah." *"I saw when you fell. What happened?"* "It's nothing." *"Come on,"* he

urged, *"Tell me."* Embarrassed, I admitted, "I ran into the clothes line." *"You fell twice."* "I ran into two clothes lines." He looked genuinely concerned for my safety. *"Are you hurt?"* "No, the only thing that got hurt was my pride. I heard you were arguing with your mom after I left."

"Yeah, my mom thinks I'm still a child. That's why I'm going to leave." "Where are you going to go?" *"Miami."* "So what's going to happen to us?" He looked at me with a dubious look on his face, *"You still want to be with me after what mom said to you?"* he asked. "It wasn't you who did it to me. Do you have any control over your mom?" *"No. I need to move out though. I can't live at my mom's place forever."* "I understand, but I don't want you to go to Miami." *"So where am I going to go?"* "You can find a place here to rent."

"Would you come to live with me if I rented somewhere?" "I'm still going to school." I guess both of us forgot that I was still high school age and needing to graduate. *"What does that mean?"* "It means I'm going to have to stay at my parents home until I'm finished." *"What are you going to school to become?"* I shrugged, "I don't know. "I haven't thought about it." *"Don't you think it's time for you to think about it?"* "I'm still young." *"Yeah, but you won't remain that way forever."*

"I don't want you to quarrel with your mom because of me." *"I guess it's too late."* "So what are you saying? You can't go back to her house?" *"I can, but she'll give me the silent treatment. You sure you don't hate me?"* "I'm sure I don't hate you. I can't hate you." *"It's a lucky thing you didn't take your clothes off. I only opened your blouse a little, but,* Veronica, you're a sexy woman, you know."

"Am I?" I asked, looking at him with a smile on my lips. "Yeah, why do you think those guys were calling you Billy Jean? It's because they say you're sexy and cute." "Are you sure that they're talking about me?" I asked, while smiling inwardly. I never thought the day would have come when someone would be referring to me as cute. I had always thought I was ugly.

"Yes, I'm sure," he said punching me playfully on *my arm. How come you don't have any confidence in yourself?"* "Who said that I don't?" *"You don't believe you're cute."* "I do," I lied.

"Veronica, if we're going to be together, you're going to have to think seriously about us making love; you can't keep fighting me off." I knew I wouldn't be able to keep him off for much longer. Maybe now was the time for me to tell him I wasn't a virgin. I had to tell him this one lie so that he wouldn't question me when it happened.

"John, I'm not a virgin," I began. My heart was racing in my chest. Was he going to hate me for this? I couldn't live with myself if he hated me. *"I thought you told me you never had a boyfriend."* "Not a real one. A guy and I were just playing around and things happened." *"So why didn't you tell me the truth from the beginning?"* "I don't know, I was scared you wouldn't want to talk to me."

"How long did the relationship last between you and this guy?" "Not very long." *"Who was he? A student?"* "Yeah." *"Where is he from?"* "Tampa." *"Well, it's okay, as long as you guys are not communicating still."* "We are not." *"Well, there is nothing to worry about. I trust you."* I sighed. I could feel my heart calming down. All along it felt as if it were beating with a vengeance in my chest, anticipating disaster. I loathed lying, but I couldn't tell him what my dad had done to me. As poignant as it would have been, I would have preferred to lose his love over a lie, rather than by telling him the truth. At the time, my dad's indiscretion was something I wanted to keep to myself, and as long

as it was up to me, I figured I would just sweep it under the carpet and leave it there for as long as I could.

Chapter 15

I was going to give in to John, but I wanted the occasion to be special. I wanted it to happen at a hotel. I had never been to one, but I had heard a lot about it. I heard how one could just lie in the bath and have a lot of warm water, and it came from the tap, too. It was just like how it was at Mrs. Gloria's home. I missed that woman. She was such a nice lady who didn't deserve to die the way she did. I do believe Mrs. Gloria was legally separated from her husband, but somehow he gained access to the home, killing both Mrs. Gloria and their one and only child who was in his early twenties.

I remember hearing my mom talking to another sister from the church about the police finding their chopped up bodies under the mattress in the master bedroom. For years, I grieved over their deaths because Mrs. Gloria made me feel special, almost to the point of discomfort. Not many people in my life validated my worth, and I'll never forget Mrs. Gloria. RIP!

I was now seventeen and soon I would be going into grade twelve. I couldn't wait until it was my time to graduate. I wanted so much to have a life with John, and I also wanted badly to leave my dad's home. We still weren't getting along. He was getting on my nerves and I was getting on his, and it was looking as if there were no end to this feud. Mom had decided to get herself from between us because nothing seemed to be working out where we were concerned. I know it made her sad to leave us to ourselves because she loved both of us. She must have felt helpless being in the middle, since she couldn't see her husband from her wounded daughter's perspective.

Monica knew I wasn't going to graduate because I was missing out on more days than I was supposed to. You were allowed five absent days from school during a semester and I had upwards of eight for the past few semesters. The truth of the matter was that I had no plans to change that, even at the risk of failing to graduate. What was I thinking? I just abhorred school that much. But if I wanted to graduate, I needed to up my grades because they were terrible. As I had said before, my mom and dad didn't put a value on education, and neither did I. Surely "the apple didn't fall far from the tree" in my case! If it were left up to me, there would be no school. At least that was the way I felt at the time. Now, you can believe I know better.

Of course my friend Monica, who was doing much better than I was in school, was about to let me in on a little secret -- one I knew all too well. She knew about my grades because we exchanged looks after glancing at our reports each time they came out. Her face was always positive and happy because hers were good. She was getting A's and B's, while mine were C's and worse. She often told me that I needed to up my grades if I wanted to graduate, and she also told me about the amount of days I was absent too, both of which directly affected my graduation. That day at lunch in the cafeteria she confronted me.

"Have you decided what you're going to do with your life?" she asked. Monica had grown into a beautiful girl. She could have had any boy she wanted, but I

think she was more of an introvert than I was, and maybe that was a good thing. It was hard for her to deal with people, so she found solace in her books, which was why she was so good in school.

I looked at her, "What do you mean?" I asked, pretending to be a bit perplexed. My mind wasn't there, and maybe that was what she meant. My mind was never at school, which was where it should have been in order for me to get an education; but in my situation, I didn't care about education. I just wanted to grow up and leave home to be anywhere away from my dad.

"You're not improving on your grades, and you know you won't graduate if you don't have C's and higher." "I don't care, I just want to get out of here," I said adamantly. "I'll be glad when this is over." She looked at me with a look that said she had a purpose for her life. *"I want to go to college."* "Good luck," I said sarcastically. Actually, I was jealous of the fact that she knew what she wanted and it far exceeded getting away from a dirty old dad.

"I want to be a doctor so that I can take care of my mom." "Are you guys going to leave Clewiston?" *"I want to."* "Where are you going to go?" I asked a little sad at the thought of not seeing Monica every day. *"Maybe to Palm Beach."* "Palm Beach is expensive," *"Well, if I'm a doctor, I'll be able to afford it."* "How do you know that?" Of course she could afford to live absolutely anywhere if she became a doctor! *"I heard that doctors make a lot of money."* "But do you see the things they have to do?" *"Like what?"* I shrugged evasively, "I don't know; they do gross things." *"Doctors take care of people."* Monica smiled as if to say she would not be dissuaded by my negativity.

"Well, they do gross things to me." Isn't it funny the way life is? When the fox couldn't reach the grapes, he said that they were sour; it is the same thing with human beings. I was finding so many things wrong with being a doctor because I knew I wouldn't be able to achieve the requirements needed to attain that level of excellence. On the other hand, the idea of becoming a doctor was exciting to Monica because the possibility existed that if she applied herself, she could achieve that goal. She loved reading and studying. I hated both!

Sandra and Gary had gone further in their relationship, to my chagrin. I was hoping she would have left him, but apparently he had learned a lesson from that last experience when he was taken to jail. After that, he promised not to beat her, and so far, he hadn't. He had moved her and her mom away from the old house they lived in, and they were all now living in a nice two-bedroom trailer.

She even had herself a baby! I was hoping the child didn't come to look like her father, and it so happened that the child was a girl. I had gone to see her on a couple of occasions when the baby was much younger. The baby was cute, as all babies are, and didn't look anything like her father. I knew Sandra was thankful for that.

On this day I arrived to see her sitting on the back steps of her trailer alone, and she was smoking a cigarette instead of smoking a joint. As soon as she saw me, she put it out, and threw away the butt. Sandra was only seventeen, going on eighteen, but she was looking like a real woman now. She had quit school awhile back, saying she didn't think she was getting anything out of going. I wished that I could quit school too.

Sandra moved over a little on the stairs and I sat beside her. "How is the baby?" I asked as I sat. *"She is okay."* "Have any regrets?" *"I love my baby, but she is a pain in the butt."* "Why do you say that?" She looked a little annoyed at my question, but how else could I truly understand what mothers and new babies do throughout the night? *"You know how many times during the night I have to get up to feed her?"* "I heard they take a lot of feeding during the nights." *"I got up last night, fed her; she was satisfied, so I put her to sleep. Two hours later she was up and crying."*

"I never asked you this before, but how did it feel the first time you knew you were pregnant?" *"I started feeling sick all the time. I knew something was wrong when I couldn't keep anything down. I was throwing up all the time."* "What about when you were having the baby?" *"My God, that was the worst. I didn't think that I could have made it because the pain was unbearable."*

"Are you going to have any more kids?" I was asking that question for both of us, though she had no idea I was considering going all the way with John, which could lead to my being pregnant and having a baby. *"No, no more for me,"* she said shaking her head. "How has Gary been treating you?" *"Great. He hasn't laid a hand on me since the last time. And he loves his daughter."* "Is this his first kid?" *"That's what he said."* "You don't believe him?" *"I don't know."*

"Are you going to stay with him for the rest of your life?" *"No, I don't think so."* "What if he asks you to marry him?" She didn't hesitate to respond immediately. *"I won't."* "Isn't that going to make him mad?" I asked. *"Look, I'm not afraid of him anymore."* "It doesn't matter whether you're afraid of him or not; he can still hurt you." *"I won't let him. I'll threaten to leave him and take the baby with me. He would hate that."*

After a moment of silence between Sandra and me, she changed the subject. *"Hey, how come you never told me what happened to you when you went to John's home the other night?"* "Because it was too embarrassing, and it happened a while back anyway." *"Well, I am just hearing about it. I heard you ran from*

Mother Jones." I told you news in Clewiston travels faster than the speed of light!

"Girl, I was so scared. My heart felt like it was going to jump out of my chest." I had to grin slightly while describing the scene that, at the time, really did cause my heart to beat fast enough to leave my body. *"Was that the first time you had seen her?"* "I had seen her before, but not up close… and not so personally. She looked at me with such disdain." Sandra laughed, *"Yeah, I heard she can be threatening all right. I heard she once scared his baby mother too."* "I'm not surprised to hear that."

"What are you going to do when you graduate high school?" "*If* I graduate, you mean." *"Why don't you think you're going to graduate?"* Sandra sounded concerned. She had no idea about my excessive absences or terrible grades. "Sandra, my grades are low and my attendance is terrible. I just know I might not graduate." *"I'm glad I quit; I didn't like it."* "The good thing is that you have support." *"What about your father? That man has more money than anyone else in this town."* "Well, I think we're the only ones who are not feeling the effect of his wealth!" It was no secret to those close to me that I often complained about Dad having more money than most people in Clewiston, and yet he allowed his family to live a depraved existence.

"He needs to get rid of that trailer." "Yeah, when you have the time, tell him." I certainly was in no position to advise my father on any matter. Our conversation had just hit a sour note. Whenever I was having a chat with anyone and the mention of my dad came up, I had to find a way to stop it. I knew I had to go back home to see him, and that was okay for now because I had plans to leave one day.

It seemed everyone was on my case about graduation. One evening mom came into our room carrying one of my report cards. *"If you want to graduate you need to up your grades, you know,"* she said in a matter-of-fact tone.

I was feeling bitchy; all these years she had never paid any attention to my reports and now she was showing interest? "Too little, too late, I thought to myself. "Why the sudden interest?" I asked, hoping my attempt at throwing a little guilt her way would make her stop talking about this subject. *"Because I don't want you to end up on the street. What are you going to do with your life?"* I know she was speaking from the heart of a mother who didn't want her daughter to learn a hard lesson that only a hard life could teach her. "I don't know; the only thing I know is that I have to get away from here." I said I was in a bitchy mood.

Mom got right to the heart of the matter. *"You can't allow your hatred for your father to cause you to go on the street before you're ready to assume the role of a responsible adult."* "I've always been ready to leave this place, Mom. I gave you a thousand reasons why, but your main concern was always peace in the house. My heart is broken and this doesn't feel like home to me." My mother appeared wounded, too, and her eyes fell to a spot on the floor. *"This is your only home,"* she said quietly. I didn't understand at the time, but now that I'm grown, I can sort of see the conflict that was inside my mother from the time I was a small child until that moment. She always knew the truth, but all she had the stomach, and maybe the heart for, was peace.

She looked at my report again. *"Where do you go when you don't go to school?"* she asked. *"It says here you were absent for eight days."* "Mom, let's not go into this," I said. At this stage of my life, I didn't feel like answering any question I didn't want to answer, and I didn't feel like answering this one. She sighed, *"It's your future,"* she said. She gave me one long stare that almost melted my heart. But I fought past the urge to cry out loud and embrace her. Instead, I looked back at her as if she were right that whatever I was doing was affecting MY future. She turned and left the room.

It was my future all right, and I knew what I wanted to do with it. I wanted to spend it with John. I knew my mom cared for me, and she still does, but she had a crude way of showing it. I wished my mom were the type of person who could have forced my dad to do what he was supposed to do. It wasn't easy being one of the daughters of the richest man in our little "Harlem," and yet having nothing to show for it. Other people who were less fortunate than us were living better lives than we were. Those were the things I looked at and realized that I couldn't forgive my dad at that time. Later in my life, I'm happy to say that, by God's grace, I would learn to forgive my father for every cruel act he committed against his baby girl.

Chapter 16

If you could have seen my living condition, then you would have understood why I wanted to leave my home so badly. I was born in this trailer, and no kind of repairs had ever been done to it. I was seventeen and still sharing a room with the rest of my siblings. One thing I could say was that whoever built that trailer did a fine job. It was still standing after more than twenty years.

I knew John was getting impatient waiting for me to do the thing I had dreaded for so long. He just figured I was nervous about losing my virginity, but he had no idea what was really going through my mind. I wasn't even sure I could truly enjoy the act because ugly thoughts about my father were bound to come rushing into my head during a time when I should be experiencing pleasure. Still, it was now or never.

John told me about a hotel in uptown Clewiston, and we could go there. I had previously told him that I wanted out first time to be special, and he agreed. Once he took the next step to locate the environment I claimed I wanted, I wanted to back out. But I knew I had no excuse left. As usual, we met at our regular spot. By now everyone knew we were dating so we had nothing to hide anymore.

We went uptown and checked into the hotel. This wasn't the kind of hotel I had anticipated. I was expecting one like I had seen on television, but this one was small and neat. We went to our room. There was a big bed in the middle of the room. The place smelled fresh. I looked into the bathroom, which had a nice bathtub. John looked a bit impatient. He was already lying on the bed with his shirt off.

I stood at the door of the bathroom and asked, "You don't mind if I take a bath, do you?" It had been a while since I sat in a bath and had felt the warm water against my skin. *"Didn't you have a bath today?"* "Sure, but it was earlier today. I feel sticky." *"Okay, go ahead, but don't be too long."*

I was there in the bathtub just relaxing, or trying to relax. My heart was racing in anticipation of what was about to happen. I was wondering if I were going to be able to please him. What if after tonight he didn't want to see me again? Those were some of the thoughts going through my mind. I don't know why I locked the door, considering the intimate time we were about to have together. I saw the knob turn, as John asked, *"Are you all right in there?"* "Yeah." *"Are you going to come out any time soon?"* I could feel the impatience in his voice, though he tried to control it. He was about to get the prize he desired for a very long time, and he knew better than to mess it up with obvious impatience.

When I came out a few minutes later, I had a towel wrapped around me. John was on the bed, stripped down to his underwear. He looked at me and smiled, "Are you getting cold feet?" he asked jokingly. I was really glad that at that moment he could not hear the beating of my heart or he probably would have thought I was having a heart attack. I lay on the bed beside him with the towel still wrapped around me. He got up and turned off the light, and lay back on the bed beside me. He started to take the towel off of me, but I held onto it for a while before I finally released it. I was thankful that the room was a little dark.

As his hand started to go over my body, I suddenly felt as my body started to stiffen. It was like I couldn't breathe. I couldn't relax. My heart started beating even faster. I pushed him away and turned my back. John was being gentle, so we both knew the problem was all in my head. He lay on his back where he had fallen after I pushed him. *"Are you all right?"* he asked.

"I'm fine; I just need a little breather." He chuckled, *"If you hadn't told me that you had had sex before, I would have thought you were a virgin the way you're acting so nervous."* "I'll be fine; just let me relax a little." He sat up a bit, leaning on his elbows and looking from my face to my naked body. *"Go ahead; we have the room for the rest of the night."* "I hope you don't think I don't want you." I didn't want to disappoint him, but I felt I needed more time to be fully ready for the sex act.

"How did it happen with you and that guy? Were you this nervous?" "Do you mind if we don't talk about that?" *"Okay, I'm just trying to calm you."* I finally calmed myself down and relaxed a little, but John had to do all the work. I was as stiff as a log, and besides, what did I know about sex to react in any other way? Every other man had taken what he wanted, so I had no idea how to give pleasure. Truthfully, I wasn't sure how to receive it either. What was I supposed to experience, anyway?

We completed the act, and I knew John was satisfied. After we wiped ourselves off, John lay back on the bed and was almost off to sleep instantly, lying on his back. As I lay on the bed and listened to him snoring softly, I wondered if everything had gone the

191

way he anticipated. I felt like something was seriously wrong with me. I felt like damaged goods because I didn't experience the fireworks shooting off during or after sex. I just felt wet and nasty. I had heard so much about sex, how you feel on top of the world, especially when you are with the one you love, but this had done nothing for me.

All it did was to remind me of what my dad had done to me. Well, that answered my silent question that I might not experience bliss, but only disgust because Dad's dirty exploits would fill my mind during sex with someone I truly cared for. What a double portion of cruelty he had gained, and he didn't even know it!

It seemed like John enjoyed it, and I sincerely hoped that he did because I had fallen in love with John and I didn't want this to be out last night together. It was later in the night when I felt his arm around me, and once again my body stiffened. I knew he could feel it. *"Relax; I'm not going to do anything you don't want me to do,"* he whispered softly and reassuringly. That was comforting. I had fallen asleep with my back turned to him. Fully awake now, I sensed that I hadn't completely disappointed him. "How was it?" I asked unabashedly. *"It was good, but you need to relax."* "I'm trying." *"Even now you're stiff to my touch."* "I said I'm trying." He pushed his body up against me and hugged me tighter.

We didn't talk much after leaving the hotel. That to me was an indication that everything had not gone the way he planned. It scared me to think that I wouldn't see him again. After that, John wasn't as enthusiastic to see me as he had always been, and I felt as if what we had was over. At the time he was working at one of the sugar factories in Clewiston. He used to work pretty hard, but before this he always found time to be with me, but now he was making all kinds of excuses about being tired and not having any time for himself. I didn't want to think like so many women that, once the man gets what he wants, he no longer wants what he got. I pushed that thought to the depths of my mind and continued to hope John and I had love going for us, and our love would outlast everything.

Two weeks later I missed my period. At the time I didn't think about it because, in my mind I didn't think that having sex just one time could end up getting someone pregnant. It bothered me that I wasn't seeing John as much as I would have liked, but I knew I had to move on. I had my graduation to look forward to, even though I knew that with my poor grades and attendance there was a likely chance that I might not graduate.

I went to see Sandra a few days after John and I had gone to the hotel. As usual she was home alone. She had just put her baby to bed and was seated on the back steps smoking. When she saw me approaching she put it out. She was decent that way; she never liked to talk while smoking. "Hi," I said as I approached her. *"Hi, yourself, what's going on?"* she asked with a smile. She pulled up on the step so I could sit. "Nothing much," I responded. She could see by the look on my face that I wasn't completely happy.

"Are you okay?" "Yeah." I guess I was not convincing. She looked at me and shook her head. *"Something is wrong."* I hesitated for a minute, but I really needed some answers to sex questions, and Sandra was certainly a knowledgeable young woman! "How was it your first time?" I asked. A big smile overshadowed her face as she looked at me. *"Oh my God, you finally did it!"* "Yeah, and it was not what I had expected."

"Girl, don't follow those romantic movies; the first time is never the way they describe it. It's painful and makes you feel as if you don't want to go back." In my mind I thought about how my first time and all the times

after that were painful. My daddy had certainly done a number on me. The memories brought back tears to my eyes. Sandra saw it and embraced me. *"Oh come on, Veronica; everyone feels the same way about the first time. It's not the end of the world. Trust me, it gets better the second time around."*

"He is not talking to me the way he used to." I dried my eyes and pulled away from Sandra. *"Why?"* "I don't know; maybe he doesn't like someone who doesn't have any experience." *"That's crap. He knew you were a virgin when he was dating you."* Well, apparently she was one person I fooled. I didn't know where she got the idea that I was a virgin while dating John. Maybe it stemmed from the fact that I wasn't the run-around type person while growing up. As much as I hated the place where I was living, I would mostly stay there whenever I didn't have to go to school or church. It was because of John that I was staying out as late as I was. I didn't bother to correct her.

"Have you two spoken about it since it happened?" she asked. "We haven't spoken much since then, and to tell you the truth, it is something I would like to forget." *"Girl, I'm sure every woman would like to forget her first time."* Not as much as I would have liked to forget mine; it was not with someone who had gotten my consent. That was for sure!

Right then I wished there was a way I didn't have to remember what my dad had done to me. It was terrible; what was supposed to be the most delightful time of a person's life was for me a time that would bring back poignant memories. My secret fear was whether or not I could ever have a normal sex life with a partner whom I really love and trusted. Would I always regress to that awful time and place where my father invaded my most personal space and changed my life forever? Every time I felt too uncomfortable to continue

194

talking to anyone, I found the way to retreat. So I told Sandra I had to go, and I left, right in the middle of our conversation.

I felt grudgingly towards Monica for the enthusiasm she had for school. I wished I were like her. There was never a day during school days when she wasn't in school. She was getting good grades and was looking forward to graduating. For me, it was all about being sad again. I had thought that things were working out so well with John and I, but now it seemed like they weren't. I couldn't see him at the spot where we would normally meet up. It was like he was avoiding me. In those days there were no cell phone, so I couldn't call him. People only had home phones, and John had never given me the number for his. The other thing was that we never had one at our home, so if I wanted to call someone, I would have to use the phone in the phone booths, and at any given time there were always too many people there waiting on the phone.

Well, according to Monica, Andrew was still interested in me, even though I had never given him the time of day. I didn't know what it was, but lately guys were really getting interested in me. I was aware that something was happening to me, and I was beginning to be a little bit more confident.

I found out a month later why John was so patient with me prior to us having sex. According to Sandra, he had himself two ladies on the side while we were dating. She was trying to explain to me why men could not be trusted. I had gone to see her to find out why I was feeling the way I was lately. I had not seen my period, and I was feeling sick and always throwing up. When I approached her, she didn't even give me the chance to tell her what I wanted to say. Apparently she had heard something she wanted to tell me.

"Did you know that John had two other girls while he was dating you?" she began. "Where did you hear that from?" I asked. I had suspected something. I believed he was still having a relationship with the woman who had his two kids, and I didn't know who else he was having a relationship with, but I had a feeling I was about to hear who it was. *"You didn't know that?"* she asked, looking at me as if she were looking at someone who was super naïve.

"I suspected, but I didn't have any proof." *"I think he is still having an affair with his Baby Mama, and someone told me he was also dealing with Marva White." Everyone in town knew Marva White.* I knew who she was. She was this attractive woman, whom all the guys in town seemed to want to date. She was an older woman but she was hot, and quite a dresser. I was sure quite a few women envied her. Maybe that included me, but right now, I was just confused and angry.

"I didn't know he was having an affair with Marva White," I responded innocently. *"Child, where have you been?"* she asked. Then looking at my face she knew something was wrong. *"Are you all right?"* "I don't think so," I said. I sat on the step. *"What happened?"* "I've been feeling real sick lately, and I can't seem to keep anything down." *"When was the last time you saw your period?"* "Not since John and I did it." *"Sounds like you're pregnant."*

I was shocked. I looked at her hoping to see a glimpse of a smile, something that would indicate she was pulling my leg, but there was none. "You're kidding, aren't you?" I finally asked. *"That was the same way I felt when I was pregnant with my daughter. I couldn't keep anything down."* "But that was my first time." I wanted to add "with John," but I was sure she would have wanted to know who the persons before John

196

were. As much as I hated lying to protect myself, sometimes I wished I didn't have to. *"It doesn't matter; all it takes is one time, as long as he didn't use a condom, and you didn't use protection."* Suddenly my friend Sandra had become an expert on pregnancy, and how to prevent it. Why had I never learned the prevention piece, and why WAS I so naïve that I foolishly thought a woman got a "pass" from God the first time she had intercourse?

"Damn, what am I going to do?" *"Call him and let him know."* I had started talking to John again and we had resumed where we had left off. He wasn't angry with me, just busy. But for me, it was like he had decided not to talk to me again. I guess that was my mind playing tricks on me. He told me he enjoyed that night we spent together. He hadn't tried to bring me back there, and when I asked why, he told me I needed to learn how to relax first. I needed to relax all right, and I was glad he hadn't tried again.

I was really scared of what Sandra was telling me right now, and I didn't want to tell John I was pregnant. What if he weren't ready for a baby from me? He had two sons already, so did he really want another child? I thought he had decided not to talk to me after our first night together, and I was devastated. I tried to see him a few nights later, and when I couldn't see him, it was like my world was about to end. What if he decided that this was too much for him, and he resolved not to see me again this time… for real?

I pondered these things in my mind and told myself that I would wait until I was certain that I was pregnant. After all, Sandra wasn't a doctor. She was just a normal person like me. I ended the discussion by announcing to Sandra that I would wait until I was certain before telling John anything. In my heart, I added that I might not tell him anything even then. I was hurt about his having affairs with other women, but I was too young and immature at that time to realize that what men show you early in the relationship is who they will be if that relationship matures. John would always cheat on me. All I could see was that I loved him and would do about anything to keep him loving me.

My parents and my teachers were still on my case about graduation. I knew I wasn't a dunce, just lazy and didn't like school. But if I set my mind to it, I knew I could easily up my grades. I was about to enter the twelfth grade, and so I still had a whole year to catch up on my lessons. Another mistake of my youth was thinking that I had my whole senior year to do what I needed to do all four years of high school, if I ever wanted to get accepted into college.

That whole summer was a drag. I knew I was pregnant, but I hadn't let anyone else in on my secret. I was always sick and throwing up, but I was careful enough not to do it when anyone was around to get suspicious. I hadn't seen my period since that night with John, and so that's how I knew for sure I was pregnant. Sandra was the one who made me feel that I wasn't going to die, because she had been through it already and knew what my problem was. I went back to see her again one day in the summer, and she wanted to know when I was going to tell my parents.

We were seated at our regular spot at the back of her house. I sighed resignedly before I answered her. "Sandra, I don't know what I'm going to do; I didn't want to get pregnant now. I wanted to wait until I was out of school." *"Well, it's too late for that now,"* she said. "What if I get an abortion?" *"Abortions are too risky."* "But people have been through it, and they came out all right." *"Not everybody's luck is the same."* "I can't tell my parents." *"Why not?"* "What if they kick me out?" *"Why would they kick you out?"* Clearly Sandra had never seen the evil side of my parents, especially my father. "I don't know. They might think that I let them down."

"Have you told John as yet?" "I don't want him to get mad at me. I'm scared. After that first time a the hotel, he didn't talk to me for three days, and I felt like my world was falling apart." *"Girl, you weren't the one who got yourself pregnant. He was the one who did, and he should share in the responsibility."* "I know." *"You're going back to school, aren't you?"* "Yeah." *"You had better make sure you graduate."*

I left Sandra thinking about how I would be able to bring my grades up, hide my pregnancy, and then miraculously deliver my baby without anyone knowing, and *finally* walk across the stage on graduation day. What in the world was I going to do?

Chapter 17

Sandra and I were the same age, but she was acting more like an adult than I was. I guess having a baby really changed someone. She was no longer hanging out with the friends she had previously. Gary had asked that she get rid of them, and I guess that was what she did. She wasn't into smoking weed anymore either. She had stopped after realizing that she was pregnant.

The thing I really liked about her was that she kept anything I told her between us, and that was how I liked it. Only the two of us knew that I was pregnant. I could talk to her about anything. There were times when I felt like I was mad at the world, and when I told her how I was feeling, she always understood.

When John and I had just met, I had given him a wrong age because it was important for me to make him feel that I was close to being a woman. He found out that I had tricked him, but he wasn't angry with me. In fact, he told me that he understood why I did it. We were in his car at our regular spot beside the lake. I wanted to tell him about the pregnancy, but I was really scared. I didn't want to lose him, and I knew so many girls and women lost their men once they learned that *we* were pregnant. You'd think we got that way all by ourselves!

John was making fun of what had happened at the hotel that night; he was always making fun of that night. When I asked him why, he said he wanted me to laugh at myself, and to learn to relax. *"If you hadn't told me you weren't a virgin, I would not have known,"* he said. I guess he was trying to make me feel good, but all I was feeling was resentment. "Why?" I asked, looking at him strangely. All he said in response was, *"It didn't feel that way."*

"I was too tense." *"That's why I said that you've got to relax."* "And I said I'm trying," I snapped. He was suddenly beginning to annoy me. *"Are you okay?"* he asked. "Yes, I'm fine." I wasn't looking at him. I was looking through the window, not sure if I wanted to cry or vomit from morning sickness. I wasn't feeling good. I felt as if I wanted to throw up, but I was hoping it wouldn't happen because that might surely have tipped John off that I was carrying his child.

It was night, but would you believe the sickness was called "morning sickness." Why did feel as if I wanted to throw up now? I didn't understand what was happening, but I was hoping that I wouldn't throw up while he was there beside me. He was quiet, thinking of what to say next that wouldn't offend me. How could he know what to say and what not to say right now, since I didn't even know what would offend me. Maybe everything he said would offend me until I shared my secret with him. Still, I wasn't ready.

"You have been moody lately, haven't you?" he asked suddenly. I looked at him quickly, "What do you mean?" I asked, trying to appear innocent. He shrugged. *"I don't know; you sure you're not pregnant?"* "Pregnant? Why would I be pregnant?" I asked, trying to look shocked. I heard a slight tremble in my voice, but quickly suppressed that in favor of a steady, strong look of denial on my face. I should have used this

opportunity to tell him that I was, but I was scared, really scared.

"You're not acting like yourself. You used to be so happy." Of course, he was right, but I had a retort. "A few times I have been sad." *"Yeah, but you quickly got over them."* "I'm okay," I said, forcing a smile. I pretended to check the time, giving some lame excuse for why he needed to bring me home. He complied, but I knew he wanted to talk more. I didn't!

I didn't spend much time with Monica during that summer before my senior year. I didn't want her to know I was pregnant. I knew that it was going to become evident as the weeks and months progressed, but for now I was willing to keep it between Sandra and me. I spent more time with Sandra than anyone else I knew, including John.

"John knows that I'm pregnant," I said to Sandra that evening when we met at her home. *"Did he get angry with you?"* "I didn't say that I told him; I said he knows." *"Are you saying that you didn't admit that you are?"* "Exactly." *"So how did he suspect that you are?"* "From my bitchy attitude!" *"Welcome to the world of pregnancy,"* Sandra said without blinking an eye.

"God, I feel so terrible sometimes; all I want to do is snap at everyone." *"You've got to go the doctor you know?"* "You want to come with me?" *"Me? Why don't you ask your mother?"* "Because I haven't told her as yet, and I don't think I want to tell her."

"You're going to have to tell someone besides me, you know." Sandra was right, of course. I felt cowardly telling anyone except her. I don't know why I dreaded telling my mother, since I didn't fear that she would understand what happened and I knew she would never abandon me. But, oh, if she told my father, he might strike me out of rage that someone besides him dared to invade "his" territory. I said I was "bitchy,"

so maybe he had learned his lesson and wouldn't care about me being pregnant. My mind was a jumble of scenarios.

I hadn't noticed that there was a long pause in our conversation while I raced through potential conversations in my mind. I returned to the moment and said, *"I'll keep it between us for as long as I can."* *"So when it starts showing, what are you going to say?"* I shrugged evasively with a mischievous smile on my face. "I don't know, maybe I'll tell them that I have just eaten and my tummy is just too full." Sandra looked at me with a serious look on her face, *"Come on Veronica, be serious!"* I guess I was just trying to downplay the seriousness of my situation with a little humor, but this was serious -- dead serious.

I wasn't looking forward to school, and when it started back, I was really beginning to feel the effects of the pregnancy. I hadn't told anyone else about it yet, and obviously whatever I had been doing to keep it a secret was working because no one seemed to be the wiser where that was concerned.

I had resolved to make my grades better, and my attendance too, but still I had this uncanny urge to stay away from school. Maybe it was the fact that I knew my pregnancy was going to be obvious pretty soon, and as a result I was feeling a little embarrassed. I should have been thinking about upping my grades and my attendance, but instead something else happened. It was like throwing in another piece of complication into a life that was already complicated. Monica wanted to know why she hadn't seen much of me during the summer. I knew she was going to ask me, so I had already planned what I was going to tell her. The complication was that I might not be able to pull the lie off this time. Monica and I had been friends for so long that she could look at me and tell when something wasn't right. Hence, I was deliberately looking away from her when we spoke.

It seemed like the summer had done her well; she was looking refreshed. When she approached me in the cafeteria, she looked bubbly. *"Hi, stranger,"* she said as she sat in front of me. She had a big smile on her face. *"How are you doing?"* I gave my rehearsed answer. "Fine, how are you?" I was feeling terrible, but I was trying not to let her see it. I had a smile on my face, but it was forced and not a reflection of what I was feeling inside. I pretended to see something on the floor as my excuse to focus my eyes there.

"Didn't see much of you during the summer. Where were you?" "I was all over the place; I went back to Tampa, and then I was in Miami for a while." *"I didn't know you had relatives in Miami."* "I was with a friend." *"A boyfriend?"* she asked with a twinkle in her eyes. "No, just a regular friend who is a girl." I was correct in saying that, except the friend didn't live in Miami. Sandra was right around the corner.

"Oh, so you dumped me for another girl," she said. It was obvious that she was joking because she still had a big smile on her face. I was beginning to feel as if I were about to throw up, so I quickly asked to be excused and rushed out to the bathroom. I made it just in time. As soon as I closed the stall, I threw up into the bowl. There were a few other girls in the bathroom. I was sure they must have seen my haste when I passed by them, and I knew they heard me retching inside the stall. I was bringing up something all right -- all the food I had just eaten at lunch, which wasn't much. Most of the food I had bought was left on the plate, which was still in front of Monica.

Thankfully, there was no one in the bathroom when I got out of the stall. I washed out my mouth and went back out to join Monica. She saw the distressed look on my face and asked, *"Are you okay?"* "Yeah, I'm fine," I said as I sat back where I previously was, in front of my half eaten lunch. I wasn't hungry any longer, and dared not try to take another bite. So I began to place my paper napkin over a portion of the plate, with the intention of covering the whole plate while Monica was distracted by our conversation.

She was still looking in my face. *"You don't look too good. Are you sure you're okay?"* "Yeah, I'm fine. I must be coming down with the flu or something." *"Maybe you need to go see the nurse."* She was trying to be helpful, but I already knew what was wrong with me. "I'm okay," I said, trying to put on a smile. I pushed away the plate from in front of me, since having the flu was a perfect reason to stop eating. Truth was, just looking at the food was making me sick. If Monica suspected anything more than me being sick, she didn't show it and we both went to our next class after lunch.

"How did you do it?" I asked Sandra that evening on my way home from school. *"Do what?"* Sandra asked. "Carry the pregnancy." *"What's happening to you?"* I sensed a little impatience. "I can't keep anything down and just looking at food makes me sick." *"It will pass,"* she answered casually. "But when?" I urged. *"I don't know, everyone goes through it differently and it lasts depending on who the individual is."* "Man, I hate this." *"Yes, this is what you get for not protecting yourself."*

What did I know about protection? The way I felt about sex then, if it were left up to me, I wouldn't have it. I know that in every intimate relationship between a man and a woman sex is very important, but I wished that it didn't have to happen to me. Of course I knew that John was thinking differently. I was sure that he would have liked it every day if it were left up to him. But then again, he hadn't been through what I had.

"Does Monica know you're pregnant?" Sandra asked. "No, I was sitting in front of her today when I jetted out of the cafeteria to get to the bathroom." *"Did you get there in time?"* "Just barely." *"And she didn't suspect anything?"* "I don't think so." *"Girl, I don't know how long you're going to continue to hide this. It's going to come out one day soon, and you're running out of time."*

"So what do you suggest? That I start advertising it from now?" I knew I shouldn't have been sarcastic, and I apologized to her. *"That's okay, I understand. Sometimes you feel like you just want to bite off somebody's head."* "Damn, sometimes I wonder why women bother to have kids when they have to go through all these things." *"Trust me, once it's over, you'll feel real good."* "Not when I'm going to have to be getting up all hours of the night to feed a baby." *"Well, who is going to do it for you?"* "The father," I said with confidence. *"Sorry, sweetheart, he hasn't got breasts to feed the baby, but you do."*

"What does Gary do when you get up to feed your baby?" *"Sometimes I wake him up, or sometimes when the baby is crying she wakes him up."* "Doesn't he get mad?" *"Why would he get mad? He is proud of his daughter."* "Does he have any other kids?" *"He said he doesn't."* "Sounds like you don't believe him." *"Honey, it's kind of hard to trust men these days."*

"You think he is cheating on you?" "I don't know; he goes from home to work, and from work to home; sometimes I wish he would stay out." "I guess he wants to keep you in check." *"I think so. He is planning on getting a telephone."* "Well, that would be good," I said excitedly. "Then I could come here and call John whenever I want him." *"If I know Gary, that phone wouldn't stop ringing long enough for you to talk to John."* The baby started to cry, which was my cue to go

206

home." Sandra went into the house and closed the door. I didn't want to go in to see what she was doing with the baby. I didn't need a reminder of what I was going to have to do very soon now. I left and went home.

I was staying out of my father's way. It was "melon time" and as a farmer he was in Miami selling his melons. Most times he would only be home on weekends. I was glad I didn't have to see him every day. I didn't know what was going to happen when I finally told my parents about this baby. I didn't really care about my dad's thoughts. I was more concerned with my mother. However, I decided I was going to wait for as long as I could before I told them. Even though I was feeling sick every day and had not had a period in a few months, I was still hoping I wasn't really pregnant.

I still saw John, but I was always wearing big clothes so he would not guess that I was pregnant until I showed so much that everyone looking at me would know I was carrying a child. John and I were in his car one night when I told him that I thought I was pregnant. His response was to laugh at me. *"How could that be? We just did it once,"* he said. "That's all it takes," I said as if I knew that fact all along. *"Look, I think you're worrying over nothing; I don't think you're pregnant."* "I haven't seen my period since that time." *"There could be lots of explanation for that."*

"Can you give me one explanation for why I haven't seen my period in two months?" I tried not to be sarcastic, but the last thing I needed was for John to be in denial about the possibility that *he* got me pregnant the first time we had sex. "Some women miss their period for longer than that, but it doesn't mean they're pregnant. I wanted to believe that I wasn't pregnant, so, I let him convince me that what I was experiencing was

my mind playing tricks on me. I wasn't pregnant at all –
really!

Chapter 18

Well, between John and me, I had convinced myself that I wasn't pregnant, and the funny thing was that I wasn't feeling the symptoms any more. I was feeling good, so I decided I wasn't going to tell my parents anything. However, I knew I still had to face up to Sandra, and I knew she was going to tell me that I was still pregnant. So I tried to avoid her.

The following Monday when I went back to school I was feeling like myself again. I was able to eat without feeling as if I wanted to throw up. Now I was convinced that it was my mind that was playing tricks on me. I decided I was going to settle down and see if I could bring up my grades to where I needed them. They weren't exactly the worst. They were like "C-," so I mused to myself that if I had ever applied myself to my studies, I would probably have been smarter than Monica and been on the Honor Roll.

I wasn't feeling the symptoms anymore, but I noticed that my period hadn't come since after that one time John and I had sex. It was almost three months since that time and no period. That was worrisome. I knew that when you're pregnant, you don't normally see your period until after you give birth, but the thing I couldn't understand was why all those sickly feelings suddenly stopped. I wasn't feeling bitchy any longer.

To make things worse, my tummy started growing. I had noticed it, but I put it down to eating too much. I was really beginning to eat a lot and still couldn't get full. I found myself eating just like when I was younger and I would search through the garbage for food. It was like I was always hungry. One night after everyone had gone to bed, I got up to get myself something to eat. I was searching through the refrigerator when my mom caught me. Apparently she had come out to get herself something to drink. *"What are you doing up?"* she asked. "I was looking for something to drink," I lied. I knew she wouldn't regard that as being greedy. After all we were living in Florida and our house didn't have central air. My mom bought that lie.

"Do you guys have the window open?" she asked. I took a bottle of soda and moved away from the fridge. "Yeah." *"It's really hot."* Mom got her drink of water, but didn't move to leave the kitchen. Still hungry, I said, "Okay, good night." I walked towards my room, but was waiting for mom to go back to her room. As soon as mom went back to her room and I was sure she was asleep, I went back out there and made myself a sandwich.

I was home one day when my dad looked at me and said, *"Don't let some good for nothing guy knock you up now. You know that would be a shame."* Honestly that smart comment hurt deeper than the years of molestation he had put me through. Can you believe the nerve of this man? I was already frustrated and feeling like I had ruined my life, and now my own father, who had done terrible things to me, was standing in front of me making this dirty remark.

I blurted out, "Well, thank God it's not yours." He slapped my face, but for some reason it was like I didn't feel it. I looked unflinchingly into his eyes, defying all I had been taught about not looking into a senior's eyes when talking to him, and I said, "There is nothing you can do to me anymore."

I knew after that comment that I better approach my mother and tell her the truth before my father shared my news in a most sarcastic manner. My mom just looked into my eyes, and then looked away from me without saying more than, *"Oh, I see that."* She never scolded me, though, but I could tell she was a little disappointed because it meant that any plans for college were snuffed out now, for sure. I guess she had known it all along but never wanted to confront me. I didn't care for my dad, so whatever he wanted to say couldn't do a thing to make me feel badly. But I did care what Mom thought, and I felt real remorse when I sensed I had let her down in terms of putting limitations on my future.

Mom and I had never had conversations about babies or menstruation, so it was easy to skip over the mother-to-daughter conversation about my obvious pregnancy. I guess after she had eight kids, who wants to talk about how babies get here? That small realization caused me to laugh out loud, although nobody heard me. Different members of the household gave me facial expressions and some words about my being pregnant, but only Dad interjected judgment and sarcasm into his comments about my situation.

Now my tummy was getting really big. I couldn't hide it anymore. One day at school Monica looked at me and asked, *"Are you pregnant, Veronica?"* I quickly denied it, "No, why did you ask?" I asked rather innocently. *"I heard a few kids talking among themselves that you were pregnant by a guy who is living with the mother of his children."* "I have a tumor, but I didn't want anybody to know." What a stupid thing to say.

"Veronica, if that's a tumor, you need to get it out; it can kill you." That was coming from "Doctor" Monica. She hadn't left for college yet and she was talking to me as if she were a doctor. "I know that it can kill, but right now I don't have insurance, so I'll have to wait." Why do people who tell ridiculous lies continue to trap themselves? I couldn't be sure Monica believed me, and now I heard I was the talk of the school. No way could I convince all of them that I had a tumor – and no insurance, with they wealth they all knew my father had. What a mess!

My tummy was really getting big and the rumors about this man with kids, all living with his mother, was really getting to me. I opted to leave school to go on "homebound instruction." This was a program for teenagers who were injured or had some disease preventing them from attending school, and also for pregnant teens. I could feel the tension in our home, so I didn't want to add to it by asking Mom to sign a form of any kind.

Well, very early in life my sisters and I got comfortable signing our own forms and not telling the parents anything. The school never checked, so we kept doing it. Also, Mom and I have the same name, so I simply scribbled something that looked like an adult signature, and it worked every time. I still hadn't gone to the doctor because I had pretty successfully convinced myself that I wasn't pregnant. Of course I was fooling myself and seemingly no one else on earth!

I was going to the store one day when one of John's sisters stopped me. This woman was about twice my age, and though I knew who she was, I had never spoken to her before. *"Are you the one who said you're pregnant by John?"* she asked. "John is my boyfriend," I responded nervously. I held my head down, not wanting to look into her face. *"Do you know that he has his baby's mother, who he lives with?"* "I know he has his baby's mother, but I didn't know he was still living with her." *"We will know who the child belongs to. Our family has strong genes, so you can't trick us."* She walked away, leaving me standing in the middle of the street, confused.

I had no intention of tricking anyone! My period hadn't come in over six months and I had yet to see a doctor for prenatal care. At least I was home now, receiving instruction twice weekly by a visiting teacher. I stayed in my room. This room was shared by five of us, but when they were not there, I could stay in there and sleep without being disturbed. I could also cook some rice and chicken with a lot of butter, and eat uninterrupted.

I was about seven months pregnant the first time I went to the clinic. I didn't have insurance and neither did John, so I decided to make an appointment at the local *Hendry County Clinic* where most low income, Medicaid people went. John had finally realized that I was, in fact, pregnant. I think he was relieved that I was finally going to the doctor. I had waited so long to see the doctor, simply because I wasn't ready to deal with being pregnant. I found out I was seven months pregnant, not six. I was a little nervous and ashamed because I had actually convinced myself that I had a tumor and not a baby inside of me. It was more acceptable for a girl to have a tumor than to be pregnant and unmarried.

John didn't go with me to the clinic on the first or any of my visits. He did, however, allow me to use his car. I liked that because I felt good driving in my boyfriend's car, pregnant and all. That basically said that we were a family in my book, but to him it mostly meant he didn't have to take me. I would drop him off about 5:00 a.m. at work, which meant I got to keep the car all day until he got off work about 6:00 p.m. I had a full tank of gas, so I drove around all day long. I wanted everybody to see me with his car, plus it had a nice sound system.

Well, it was 8:45 a.m. and I was at the *Hendry County Health Department Clinic*. By the time I made it to the sign-in window, I had already seen at least three people I wanted to avoid. That meant that by the time I left the clinic, the whole of "Little Harlem" would have known that I was pregnant.

I was finally called by the lady at the window. She asked, *"Are you here for a prenatal?"* "Yes." Her next question was, *"Is that John's baby?"* At that precise moment I felt as if I wanted to faint, but then again somebody would have told that to the community too. The Jamaican nurse was somewhat rough around the edges. She basically chewed me out because I waited so long to see a doctor. She also said I was too young to have a baby. It wasn't like I was unaware of both her points.

I hadn't seen Sandra in a while. My sisters were now talking to me about my pregnancy, telling me how it was going to hurt when I delivered the baby. They wanted to know the date of delivery. At least that got them talking to me, since, as I had mentioned before that ours was a family that wasn't good at communicating.

I was tired of this pregnancy. The bump I had in my stomach was telling the world that I was bad, and it was making me feel ashamed. Isn't it funny the way life is? The men are the ones who love to boast about their conquest, while we women are the ones who display to the world what they did.

I was told that if you were in intense pain, and you go to the emergency room they would induce labor and the baby would be born. I wanted to deliver this baby and get it over with so badly that I started feeling just a little bit of pain, and made a big fuss of it. I called John and told him what was happening. I didn't know what it was about hospitals that scared John, but he had never made the choice to take me. Anyway, I was glad he had taught me how to drive. He agreed that I could use the car, so I drove myself to *Hendry County General Hospital*. I knew that hospital did not deliver babies, but I was hoping that they would send me to a hospital that did. I was just tired of being pregnant because it was physically, emotionally and mentally exhausting. The hospital attendant just took one look at me and sent me back home. I was so hurt.

Four weeks later, while I was in bed, my water broke. I knew that this meant it was time for the baby to be born. I called John and told him what happened. He met me at the park with my little suitcase and this time he knew he had to take me to the hospital. I wasn't in labor for too long before the baby was born. Yes, it was as painful as Sandra had previously told me, but it was over with and now I was happy. My baby girl finally came into the world, and I named her "Precious." Initially I didn't feel a connection to my baby, but as time went on, I started to really love her.

After the baby was born it was time for my graduation. I was going to be finally out of school. I hated confinement, and that was what school represented to me. Now I was about to be set free. I felt like jumping for joy, but there was a problem. During the time that I was pregnant, representatives from the school would drop by and I would be given homework. Now did I do those assignments? That was another question.

I saw Sandra a few days after coming out of the hospital, and she was glad to see me. She embraced me joyously. She held me off to look at me. *"How are you? I thought you had run away,"* she said. "I felt like I wanted to." She had met me at the front of the house and we walked up to our regular spot at the back of the house. She looked at me. *"You're looking good, girl."* "Thanks," I said. *"Why didn't you come back to see me?"* "I was living in denial and didn't want to be constantly told that I was pregnant." *"And you thought that I would do that?"* I shook my head affirmatively.

"The thing is that whether you want to live in denial or not, the truth normally comes out in the end." I smiled, and responded mischievously, "And am I glad *she* did!" She smiled. *"So you have a girl?"* "Yes, I have a girl, a cute little girl." *"They are always like that when they're small, and then they become one or two, and you just feel like they are too much to handle."* "How is your daughter?" I just noticed she wasn't with her mom. *"She is one, and she is already driving me crazy."* "Where is she?" *"My mom took her with her; she is giving me a break."* It was time for me to get home to see about my own baby.

Sandra's home was within walking distance of mine. I hurried home in time to feed my baby and put her to sleep. The rule was I couldn't leave the backyard of our home unless I fed my baby and she was asleep. No family member offered to care for my child until she fell asleep, so I understood clearly that everything concerning my child was my sole responsibility. Oh, Mom didn't mind taking care of her, but she wanted me to feel the full weight of what I had done by getting pregnant before I finished high school. Lesson learned!

My only escape from motherhood was visiting Sandra. I just wanted to get out of the house for a while. It felt good coming out without pushing a big tummy in front of me. I was committed to rushing home from school to feed and change my baby, and then rock her in my arms until she fell asleep. But after that, I always wanted to leave the house to visit the only friend who truly understood my feelings. I wasn't trying to abandon my responsibilities as a mother, but I couldn't breathe at home because I always felt anxious and nervous.

I almost ran out of the house and down the street to Sandra's house. "Now I know what you mean when you were telling me about getting up the nights to feed her. I fed her and she was full, and just a little after putting her down, it was like I had to take her up again and feed her." *"Trust me; you have a lot more nights of that to go."* "When does that stop?" *"The older they get, the less they need to be fed."*

"So I don't get up that much in the night, but she is hell during the day." "Someone told me that they don't like to sleep at that age because they think that they'll miss out on something." *"Yeah, I figured that."* "Hey, Sandra, I have to leave. You know I can't stay too far from her. I just needed to get out of the house." *"Yeah, it was nice seeing you again. You look good."* "Thanks." I left her.

As I walked back home that day I had the chance to think about going back to school. Receiving "home instruction" simply meant that an insensitive teacher who needed extra money came to my home twice weekly to give and collect homework assignments. Her body language told me not to ask questions, or request that she actually teach me something. I was on my own to learn.

I never understood why no one from the school came to check on me or call to see how I was doing. Perhaps they wanted to call, but we never had a house phone during all the years of our growing up. Still, a school official could have dropped by once during my entire senior year!

Well, I was determined to show everyone that I could be a young mother and a high school senior. I didn't need any help from apathetic teachers or parents with more baggage that I seemed to have with a new baby. I managed to do just enough work from those boring homework packets to get by.

Technically, I failed my junior year because of too many absences, but I convinced my counselor that my morning sickness was extraordinary and that kept me out of school far more than I wanted to be absent. It was a lie but remember how good at lying I had become by the time I was a teenager. The counselor accepted my tearful (yes, tears fell) story and got the administration to waive this huge failure as long as I did all the work that I needed so far this last year to put me on track to graduate.

Homebound instruction was over because I was physically able to return to school the last few months of school. I had been out for about six months because of my pregnancy, delivery, and providing very early care for my child. But I knew I would have to go back to face those nosy kids. It would be a daunting experience, and something I wished I didn't have to do. Plus I had to explain the truth to Monica, whom I had lied to about my pregnancy.

I hadn't seen or spoken to Monica since leaving school for homebound instruction. I knew she was mad with me now, because we had been so close. The truth of the matter was that I was embarrassed. Monica was talking about a future, and even though we were the same age, it was like I was living my future at that very moment. I was having a family and I wasn't ready for one because I was still a child. I hadn't really begun to live the life I wanted to live, and now here I was with a child.

My mom was pretty young when she started having us, but that didn't mean I had to follow in her footsteps. I wanted to get out of school, and I would do anything to get out, but looking back on my life, I probably should have waited to have a child. Well, it was too late now. There was nothing I could do about it. I just had to make the best of my situation, and move on.

Chapter 19

Imagine my total shock when my counselor said that after I received every possible consideration, my cumulative days in school were insufficient for me to receive a State of Florida diploma. I would have to return to school for a small, but obviously significant number of days in order to fulfill the requirements to receive a diploma with the next graduating class. Oh, no!

Well, Monica left me in school. She, of course, graduated with honors and had her pick of colleges to attend. I didn't graduate that year; I had to wait until the following year. So instead of graduating in the class of '84, I ended up in the class of '85. That was humiliating, but what was even more humiliating was that the school official let me walk across the stage with my class, but I wouldn't get a diploma.

The graduation was not like what I had imagined it would have been. Maybe it was because I didn't get a diploma like the rest of the class did, or most of the class. I was sure I wasn't the only one without a diploma. However, I remember walking through the lonely cane field between my home and the school, broken-hearted because I knew and thought that everybody knew by way of an ugly rumor that I had a diploma case, but no diploma. My sadness was overwhelming. Each step I took, I got more depressed because I just knew that with all the celebrating and excitement, someone was going to ask to see my diploma.

Rumors or not, it was true -- I didn't have a diploma. That night I put on my black cap and gown, well aware of what was not in my beautifully trimmed diploma case. I held on to it for dear life, not wanting anyone to take it and look inside, thereby realizing what I was hiding -- nothing, absolutely nothing!

I had already come up with a lie to explain why I couldn't show them my diploma. I would say that I wanted it to be special when I told my mom. She was not able to make it to the graduation, so if they asked me, I was planning on telling them that I wanted her to be the first one to open it. You know how good I had become at covering things up. I could become a professional liar, and that fact made me sadder than I was a moment before I gave myself a promising career!

I didn't really remember my mom ever saying much about me graduating. Not once did she say, "Good job." She never gave me a nickname or term of endearment like "honey" or "baby." Maybe she had invested all her emotional capital birthing and raising all of us, plus looking the other way when or dad did inappropriate things. So a genuine show of affection towards me when I reached the milestone of high school graduation was an unrealistic expectation. I swallowed hard and kept moving forward.

Now the night of the graduation my second eldest sister came along with some other people. I spotted four of them all together, but I purposely avoided going towards them. I was scared they might say something harmlessly and make me cry. I was an emotional wreck, very near the edge of losing control,

221

and the least little thing could open the floodgates of uncontrollable tears.

When I saw my sister I went the opposite way. However, she saw me and came over to congratulate me. That should have made me happy, but instead it made me even sadder. In my mind I was thinking of how embarrassed she was going to be when her little sister's name was called and there was no diploma for her to collect.

John was there, but he was not there particularly to see me. He had about 5 family members who were graduating that night. Not once did he come over to see me, but I knew he was there because I had seen him. I had been wearing this fake smile since early evening, and it was beginning to wear me out. It was like my heart, mind and spirit were dragging the floor, but I forced myself to smile. I remember feeling like I couldn't breathe. I remember counting the steps and judging the amount of screams and good lucks coming from people for loved ones who were graduating. I heard the people who came for me shouting, *"We are so proud of you, Veronica."* That proud comment made my heart sink even further, because Veronica had no diploma.

My name was called and you could hear my four supporters. There were some kind folks there who sensed that my four supporters needed help, so they all started yelling for me. OMG, it made me feel worse; my supporters were screaming for me, and that included people I didn't even know. I felt like a bum for real. That was one of the worst days of my life.

I quickly lost myself among the people as all the families and friends flooded the school auditorium to give their loved ones their official and final congrats. That was a perfect cover for me, as I navigated my way inconspicuously through the crowd and made it to the parking lot undetected. I didn't know how I was going to get home because John was nowhere in sight and I had hidden myself away from my sister, her husband and her two young children.

I began walking past the parking lot and ended up running into John. I was so hurt, not because he wasn't there to support me, but because I felt dead inside and scared of what was to come next. Yes, I would have to go back to CHS to make up for the missed days, and then I would get my diploma. But what was I supposed to do now? John surely had no plans for himself. He still lived at his mom's one-bedroom apartment in the laundry room where he slept on a twin bed. That was where he called his room.

I knew I had to leave home. Never once did I see myself living in my parents' house for too much longer. Now neither of them had ever said that I couldn't, but I knew I didn't want to die in Clewiston – Little Harlem. I had to leave for that final time, heading either to Tampa or Alabama, where my dad was from.

Monica had left for college on a scholarship. She was on the road to her journey of becoming a doctor. I didn't see much of her as she was obviously living on campus, and didn't bother to make the trip back into Little Harlem during the summer. I didn't see much of her mother either. Rumors were that she was planning on going back to Atlanta, Georgia to be with her husband. Apparently they had made up. Good luck to her! My belief is that once you're an abuser, you'll always be an abuser and you'll never change.

My daughter was now one year old and had grown into such a sweet little baby. I adored her, but I didn't want the same life for her that I had had for myself. I didn't even want her to be in the same house that I had grown up in. And I didn't trust my dad with her. As much as I could, I kept her away from him. I didn't even allow him to touch her.

But I needed a life. I was an adult now at nineteen years old. I shouldn't be in a high school at this stage of my life, but it seemed as if the man of my dreams wasn't about to do anything to help me. So I needed to do something to help myself, or convince him to do something to help me.

As much as I had grown to love my daughter, I knew that I wouldn't be able to take her with me when I was leaving. The good thing about it was that my mom had really taken a liking to her, always telling me to leave her with her when I had to go anywhere. I was thinking I could leave my baby with my mother when I decided to go, because for sure I knew that I would be departing. How and to where, I didn't know, but I knew I would be taking a trek out of that little village we called Harlem, and I knew it was going to be soon.

So far, John had been a good father to our little daughter. He was kind to her, as well as to me. I felt as if I had really found the man of my dreams, but I wanted him to get away from his mother's apartment. He was no longer a child, obviously. He was working and was able to take care of himself, so what was he doing there?

One evening I met John and told him about my concerns. I told him that I wanted to leave Clewiston. *"Where do you want to go?"* he asked. "Well, we could always go to Miami." *"Have you ever been there?"* "No, but from what I've seen, I think it would be a nice place to grow up our daughter." He looked at me strangely. In my mind I felt that I had grown, but I didn't know what he was seeing when he was looking at me then. He asked me, *"Do you think you're ready for family life?"* I was almost sorry I asked my question because I felt he was belittling me.

"What do you mean?" I said with a little attitude. *"Do you think you're ready to stay home and be a mom?"* "Well, I'm already a mom, and I don't mind staying home." He looked as if he needed to choose his next words carefully because we were not connecting at all. *"It's not that easy."*

"Come on, John, the hardest part is over. I survived the pregnancy, I breast fed my daughter, and now she is able to drink from a bottle. What could be harder than doing those things?" I was remembering those nights that I had to wake up and tend to my daughter, those nights when I felt as if I'd rather be sleeping than having to get up to feed an annoying, crying child.

John chuckled, *"Trust me, when it comes to taking care of a kid, those things you have just described to me are just the beginning of child rearing, not the end."* I didn't understand what he had meant then, but I was sure to find out.

I didn't just have a desire to leave Clewiston for new adventures. I was *desperate* to leave! I wanted to get away from people whom I knew were looking at me like someone they thought was a failure. I had gotten pregnant as a teenager and had brought a child into this world out of wedlock. I had graduated high school, but I didn't have a diploma.

There were times when I walked on the street that I felt as if people were staring at me in a condescending manner. And then there was my father, who was a constant reminder of what he had done to me while I was only a child. If those reasons were not enough for me to leave, then I didn't know what was.

I hadn't been to see Sandra since my graduation. I knew she must have heard what took place there. With our community being so close, one person's dilemma was the community's news of the day or week, depending on how terrible it was.

Life can be terrible, especially for people with low self-esteem. Lots of people don't really care about your dilemma or your problems, but when you know something embarrassing has happened to you, as someone with low self-esteem, you will always get the feeling that people are laughing at you or disrespecting you. Well, I was born with low-self esteem, so you can imagine what I was going through whenever I passed a group of people and would suddenly hear laughter.

I felt as if I wanted to run and hide because I must be the one they were laughing at. I wanted to go some place where I could get a new start, a place where no one knew me. Then I could put all of this embarrassment behind me and start anew. Clewiston had too many bad memories for me. I needed desperately to get away.

A few months after graduation, I called my eldest sister to see if I could go to Jacksonville to stay for a few weeks with her. I assured her that I would not eat too much, or cause any problems and that on the day I arrive I would look for a job and pay her. I, for some reason, felt like I was a bother to everyone. Without hesitation my sister said, *"Yes, of course you can come,"* but she first had to ask Sueleene , our cousin whom she was living with.

I don't remember exactly how long it took for her to get back to me with the response from Cousin Sueleen, but it felt like forever. While waiting, all kinds of negative thoughts were playing in my head, like they are laughing at me and nobody wants me there. It's a sad fact to admit, but I never really thought about my baby. My focus was all about escaping emotionally, mentally and demographically from the place where I had been nearly all my life. I was almost at the breaking point, no longer able to deal with life as it was. I had gone back to school and gotten my diploma. Now I was a recent high school graduate with a *Diploma* in hard. I had a cute little baby girl, but I had no job and no moony.

The only thing at that time that brought me happiness was the off-and-on relationship I had had with John. Everything else seemed to be bringing me down, reinforcing the idea that I needed to get away. John didn't appear to be in any haste to leave, but I couldn't wait. It was like Clewiston was a burden and I was carrying it on my shoulders, and it was just me, and me alone!

I went to call my sister. I just couldn't wait any longer. I didn't want her to know how desperate I was, but as I waited for her to answer the phone, I could feel my heart racing in anticipation of what the response was going to be. The phone rang a couple of times before it was answered, but in my mind, it felt as it was ringing forever. Maybe they knew I was the one who was calling and they didn't want to answer me because they didn't want me there.

Anyway, finally the phone was answered. I could my heart racing. *"Hello,"* my sister said. "Hello," I responded timidly, all the while expecting her to say that she had asked our cousin Sueleene and she decided that she didn't want me there. "Did you ask cousin Sueleene if I could come there?" My sister said, *"Yes, and she said it's okay. But I won't be able to pick you up until Friday after work."*

It was Monday when I called her, so I had another four days to wait. I was happy, but I knew those days would be forever. The important thing was that she said I could come. Maybe they didn't think I was a terrible person; maybe they did like me after all.

I did everything I could to make the time pass quickly. I tried not to think about it because I realized that the more I thought about it, the longer the time appeared to be taking. Finally the day came and my sister came as she had promised. We arrived in Jacksonville, which was about a four-hour journey from Clewiston. During the whole trip I was imagining what the house looked like. I was thinking of meeting new friends, working and perhaps even finding a new boyfriend.

It wasn't working out with John. I hadn't been seeing much of him, and I hadn't told him that I was leaving. I thought that by leaving Clewiston behind, I could come here and reinvent myself. I could have a new lease on life. There was no one here who knew me as "Esther," or "Billy Jean."

The former was a name I had come to hate so much because "Billy Jean" was the name of one of my classmates who started calling me names. He said I walked around Little Harlem like "Andy Dufresne from the movie *Shawshank Redemption*," meaning I thought myself better than everyone else. If only they knew how lowly I thought of myself! Truth was I carried myself like Aunt Mazie taught me, with head up high. Funny, though, this kid caused half the people in the town to call me "Billy Jean," even today! This memory brings tears to my eyes as I write this book, but it just confirms the awesome power of God in bringing me through my journey.

Anyway, returning to my story, we arrived at this big two-story, older wooden house that looked like someone had started construction on the back some time ago, but had never completed it. The front of the house was plain, but neat. It was nothing like what I had imagined after hearing so much about Sueleene's "mansion," but nonetheless I was very happy to be there.

There was nothing striking about the outside or inside of the house, although it was a mansion with seven bedrooms. e had rented the bottom portion out to some relatives who didn't seem to pay, or at least if they did, it was never on time.

I was now in Jacksonville for a few weeks and had gotten no new connection. I had no luck finding a job, which was mostly due to lack of transportation to go job hunting because my sister had to work and Sueleene

was your typical "workaholic."

Every other week my sister would treat me to dinner at one of the local Chinese restaurants and we would eat all we could; there was not a lot of conversation, but I sure enjoyed those outings.

I had begun to hate Jacksonville. Sueleene and I didn't say much to each other, but she was nice and never made me feel as if I were in the way or not wanted there. Nevertheless, I never felt like it was home, the same way I felt about my home growing up. Now she had several kids much younger than I living there, so I shared a tiny room with my sister and kept my clothes in a box.

Jacksonville turned out to be another place where it was a nightmare for me, not because of my family. No, they really treated me well. It was because of a horrible incident involving some boys and their car, and a crazy woman with a gun. I had a "play cousin" who was dating a guy and brought a friend for me. While driving around, hanging out, a female just approached our car and started sprayed the car with bullets. I didn't care the reason -- I started screaming to let me out of the car, and my play cousin and I emerged safely.

Yes, another incident where God was watching out for me because He had specific plans for my destiny that did not include being killed by a stranger while I sat in a strange car with people I just met! I never told anyone about that one horrible night. I mean who would have believed me? Plus I felt like if I told what happened to me, it would have caused problems, both there and back home. So again I managed to suppress that night like I had learned to do my past.

I had many more restless days and sleepless nights while in Jacksonville. One day while at the restaurant with my sister, I saw this hand on a large poster pointing straight at me. *"We want you!"* it said. It was an ad for the United States Army. At that moment I felt as if I wanted to join. I just wanted to get away from a place that had become a disappointment to me. I had come here thinking I would have the chance to reinvent myself, but instead it had brought me pain and more distress. My baby was with my mother and I knew she was doing well, but I needed to make something of myself, and I realized that it wouldn't work here. I needed to leave again.

I had never considered joining the army. I was never the athletic type, and I thought that one needed to be very physical to be successful as a soldier. But at that moment I was anxious to get on with my life, and I was willing to do whatever it took to get away from Jacksonville, the place that I had thought would be somewhere I could start anew.

Chapter 20

The fact of the matter was that I didn't ever recall discussing going to college, or joining any of the Armed Services, and to be fair, I didn't even communicate my desire to do either of the two. Subsequently, I saw no reason to attend the annual college prep classes offered by the school. My thought process was that only the smart people went to college, and the mere thought of joining any one of the branches of the United States Armed Forces scared me to no end. But at this moment, getting away from the place my parents called "home" was all that was on my mind.

A few days later I found myself sitting down with a military recruiter in Duval County, West Jacksonville, Florida. Although lost, restless and desperate, I was aware that I could go to Job Corps from here, and that was what I was hoping to do. So how did I end up sitting before a military recruiter?

Basically I had already reasoned within my own mind that I wasn't a suitable candidate for the Armed Services. First, I had watched a movie about the difficult life of men and women in the military. Several things stood out, the most notable being that mean drill sergeant whose job was to make the new recruits' lives a living hell.

While sitting there waiting for my interview, I was fighting images of some militant, belligerent, narcissistic person getting all up in my face, yelling and making derogative comments about my mother. To that image, I added the physical side of military service, which included waking before dawn and undergoing grueling bodily abuse until well after the sun went down! I imagined the five-kilometer run and a slew of other cardio-targeted drills that would have challenged the stamina of the best athlete. I was born with little athletic ability, so I already knew I would be the object of the mean sergeant's daily ridicule.

I was patiently sitting in the waiting room, when out came this tall, well-manicured officer. He walked over to me and firmly shook my hand, giving me what seemed to be a sincere smile. *"We are really glad you are here."* I sensed my stress level diminishing to the degree that I felt comfortable enough to share some personal things with the recruiter.

I felt it was necessary that I paint a clear picture of how desperate I was to leave the place where I grew up, which I extended to a need to leave the whole State of Florida. I followed him into his office. The recruiter made a few phone calls, then reclined in his office chair, and turned his attention to me. With a smile he asked, *"Veronica, can you be ready in ten days?"* I replied "Yes, sir, and thank you so much."

He reclined back in his chair and started flipping through a stack of manila folders on his desk. I was excited and eager to discover where I was soon to be going. All I could think about was that this was the long awaited opportunity for me to recreate myself in hopes of improving my life. No one where I was going would know my past, so I could literally become any type of person I chose.

"You're going to Franklin, North Carolina," he mouthed as he answered the phone. I didn't know a lot of about NC, but I knew it got pretty cold during the winter months. Being a true Floridian, I didn't do well in the cold; nonetheless, I kept quiet because I suspected my departure date would be pushed back if I asked for a warmer city, and God knows I desperately wanted to leave as soon as possible.

Franklin, North Carolina was a place where nobody knew my name. There I would reinvent myself. When I went back home that day, I found my sister sitting outside on the steps in front of the house, so I eagerly shared with her every little detail of that day, and then asked if I could stay there for another week, or until I received my bus ticket. Things weren't going right in Jacksonville, and I was supposed to go back home, but I didn't want to go back to Clewiston. I didn't want to go back to my Harlem with nothing to my name. At the same time I didn't want to be a burden to my sister, so that was another reason I decided to take this opportunity to join the military.

Big Sis, "the protector," was always concerned about my well being. I knew she understood my need to leave, and therefore her answer would be yes. We had much dialogue about the trip, the what if's, the questions about how I was going to get there, and so forth, but finally with some reservation she gave her blessings. She said she understood and assured me that I could stay as long as it took for my assignment to materialize. I saw all the stations where recruiters were standing to entice youngsters like me to join each of the four branches of the military. However, I made up my mind that I was going to Job Corps.

My mood was happy, happy, happy. I cleaned while daydreaming about how Job Corps would be. I saw myself free, with lots of friends who were enthusiastic about hanging out with Veronica. Days passed until finally, I said my goodbyes to my sister and my cousin and off I went.

It was a two-hour waiting period until the bus pulled out. I was not sure if we were waiting on another bus or a lunch break for the bus driver. I was a little hungry, but knowing I had only fifty dollars to my name and didn't know what to expect once I got there, I opted not to spend anything out of it. So I just ignored the stomach noises like I had done on more than one occasion before.

The bus station had always been somewhat of a scary place to me, mostly due to all the late night scary movies I had watched as child, like the *Twilight Zone* and *Alfred Hitchcock* shows. It was like strange things always occurred at the bus station and weird people always hung out there. I guess that's what I got for disobeying my mom when she used to tell us to go to bed and turn the TV off. Obedience truly is better than sacrifice, just like the *Holy Bible* says!

Scanning the happenings around me as I sat anxiously awaiting my bus to be called, I spotted these three individuals who looked to be in their late teens or early twenties. All seemed to be relaxed in the bus terminal, while I fought back the bittersweet tears.

I had always envied people who seemed to not have any worries. I so wanted to be like them. So naturally I watched the three for a while, and then I noticed they got up when the voice over the intercom announced that the next bus was heading to North Carolina. Wow, we were going to the same place!

Once on the bus I contemplated going over to introduce myself to them, but eventually I talked myself out of it. I didn't have the confidence in myself to engage strangers in a light conversation about where we were all going. Silence was safer.

At last, the driver arrived at our destination, and I rushed to the front of the line, hoping to make it out before the three young women. I was hoping I wouldn't chicken out before I got the chance to introduce myself. Let's just say it went well, as all three individuals received me and we all ended up being close associates once we arrived at the Job Corps Center.

I finally settled in my new dorm room at LBJ Job Corps in Franklin, North Carolina. There were four girls to a room and I was assigned to a bottom bunk. The first thing that came to my mind was that they had sensed I was nobody. How else did I get the lower bed? Why wasn't I given the top bed? Once more I was beginning to doubt my worth. Would this ever end? I was so emotionally screwed up that the simplest negative thing in my life became a tremendous slap in the face. It always seemed to reach to my very core.

I had arrived with very few belongings, including my Florida-style winter boots and jacket. What I didn't know then was that North Carolina cold was a different type of cold from Florida. It chilled the bones and that little fake fur around the ankles of my leather boots would not be sufficient to keep the cold away from me. To make matters worse, I was soon to learn that the water from the ice could give me frostbite. To say I hate cold would be an extreme understatement! What had I gotten myself into? True, I had left my birthplace and the warm state in which I grew up. Yep, I got what I wished for!

Months passed, and while I reluctantly adjusted to the weather, I was beginning to miss John. He couldn't call me because I had never given him my contact information. I had considered ridding my mind of him because I thought there was no future with him. But now I was starting to realize that I was really missing him. John was the first person I had ever given myself freely to, and it seemed as if I were really falling in love with him. They say, "Absence makes the heart grows fonder," and maybe that was what was happening to me. It was never about sex for me. I had really wanted to wait until marriage, but I guess I never had a say in that, thanks to my father whom I had privately nicknamed *"Jack the Ripper"*

I was here alone, and being an introvert did not help. I had decided to punish John, but instead I was punishing myself. I saw everyone there at the Job Corps hooking up with someone else, but to me it felt as if a part of me was missing because John was nowhere around and I couldn't get in touch with him. When I said that I wanted to reinvent myself, I was thinking of leaving Clewiston and John, but now I was beginning to see my mistake.

I was sitting on my bunk bed in the dorm one day, about to write a letter, when I suddenly got frustrated and threw down the pad and pen on the bed. John hated reading; he wasn't too good at it either. If you wanted to hide something and it could be written, you only had to write it on a piece of paper and it would be safe from him. I decided that it was best to call him.

Now keep in mind that he had no house phone, so the only way to reach him was to call the operator and get the address to the only convenience store/gas station in Little Harlem, which was *K & J*. Once I got that, then I called the 411-directory, gave them the store's address, and made inquiry about the nearest pay phone. People who went to this much trouble really wanted to connect with the person they were calling. Well, I truly wanted to connect with John.

That week I left no fewer than five messages. Each time I called, I got more and more desperate to hear from him. I knew almost everybody knew whom he and his grandmother, Flossy, were. Also, his elder brother, sister and a slew of other relatives lived less than a few houses from the pay phone. So I made myself stressed over the thought of him ignoring my request to call me.

I was feeling frustrated, upset and abandoned. I had made the "statistic" of being another young, single mother who was alone. Three weeks had passed since the initial phone call, so I conjured up enough nerve to call again, telling myself that if he was not there, he had moved on and giving me a subtle message that my situation was just my baby and me.

This time when I called, I got him. When I heard the voice on the other end say, *"Veronica,"* it felt like music to my ear and to my heart. I was so glad to have heard from him that it didn't matter why he didn't call. All I cared about at that moment was that John was back in my life and life was worth living again. Unlike the many times before when I told him I loved him, this time it was without hesitation.

We exchanged contact information, and thereafter, we talked twice almost every week. Gee, he must have missed me terribly, too! I kept promising myself that I would be mature and let bygones be bygones after he left me alone to deliver and care for our baby. But I couldn't help myself because I felt incomplete without him. So one day when I was talking to him, I blurted out, "Where were you, John? I called you like a hundred times and I know they gave you the messages."

He chuckled a little and said, *"I went up the road because I needed some money. You know Okalanta is closed."* I knew it was. Working at the sugar factory was a seasonal thing, but once that was over they would close and reopen when the sugar cane was on again.

I was happy now. I was talking to John again and feeling like a million dollars. For some reason, knowing

237

that John was awaiting me when I got back home put a drive in my spirit. I felt as if I could tackle and conquer any course here at Job Corps. Several positive things were happening in my life. I got a Driver's License, completed a year course as a legal secretary, tried out and made the football squad as a cheerleader.

Man, did I love my outfit! I loved the way that little short skirt made the boys take notice, but on the flip side it wasn't worth it because the girls at LBJ had issues with me because I was so cute in my uniform.

There were four people who helped shaped my LBJ experience. We'll call them Mr. Bo-legged, Ms. Miami, Little New York, and Mr. Dorm. First there was Little New York. She was this 4'4, 98lbs, yellow female, who, for some reason, didn't like me. She literally tortured me daily for months. She would block the entrance of the door and dared me to go through, while cursing me out for no reason. Granted, I was at least twice her stature, and a good 30lb heavier. I was twenty years old then, but had never in all my years heard such profanity.

I can remember as a child how my mom occasionally used the word *"hell,"* and that alone made me cringe. It was like my world came to an end. While the words *"heifer and wretch"* were this girl's utterance of choice, even those made me feel horrible. I felt like my mom hated me when she called my siblings and I the occasional wretches back in the day, probably because I had so much respect, adoration and love for my mother. I still do!

I remember the time we witnessed Little New York beating up this 5'11, 180 pound chick who was known for being LBJ's notorious loud mouth, trash talking bully. She sometime went by the name "Tarzan."

Little New York was tiny, but she had the heart of a lion. There was this other time we watched her go toe

238

to toe with her boyfriend. I mean he hit her with intensity, and she never shed a tear. Her famous saying was, *"I don't have nothing to lose."* That girl would get right back up each time her boyfriend knocked her down and charged at him, until the dorm leader decided they had seen enough. A few months down the line Little New York and her boyfriend were arrested and hauled off to jail for selling Marijuana. I was relieved. I now realize that that young lady had had some issues and really felt like she had nothing to lose.

The second "person of great influence" in my life was "Miss Miami." She leaped down off the bus, thrust her way to the front of the group, and then motioned with her hand for all to stop. She had her lips puckered, her hands akimbo, and boldly proclaimed to be NIC, (Negro in Charge). Then she turned and walked towards the LBJ office with her suitcase in hand.

I overheard one of the dorm monitors saying, *"She's trouble,"* and believe me she was just that - TROUBLE. Miss Miami was wearing a plaid mini with shorts underneath them, and a low-cut, solid blue V-neck tank, with a pair of blue high top tennis shoes.

After she was officially checked in, this woman marched right up to the entrance of the girls' dorm, pushed opened the door and jumped dead center on top of one of the tables, where she repeated the "welcome speech" she had given outside. I am guessing that this was a reminder for those who were there, and a FYI for those who had yet to "get the memo."

After her speech, she asked to borrow a smoke, and half the smokers in the girls' dorm stood in line to light the borrowed cigarettes. As scared as I was back then, if I were a smoker, I would have gladly offered her my entire carton.

Miss Miami (Tarzan) was constantly bullying folks before she faced a showdown with Little New York. There was this one time when she took the handle of an old broom, walked over to this girl who was minding her own business, picked up a pair of her underwear with the handle of the broom, and flung it around the girls' dorm.

They called her "country" because she was from Tennessee and had a strong accent. Sad to say Country was country and that's not necessarily a bad thing in my book, but it was obvious that Country had basically made herself a target for all the bullies. How? Well, first the girl never -- and I mean never combed her hair. Her mouth was jacked up with teeth the color of butter, and Country showered no more than once a week. At any rate that still didn't give Tarzan or anyone else the right to bully her.

Watching Tarzan waiving that broom back and forth with Country's underwear hanging from the end was like watching a tennis match. Our heads were going from side to side, watching as Country played cat and mouse with the broom handle in an attempt to get what rightfully belong to her. I made it my duty to stay my distance because I felt with my luck Miss Miami could spot the fear in my eyes and change her focus from Country to me!

I'm not sure whatever happened to Country, but the word was that she was sent home or to another Job Corps center. I purposely avoided her and anybody else on the "Tarzan hit list" because I figured after they became bored with bullying and harassing the folks on their list, then naturally I would be the next target.

Miss Miami (aka Tarzan) was pretty scary in my opinion. She stood shoulder-to-shoulder with any 6'0 ft. male, had a nice figure, but was as solid as a rock. She may have had a feminine body, but she had a mouth like a sailor, and tattoos of Indian ink -- homemade tats and old keloids scars around what should have been cuts smaller in size. On top of that Tarzan was a hustler who made it her life's mission to stir up mess.

Little New York was a direct contrast, and was for the most part low-keyed, somewhat of a lone wolf. Eventually she and Tarzan got into it. And let's just say Miss Miami had more mouth than bite. It was comical how the predator soon became the prey.

Things got much better for me once Little New York had left, but in the meantime I did my best to avoid Tarzan. Both of us were on the cheering squad for LBJ. I'll never forget the day we were trying out for the varsity team. First she showed up late, never tried out, but announced she was on the team. Each time we played an away game, two things would happen. First the other team beat the stew out of our boys, and Miss Miami, without fail, found herself involved in a verbal confrontation that oftentimes got physical.

I must say I ended up liking her. I sensed in my spirit that somewhere deep inside she was gentle, but it was hard to see because she was just so loud. It was odd how she never bothered me, yet she continued to bully the other students, females as well as males.

My new friend, although I didn't trust her, was Miss Miami. I knew she would turn on you in a heartbeat, and I had no plan of fighting that giant. Often she would get into a cursing match with one of the male dorm leaders, but she never got in trouble for it.

She even bragged about *"getting what she wanted, or else."* I honestly did not get it until one day it was rumored that she and Mr. Dorm leader were seeing each other. Now we all knew that was not permitted, and if caught, the employee would be fired on the spot and the student would be sent home.

241

Mr. Dorm, the third person I want to talk about here, was a tall, handsome guy whom I had tried so hard to get to notice me. The thing that comes back to my mind is the day I put on those tight little shorts and made my way in the vicinity where he was in an attempt to get him to look at me. I wanted him to notice me the same way he seemed to see Miss Tarzan and several of the other girls. But instead he burst my bubble when he told me I needed to take those *"Hoochie Mama"* shorts off and stop trying to be somebody I was not. That thing hurt me so badly that I felt like he pimp slapped me with an ugly stick. I mean it had to be because I was ugly and unattractive, or why else would he have said that? I have never heard of him saying that to anyone else.

After that it took me a few days before I came out of the dorm during our free weekend time. That was because when he had made that statement, other people were around and heard him. So that small fact added humiliation to the equation. I purposely avoided Mr. Dorm for the remainder of my LBJ stay. Yet I heard of him flirting and sleeping with other females who made a point of wearing "hoochie mama" shorts.

I was too hurt at the time to realize that he was paying me a compliment by rejecting my attempt to look and act like those permissive females to whom he was attracted. He must have assessed that I was a "good girl." I praise God for protecting me when I didn't have the positive mindset to protect myself.

Job Corps is the nation's largest career technical training and educational program for young people. One has to be at least sixteen years of age and qualify as low income. There are approximately 125 centers nationwide. New students arrived at LBJ on a weekly basis; there was this unspoken tradition that one was to "dress up," (hair /face/clothing) and be at the bus pick -

up and delivery station or be somewhere in close proximity so as to scope out the new meat.

I didn't have a lot, but I was slim and had a half way decent figure, so I could pull off a tee shirt and jeans and still hang with the best of them. So like the others I got all dolled up, and positioned myself in the vicinity of the bus stop, waiting and watching for the newcomers to arrive.

LBJ was like a revolving door where people came every week, and for the most part people went home every other week. Job Corps didn't monkey around, or at least not Lyndon B Johnson Center, which did not tolerate foolishness. Around the time the business office announced the bus arrival time of the newcomers, I got these butterflies and knots in my stomach, which forced me to spend a lot of time in the restroom. As a result I usually didn't see the new folks until later that day.

I dreaded the mere possibility of meeting another Little New York, or worse. We all sized up the newcomers. Both genders did the same thing, but for different reasons. The girls sized up the competition, and the guys sized up their next victims, if you get my drift. In no less time than two weeks on campus almost everyone was in a relationship. It was like no female was left without a man, except me. Ironically some coupling occurred within the same sex.

Then one day I saw the fourth person I want to describe here. I saw " Bowlegs," who stood a little over 5'7, medium built, dark-skinned, nice smile. He had both dimples and bowlegs. He resembled the fictional character "Cole" on the Martin Lawrence show. Eventually, Bo and I met and started "talking." It was nothing official. We were just friends, but I liked this boy. I enjoyed every word that came out of his full lips. Bo was from Fayetteville, North Carolina. However, he pronounced it "*Fedville.*" To put it nicely, his ability to articulate was far less than perfect, and his writing skills were less than average. His overall demeanor was a cross between "country" and "Geechee."

Chapter 21

I couldn't really say that Bo was this big time communicator. He was more on the quiet side, but when he did speak, I listened intently so as to decipher what he was saying with that decidedly Southern accent of his. Plus he was pleasant to look at. A typical conversation went like this: *"My last two jobs were at a Kafaye, (Café') the maine (man) was not happy when they knew I was finda (about to) leave, because I was good at mi job, and was jist (just) about to become head cook."*

There was no question that Bo-leg butchered the English language, but his words sounded like the New York Philharmonic Orchestra to me. I was feeling like my life was changing for the better. Check me out talking to one of the "cutest" guys on campus, never mind it was the campus of Job Corps, but campus nonetheless.

And then *she* came. I knew it; it was like the forbidden tree. Bo had been there for over eight months and never dated or talked to any other girl besides me. I was the first, and then out the blue, "Ms. Red-bone" liked him. In the African-American community we learned from the days of slavery to classify ourselves from the lightest complexion (light, bright and damn-near white) to the darkest (ebony). Closest to the whitest looking women were those whose bones we assumed were "red." Hence, the name given them. Our men were first drawn to the light-skinned women and lastly to women of my dark complexion. See the problem?

Now due to the fact that Bo and I were not officially dating, this lovely and prissy thing was within her rights to go after him, and plus I felt like I didn't have a chance in hell to keep him, once she arrived on the scene. This girl was cute, and also popular with both the girls and the guys. As a matter of fact most of the guys and some of the girls wanted to date her. So I did the honorable thing. I backed away, and once again -- you guessed it -- the two of them became an item and were with each other seven days a week. Folks started calling her "Ms. Bo," and like they say, "if you can't beat 'em then join 'em."

So I, too, addressed her as Ms. Bo, but Lord knows I felt so rejected. It felt as if she had stolen my man, even though we were not dating, nor had he deceived me about our relationship. I was devastated, wondering if I would always have to give up "my man" as soon as a light-skinned beauty showed up. It was all so unfair! How could the legacy of slavery be so painful four hundred years after it supposedly ended?

I had learned early in life not to show emotions. My motto used to be, "never let 'em see you sweat." Many nights I cried, and not necessarily over Bo. I just cried. It seemed at that point that crying without defining my pain was the only way I could feel something. Certainly I wasn't in love with Bo; heck, I didn't even know him at all. We never even kissed. I was more upset with the feeling of inferiority that engulfed me when he chose another woman. Once again I felt rejected, as if everyone were laughing behind my back.

A few months down the line I heard that Mr. and Ms. Bo-legs were no longer an item. The word on the street was that she broke up with Bo, and left him for his best friend's girlfriend. Yep, you heard right. She was, or became a lesbian.

Honestly I was happy to hear that. I felt he deserved it because, in my mind, he dumped me for her. Some more time passed and I would occasionally see Bo walking with a group of men and sometimes women, but where I stood and the unsolicited information I got from what we called "LBJ big mouths," was that Bo had several girls interested in him, but he didn't appear to be interested in them. Wow, she must have hurt him immeasurably. I felt a slight bit of compassion for him.

Then one day I heard someone call my name. I quickly turned and I saw that it was Bo. I had acted uninterested for several weeks, but he pursued me and I finally gave in. I was still not dating, so I agreed to go out with him that Valentine's weekend. I was super excited. I eagerly shared the info with my friend, Miss Miami.

I was in my bed cutting out photos of the beauty of the month from an old *Jet* magazine. I had never really considered myself a beauty queen, but the way I was feeling at that time, I could have been featured as the beauty of the month. I figured 38-28-38 was pretty close to perfect.

There was to be a dance at the Job Corps Centre pretty soon. One early February morning, I overheard some girls discussing sex and scheming up a plan to sneak their boyfriends into the girls' dorm the night of the dance. They were planning on having sex while the monitors and staff members were out chaperoning some of the girls.

Now somewhere between the scheme and the execution, one of the girls informed me that Bo was a part of the plan. God knows I wasn't that bold (nor that man-crazy) to take a guy to my dorm to have sex with me, but neither was I a snitch. Deep down inside I was pleased, and yet somewhat surprised that he said yes when I asked him about the plan. I wasn't expecting it, since I didn't take him for the "brave heart" type.

Perhaps he felt pressured, or it could have been that he, too, wanted to fit in. Either way I really didn't care, nor did I spend a lot of time thinking why he had said yes. I was just glad, because I really liked him. I thought he was cute, a little shy, and as fine as they come.

That boy didn't owe *Levi 501* anything. They should have offered him a contract for doing such an incredible job advertising their jeans. He had a masculine body with a tight ass and a sexy bulge where the seams of those jeans met. So for the next few days, all I could think about was me and Bo, hugging, hunching and kissing.

Never did I claim to be one of the five virgins, (virginity taken, not by choice) and I had a beautiful baby girl named Precious back home. In terms of my Precious, the lesson learned was that you can get pregnant the first time, even if you don't go all the way. I later read something about a woman ovulating and a man easily impregnating her at that time. I must have been ovulating, but, quite simply, when you play, you pay!

But you had better know that if I were going to do dirt, or have sex, trust me, it would not be in the company of girls or guys who were given to gossiping and divulging personal information about others, whether it was the truth or fiction.

I had no intention of sleeping with Bo, planning to make myself content with a kiss, a hug, and a hunch. For readers who don't know what a "hunch" is, it is the act of rotating the pelvis in an erotically suggestive way -- aka "hunch."

LBJ was well known for its gossip; everybody talked, the girls, the boys, and the staff. Not a week went by without one hearing something about a girl or a guy getting caught, and sometimes it was a staff member sleeping with another staff member, and often you would hear about staff sleeping with one of the students, both the males and the females. In short, it was a place where soap opera material was developed.

It was night. I could hear my roommates in the bunk above, and in our quarters there were about eight of us altogether. I was nervous because Bo was not there as yet. I whispered a prayer, "Lord, please let him come; I promise you we will not go all the way. I just don't want to be taunted for the rest of my stay at LBJ." I preferred to be an invisible spectator and not the focal point.

Just about the time my emotions were about to overcome me, suddenly I heard what sounded like a tap or a thumping sound. I quickly pulled myself together, got out of my bed, and held my breath, hoping it was Bo and not one of LBJ's authorities. With heart pounding, I listened for a voice. I opened the door and it was he. I invited him inside, closed the door, and we crawled into my bed.

Bo was not a serious communicator. The few times we had spoken, I would get a "yes" or a "no" out of him, but that was about the extent of it. Ironically, we started out in bed with legs crossed Indian-style, listening to the others. Let's just say they had no shame in their game and didn't try to hide the noise. I think at that point we both knew there was not going to be any sex between the two of us.

To tell the truth, I think both of us felt very uncomfortable. I was in bed with my matching candy apple red bra and French cut underwear, feeling like a slut. All my life I had a check in my spirit, even when I tried to be like everybody else and sometimes be like myself. I was condemned by an invisible finger! I just couldn't get away with much without repenting, or at least saying I was sorry.

Slut or not, I still wanted to kiss him. I figured that was the least I could do without crossing the line, so I pulled the thin, fake silk robe up and tied it snuggly around my waist. Eventually the anticipated kiss came. He stumbled to find my lips, but once we got past that, we kissed, French all the way. For me to describe my emotions right after that deep throat kiss is to just say everything that glitters is not gold. This boy had no idea how to kiss! He possessed bona fide soup warmers, "full thick lips," but he literally gave me all his "suga," and I ended up with a mouth full of spit.

I didn't know what to do so I hung in there as long as I could. But eventually I had to spit and there was no place for me to expectorate except the bed sheet. Well that ended our date. Bo was the last to arrive and the first to leave.

The next day and thereafter, until the day he left, we never mentioned that night and neither did we ever speak again. He avoided me at all cost, and I did the same. I didn't care if I hurt his feelings or bruised his ego that night he filled my mouth with spit. We both knew in an instant that he had no kissing finesse and he didn't want that information to get out.

The strange thing about the whole situation was nobody, and I mean *no one* asked about our night, nor did they inquire about why we no longer spoke or

250

avoided each other after the night in the dorm when most girls made sure they saw their men again and often. Three months later Bo's tour was over. I think he had reached the age limit. He had obviously gotten older, or he would not have what they called "aged out." Bye, bye Bo!

Chapter 22

It was time to go back home to Clewiston. I, too, had finished my time there and now I was leaving. Everything I owned was in two old *Sampsonite* suitcases. I was not sure what I would encounter once there. I hated Clewiston and wished that I didn't have to go back, but the two most important people to me were there -- my daughter and the love of my life. I was very anxious to see the latter. We had been communicating twice a week via telephone for the last 10 months, and not only that, but he had been sending me $50-$60 every month, and God knows I needed and appreciated it. Now LBJ gave us about $75 a month for personal hygiene and toiletries, and a little extra for clothing, so it all added up to taking care of my needs and a few of my wants.

John and I were back to being girlfriend and boyfriend, and I couldn't wait to see him. The bus ride back home seemed as if it were taking forever. He knew I was coming, and he had told me how excited he was about seeing me again. We hadn't seen each other in over two years, and I was aching for his touch. I was seated on the bus, looking through the window with a big smile on my face. I was hoping no one was seeing it, because they would have thought that I had lost it for sure.

My mind went back to the conversation we had had the night before. *"Are you longing to see me?"* he had asked. "You bet," I said with a big smile on my face. *"It has been a while, hasn't it?"* "Yeah, are you longing to see me?" *"Of course, what do you think? I don't think you know how much I missed you."* "Well, we'll be back together tomorrow. Have you had a chance to see our daughter, Precious?" *"I have been so busy."*

I was disappointed with his response. "She lives in Clewiston. I'm sure you could have gone to see her." *"Well, we can go see her when you come. I don't think your mom likes me."* If he had said my dad, I would have understood, but I don't think my mom hated him. He was just trying to find excuses. I didn't like where the conversation was going, so I changed it back to the more pleasant way it was before. "I'm really longing to see you," I said before hanging up.

I was glad I was leaving LBJ. There was no more restriction on my life, and I loathed restriction. LBJ was like a school, since we had classrooms and everything, but for some reason I was more tolerant of it there. I couldn't hide away like I did when I was in high school, because there were always roll calls, and one had to account for where one was, and there were stiff penalties for breaking one of their rules.

In my heart I was sure John was seeing someone else, but nonetheless, I was still glad to be seeing him soon. As the *Greyhound* bus turned the corner and pulled up into its stop, I could see John's Hunter green *Ford Granada* in the parking lot. I was pretty excited. I checked my hair to make sure it was in place and reapplied my strawberry lipstick and gloss. I got off the bus, pretending I hadn't already spotted him, so that I could act surprised when he approached me.

253

I was standing beside my two suitcases when he approached me. We gladly embraced each other. We were smiling, showing all our teeth and then some. He held me off and looked at me. *"You look good,"* he said, turning me around so that he could get a good look at me. I knew I had put on a little weight. I could feel my jeans fitting more snuggly than they had before. He wasn't looking bad himself; however, he hadn't changed. He was the same lanky person he had always been.

"I really missed you, you know," he said, looking into my eyes. *"You didn't cheat on me, did you?"* "Of course not, why would I? Did you cheat on me?" I asked. *"Honey, I'm as hard as diamond."* In my heart I knew that meant he had not waited for me. I was hurt, but I brushed it off. When I had left Clewiston we were not on good terms, so I couldn't blame him for that. As he took my suitcases and we walked to the car, I gave him a rundown of a few things that had taken place at the Job Corps.

I was glad to see my daughter. I had really missed her. She was walking and looking really pretty. My mom had obviously done a good job with her while I was away. I was now twenty-three years old, clearly an adult. I saw my dad, but I had vowed never to talk to him again, which I didn't. I avoided him as much as it was humanly possible.

I went to find my friend, Sandra, but I saw a new lady in the trailer where she used to live. When I asked her where she was, the lady told me she didn't know her. I left, wishing I had made more of an effort to keep in touch while I was away. I never saw her again.

John and I spent a lot of time together, just hanging out doing nothing. At first I didn't care, but then I started getting bored. I knew a change had to be made, but I didn't have a clue how it would be done. All

I knew for certain was that I was slowly dying in Clewiston.

A few months after returning to Clewiston, John told me that Joan, the mother of his two kids, was moving to Jacksonville, Florida. I was really glad to hear that because I always thought they were still messing around, even though he had denied it emphatically. I had this underlining fear that they would be getting back together because of the kids, or perhaps he would eventually move there after awhile.

I could tell he was restless and that meant he was ready to run. I knew of his history, not by way of actually experiencing it, but it was something I had picked up listening to his many conversations. I struggled with the thought of him leaving because I wasn't sure if I were a part of the plan. I was reluctant to bring it up because I had learned earlier in the relationship that John was primarily an avoider when it came to real life situations, or anything that might cause an argument or required an intelligent decision. He was just the kind of person who would leave without even considering the matter or the consequences.

One day we were all at the park when I heard one of his friends said to him, *"Man, when are you leaving?"* My eyes got big as a saucer and my heart started palpitating. A feeling of hurt and abandonment flooded my mind, but I managed to keep it in check. At that moment, he didn't answer his friend. I guess the look he gave him was an indication that I wasn't aware of what was happening and he didn't want me to know. But it was too late because I had already heard.

That evening when we were by ourselves, I brought up the conversation. "When were you going to tell me that you were leaving?" I asked. *"I wasn't going to leave without telling you,"* he responded. "So that means you're planning on leaving, aren't you?" He shrugged, *"I don't know what I'm going to do. I need a woman in my life, a strong woman."* "So you don't think I can be that woman?" I asked. *"I'm not saying you can't, but you don't have any experience. I need to think."*

"What do you want me to do in the meantime?" *"I'm not pushing you away from me, you know."* "Then why do I feel this way?" I said softly, more to myself than to him. This conversation was getting me more depressed. In my mind I was building a future with John and I, but it seemed as if his mind was somewhere else. He was my ticket out of Clewiston, but it appeared that the price for it was about to go up to more than what I could afford, and it was getting me down, way down.

We met after that, but each time he saw me he could tell that something was wrong. This evening as I was sitting in his car, he looked at me and said, *"Look, I've made up my mind. I'm going to Miami, and I'm taking you with me. How soon can you be ready?"* I couldn't believe what I was hearing. I looked seriously at him, "Are you serious?" *"Yes, I'm serious. I'm as desperate to leave this place as you are."* I quickly hugged him. "I'm so happy. You'll never regret this, I promise you."

"Can you be ready tomorrow?" "John, I'm ready now. I can't wait to leave Clewiston." *"Okay, we leave tomorrow. You meet me here tomorrow at 8:00 in the morning and we will leave for Miami then."* I hugged John again, screaming with delight. I didn't care where we were going to stay in Miami. All I knew was that I was leaving Clewiston, a place I had grown to detest.

We arrived in Miami according to John's plan. I was so excited, yet a little nervous. I wasn't sure if I fit in. You see, I had been a fan of *Miami Vice*, (the Hit TV program) and they were always in full makeup, wearing the latest clothes, and sporting bodies to die for. Also I had the fear that John was going to cheat on me with one of these beautiful women. I mean, he had a lot of women in small town Clewiston, so I could only imagine what it would like in a big city like Miami.

Sadly I lived with that fear during our entire stay in Miami, to the degree that I became extremely suspicious and jealous. I already had self-esteem issues and now my confidence was dragging the ground.

It was then that I met "Aunt Lucky," John's biological aunt. She was not happy about John bringing me with him to Miami, so apparently he told neither of us hat we were going to live with His Aunt Lucky and her grandchild, Debbie Lee

I was very upset because I was not aware of this living arrangement, plus it didn't look good. It was pretty obvious we were sexually active, and we had a child together. Aunt Lucky agreed to let us stay after she laid the law, and I mean she didn't use a chaser.

John and I would get into low tone augments because I stopped sleeping with him. You see, I had made up my mind to wait until he married me, or at least until we moved out of this women's house before we slept together again. The way I was brought up, it didn't sit right with me doing it in one room while an adult was next door and could hear us.

RIP Aunt Lucky She died many years after we left Miami, but OMG, let's just say she was a straight Hellion, even though she confessed to being a Christian. The things she did and the foul language she sometimes used was not what one would expect from a Christian.

However, John's cousin Debbie Lee was like a breath of fresh air. She was very nice and she was willing to share her room and everything she had with me. A few weeks after moving in, Debbie Lee got me a job at McDonalds and we had a blast working together. Debbie Lee was about 5"4, 120lbs, flawless beautiful dark skin, and shoulder length hair tinted in a light burgundy color. All the guys at McDonalds seemed to like her. Three weeks into the job I found a one-bedroom apartment off the Causeway very close to the beach, so I rushed home and shared the news with John. I begged him not to tell Aunt Lucky because by the time she was finished speaking negative things about the apartment, the job, and everything else, we would have second-guessed the move. So one Sunday I moved while she was at church, and never did I visit her again during the ten plus years we stayed in Miami.

PLEASE REMOVE (Veronica, this seems to be unnecessary information, unless you are going to connect it somewhere by the end of your book. If you agree, delete this paragraph.) We had moved several times already due to pending eviction, and each time we moved it was during the night, thus we mastered the art of night moving. I had left McDonalds and was now working at Popeye Chicken due to the fact that we moved from Carol City to N Miami Beach, and it was too far to try to stay McDonalds.

Things were going pretty good. Both John and I were working full time jobs, and we had an apartment for which we managed to pay the rent before the 15th of each month. It was always late, but the landlord never complained, probably because we just paid the $50 late fee and called it a day.

One day John came home from work, showered and while sitting on the sofa that we had gotten from off the side of the road, he reached into his pocket and produced a diamond ring. He told me that he had found it in a parking lot. I eagerly tried it on because that was my first time seeing a diamond. I had heard that it was a girl's best friend. However, I was unable to try it on because it was bent, so I just looked at it, and the truth of matter was that it looked like a cubic zircon.

A few weeks later I got a phone call from John while at work. *"Hey, guess what? I got the ring fixed,"* he said. He sounded excited, *"You wanna give it a shot?"* I was excited, "Do you mean marriage?" I asked. I had the biggest smile ever on my face. This was what I was hoping to hear a long time ago. Now I could have a real family. *"Yeah, that's what I'm talking about; you think you're ready?"* *"Sweetheart, this is what I was born for,"* I said. I'm sure he could hear the excitement in my voice.

"Ok, have you got your half?" He was referring to the money we had to pay at the courthouse to be married. "Yes," I said quickly. We had called the court on several occasions to check the price of a courthouse wedding. So five days later we each paid our half totaling $60. We were seated beside each other in the chapel, holding hands and waiting for our time, when John said, *"Well, here's your chance to turn back."*

I looked nervously at him, hoping he didn't want me to turn back. I never thought I would have seen this day. I took a deep breath, trying to calm myself, "Do you really want me to turn back?" I asked. *"No, if it works, it works, if not, at least we can say we gave it a try."*

It's kind of comical now, but back then those were the most beautiful words I had ever heard. I felt I had come a long way. I was someone who at one time in my life felt as if I were trash, and now here I was being married to the man of my dreams. It may not have been the type of wedding I had dreamt of, but it was a wedding anyway, and it was mine.

Years after moving to Miami, I ran into "Miss Miami" from Job Corp. We hugged, laughed and caught up on old times. I found out that one of the girls I went to LBJ with was seen in a Miami prostitution ring. One guy got shot trying to rob a bank. Several others were doing good. A few ended up getting married and moving back to their hometown, and a girl named Veronique lost her long-term boyfriend and he ended up living with a woman. All these things were told to me by Miss Miami.

But what I saw did not line up with the story Miss Miami was telling me about herself. Something wasn't quite right. This woman looked as if she had the HIV virus, as she was pale, thin, and I could see several bottles of medications with just letters of the Alphabet. Having worked for Dr. Goodgame at the Infectious Disease/HIV Research Centre, I was aware that those bottles carried drugs for the HIV virus.

Several weeks had passed since our last conversation. I decided to pay her a visit to see how she was doing, and also to confirm my suspicion. We somewhat kept in touch via pager/phone, so this would be the first time I paid her a house visit. I wrote down the address she gave me and called to confirm I had the correct apartment name and number, because from where I was standing it looked to be condemned. It was not far from the Pork-n-Bean projects off of 62nd St. in Miami Dade Liberty City.

I was startled at first glance, but I managed to keep a straight face and not make her uncomfortable. I forced out a "Hi, how are you?" and without giving her a chance to answer, I immediately started reminiscing about Job Corps and the great times we had had. Once again I felt the need to change the subject. It wasn't until later that I understood the sudden change in her facial expression. After that both of us continued to struggle in conversation until she finally admitted to being exhausted and we said our goodbyes.

I was about to walk out when she said with much effort, *"Girlfriend, don't forget about me; come back and see me."* I looked at her and all I could see was a shadow of the girl I had come to know as "Miss Miami." She looked piteous. I quickly changed my blank stare to the words, "Yeah, I promise." As I walked away, I felt heavy in my heart. Perhaps it was the "female cancer" that she said she was recently diagnosed with that had spread. Therefore, I purposed in my heart to go back and see her.

For the rest of the weekend it was hard to get Miss Miami out of my head. I couldn't shake the sick feeling in my stomach, remembering how she was sleeping on the floor of what should have been a condemned building, and the difficulty she had just trying to raise her head.

A few days passed and I called her to confirm a good day and time to visit. We talked for about thirty minutes. Within that short time, she sounded winded – short of breath. The following week I went to see her, but once I arrived, the apartment was empty. As I proceeded to leave, I heard, *"Hey, Job Corps."* I turned and it was her cousin who also attended LBJ with us. No big time hugs, just a quick hello and before I got my hello out she told me about how her cousin, Miss Miami, lost her two-year battle against AIDS.

The cousin shared with me how over ten former students at LBJ were contacted by the Center for Disease Control because all of them, plus Miss Miami, were connected in some way to "Mr. Dorm," who had died of AIDS five months prior to revealing all his sexual partners, or at least the ones he remembered. Oh, my, and to think I thought I had lost something precious when Miss Miami just swept Mr. Dorm off his feet, and both of them dismissed me like yesterday's newspaper. All I knew about the AIDS virus was that once you contracted it, in time, you died. However, today I know that's not the case and there are options to dying.

Once home I started reminiscing on the experiences I had had at LBJ. I thought about how it seemed as if Mr. Dorm had favored Miss Miami and allowed her lots of extras. There were lots of rumors about the two of them, and on more than one occasion Miss Miami would have outbursts and verbal confrontations with him, yet never did she get into trouble like the rest of us were guaranteed to receive. I realized God had protected me from Mr. Dorm, and now I was glad he didn't find me attractive. Somewhere in the *Holy Bible* it speaks to situations where men mean us harm, but God turns it into our favor. God had been saving me from dangers seen and unseen for years, but this conformation gave me added reason to tell my story by writing a book to bear witness!

Chapter 23

John and I had been married for quite awhile now, and like any other married couple we were having our fair share of arguments. There were certain things he had come to learn about me that didn't sit well with him, and vice versa. But for my part, I was learning to accept his faults because I wanted this relationship to work. I always wanted to finish something that I had started, because if not, it always made me feel like a failure, and I hated feeling that way.

I had left Clewiston for a better life, and I didn't want to go back there looking like a dog who had returned to its master, begging for forgiveness. Things were looking up for me in the job department. I was now working for a group of urologists. The company was called *Urological Consultants of Miami Beach*. I knew John was getting frustrated.

There were times when I would go home expecting just to see the house and no John in it. I was praying that it wouldn't happen, but by listening to him sometimes when we were lying together on the bed, it seemed as if it were inevitable that he would leave me. I should have sensed from his pattern of abruptly leaving one place for another that his restless spirit would call him away from me – it was just a matter of time. But love is truly and completely blind, as they say.

Sometimes I felt as if I were the problem in the marriage, even though he would try to make me feel better by saying, *"It's not you, it's just me; I think I need to see a little more of the world."* But that wasn't doing anything to comfort me. I knew he wanted to get out of this marriage. Maybe the way I had felt about him wasn't the way he had ever felt about me, but he insisted that he was the cause of our problems. In my book, the end result was going to be the same, whether it was my fault or his. He was going to leave me and our daughter. He never really bonded with her like you would expect a father to bond with his child. My father-daughter relationship was vulgar and unnatural, but John had a real chance to be a worthy father and husband. No, I was going to be left alone – again – and there was nothing I could do to change that fact.

All my life I felt as if I were alone. I had carried since my early childhood a huge burden -- one I couldn't share with anyone because it made me feel as if I were worth nothing. It wasn't my fault, but it didn't matter. I still felt sometimes as if I were nothing, which gave way to deeper feelings as I grew up, that told me everything that was happening around me was *my* fault.

There were times when I found myself at work doing what I'm supposed to do, but my mind was not where I was. It was at my home, wondering what I could do to make things better. As I sat there in the office one particular day, my mind went back to that morning when we had the conversation that always seemed to make me want to cry.

I remember asking John why he didn't want to be married. "Did you ever love me? Please stay and let's work things out." Regardless of the tenderness of my words, which I tried desperately to sound as if there were no judgments in them, our discussions always ended up with him being frustrated because he really

264

didn't want to stay married. My self-esteem was already as low as it could go, and yet I had to ask myself if he just didn't want to stay married to *ME!* Oh, he was always careful to say he wasn't trying to hurt me, but his words were killing me with a force greater than his fist could ever manage.

Why did my life come to this? I really loved John. I loved him with all my heart, but that love was not reciprocated. One thing about me was that, no matter what was going on inside of me, I always got my job done well and efficiently. I understood the importance of a good work ethic in affording me the money for food and shelter, especially since I couldn't depend on John not to up and leave on a whim.

So I worked as hard as possible, doing the work of two people, just to insure myself of steady employment because I was too valuable to let go. What hurt me the most about my marriage is that it was apparent that John wasn't willing to fight for it. I always saw our marriage as something worth fighting to preserve, but that takes equal effort on the part of both partners.

It was 5:00 a.m. and I had been awake for hours, unable to sleep. My heart was heavy and I wasn't sure exactly of the ramifications of that feeling. For a while now, John hadn't been the loving person he used to be, but I couldn't seem to get anything out of him. He wouldn't tell me what was wrong, just kept giving me that insincere phrase that "he was the problem, not me."

I was lying there in the bed that morning. He was beside me with his back turned to me. I reflected silently on how much we came to enjoy intimacy, so I missed it when it left our bedroom. Now things weren't good, not good at all. I wanted to put my arms around him, but every time I did that, we always ended up arguing over something insignificant. I didn't have the "marriage maturity" to recognize that the argument was a diversion to avoid talking about the problem of his lack of affection in bed. He never said he didn't love me, but I felt the need to ask the pointed question: "John, do you still love me? Did you ever love me? Maybe I better limit myself to one question.

So I reached over and touched him. "John, do you love me?" I asked. He rolled over and said, *"Look, I don't want to start an argument now; I'm tired."* He then rolled over with his back to me once again. Truthfully, I had the answer to my question, but I chose to think he would reveal the answer in time. I was wrong.

I got out of bed as John fell back to sleep and release a soft snore to let me know I was free to get up and do whatever I wanted. I went into the bathroom and closed the door. I involuntarily fell to my knees. I didn't know how to pray, so I just cried. I remembered those days when I used to go to church, but what did I learn? I was a kid then, and I had only gone there to get away from where I lived. It was just a haven. Why had I not paid attention to biblical scriptures or life lessons coming from the pulpit? I sure needed one of those lessons to come to the front of my mind right about now. I didn't know how merciful God is, and I rose from the bathroom floor thinking He probably was too busy to hear the awkward prayers of someone who didn't know Him "like that." I tried to go on with my day and not feel utterly defeated. That day turned into another, as the burden I carried daily grew heavier and heavier.

One day I paged John with 43770-`123 (pager code for hello - I love you). I got no return page. I was devastated because I knew something was wrong. I felt this sharp, piercing pain that just wouldn't go away, but like always I made myself suppress it. In my mind I just needed to make it to 5:00 p.m. and then I could let it all out once I got home. I started crying on the inside at 5:01 p.m., determined not to actually cry or have puffy eyes when I walked through the door. John hated to see me cry. When I cried, and unfortunately it was often, he would have this look of sheer disgust. I would hear, *"Crying all the time like a weak fool; you make me sick."*

Now I didn't want to appear weak in his eyes. He liked strong women, and that day I needed him to like me, to love me with all my exposed weaknesses. I wanted our marriage to work, and I just couldn't deal with not being good enough to even keep my marriage. My mind was flooded with thoughts that something must be wrong with me. I just wasn't normal. I felt that I was broken, inferior, "a gamble girl," but I sensed in my heart that he had left a long time ago, and now he was about the leave… for real.

The next morning breakfast was over, and I left for work. I was good at functioning in survival mode. At 4:45p.m., the dark cloud returned and all I wanted to do was make it out of the building and, let the tears roll while driving home. I had wildly contrasting thoughts about the meaning of the word "home" to me growing up, and to me as a wife trying to make a good home for her family.

I had just enough drive time to fix myself up before I walked through that door. I gave a quick glance in the mirror while still in the car; my eyes looked ok. I pulled up outside the house, but I didn't see his truck. I told myself that he was just running late, but I sensed that it wasn't so.

I unlocked the apartment door, and walked straight back to the bedroom. I swung opened the closet door, and, you guessed it, all of his stuff was gone. There was no note explaining anything. He and his clothes were just gone. This was what I was afraid of, and now it had happened. Could my daily anticipation of this action caused it to be less dramatic and painful than I expected?

I shed no tears. It was like something inside of me went numb for a second, but yet I felt this surge of courage and strength come upon me. I knew I had to survive. Maybe this was my life; maybe this was the way things were supposed to happen to me. I was not supposed to be happy, since, from the moment I was born there was sadness in my life.

I thought about those things, and I didn't cry. I can't explain it, but I felt a sense of relief, empowerment and strength. I had an attitude that screamed, "I will make it, and no matter what, I am not going back to my parents' home. I'll get a room if needed, but I will not move back to Clewiston, Florida!"

I sat on the bed silently for a while, and then it was like my mind started thinking of the bills, rent, lights, car insurance. Will I be able to meet my monthly obligations? Somewhere inside of me I heard, *"YES, you can, and yes, you will be ok."* I had remembered way back a long time ago that a preacher spoke about the "audible voice of God." I thought it would be so strange if anyone actually heart God's voice because that would mean you're dead! But here I was, very much alive, though in pain, hearing the audible voice of God as if he were sitting on the bed with me. Wait a minute! He *was* sitting on the bed with me!

I had started going to a church in Miami, but after what happened between John and me, I decided I wasn't going back. What was I going tell them? Now my Mondays through Fridays consisted of working from 9:00 a.m. to 5:00 p.m., and sleeping from 6:00 p.m. until the next morning. My sleep was never comfortable or restful. It was the unhealthy kind of sleep that comes when you want to escape reality.

My Saturdays and Sundays were about the same. I had breakfast at home. I had no strength or desire to go out, other than to the local store to pick up Nyquil to get me through the weekend. Today, I understand that my behavior could have easily been the textbook definition of "clinical depression," but since I was so used to suppressing everything negative that was important in my life, I figured there was no situation I couldn't handle. I was so very wrong because I sank deeper and deeper into the kind of depression that leads to suicide, but I was unaware of the evil spirits attached to depression. Thankfully, my daughter, Precious, was with my mother, since she could do a better job raising her than I could – that's what I reasoned in my sad mind.

Eight months elapsed, as I followed this common routine, with no one in my life interrupting it with a little joy or concern for my welfare. Still no phone call, letter, note or page from John. I wasn't sure where he was, and I tried not to think about it. Now when I called my daughter, Precious, and Mom put her on the phone. I managed to sound happy and let her know that her daddy loved her so much.

I was home one day when finally the pager beeped. Since I had no home phone, I got into my car, drove and found a payphone. Excitedly I picked up the phone and deposited the required amount of money. In my excitement to get to a phone, I hadn't taken enough money. I dialed the number I got on the pager. When he answered, I said, "Hi, where are you?" *"Orlando,"* he responded calmly. "You got your own place?" *"I'm going to get a place soon, but I need about $800.00 more; the apartments here cost a lot of money."*

I wanted to ask with whom he was staying, but I knew my heart couldn't take hearing that he went back once more to the woman who had his two kids. And I couldn't bear to hear about yet another new woman in his life. So I kept the conversation light. "What are you doing?" *"Nothing, you still got the apartment?"* "Yes." *"Isn't the lease up soon?"* "No, I just signed a new one two months ago. Why do you ask?" He paused, *"Why don't you come down here and we can get an apartment together? We can try to work it out."*

"Ok, talk to you later. I'll call you back tonight. I am running out of change and I hear the lady on the phone asking for more money." Everything in me wanted to stay on the phone forever. I wanted him to come through the phone line and stand next to me in that phone booth and kiss me like he cherished me. All I could do was say, "Bye, hey, wait, hello?" *"What?"* he asked. "I just wanted to say I love you." I heard a click. "Hello, hello, you still there?" I heard the automated voice say, *"Please hang up, and try again."* It seemed I had run out of money. I was too in love and too blind to see that I had run out of hope!

I was excited when I hung up the phone, telling myself that I was getting back with John again. Without thinking, I resigned my job. Nothing could be more important than getting back with the man I loved. When I was leaving my job, I got hugs, kisses and goodbyes, and best wishes. My boss said, *"Here's your letter of recommendation, and if you need anything, don't hesitate to call us. If you decide to move back to Miami, you have got a job always. We're going to miss you."* After working with them for ten years I walked out the door, not really sure what the future would be.

I called around to find a moving company, but the cost was prohibitive. The only thing left for me to do was to rent a U-Haul truck. My landlady was aware that I needed to get out of the lease and was very understanding. John came into town early Saturday morning, attached our white *Cougar* to the *U-Haul* car hitch, packed up all the stuff we were able to load into the car and on the small *U-Haul* truck, and threw the rest away. You see, I had learned not to buy anything of real value, because you never knew when you were going to have to move out by morning taking only the essentials.

We were on our way to West Orlando. I was sitting beside John, just where I had always wanted to be, and he seemed like the John who was my one true love. And I was happy. I had already forgiven him for all the wrongs he had done to me, and was ready to start anew again with him. I wanted to know where we were going because he hadn't told me.

"We are going to go by my niece, Faye, and stay the night, and then go sign the paperwork to our new apartment." I was one hundred percent ok with that. It showed me that he was taking charge, which was actually the first time John was taking the lead. I was always the one finding the apartments, so it was good that he was the one who had found this one.

We arrived at the Johnson's place, Sewell Place apartment off of Pine Hills Road in West Orlando. John had the key to the apartment. He parked the truck in the driveway and we entered. He then informed me the Johnsons were not home, but they would be back on Sunday. While in the house, the phone rang and I picked it up. "Hello," I said. *"Who is this?"* the female on the other end asked. "I'm John's wife," I responded.

"Oh, I thought you guys were still in Miami. Are you down for the weekend? Make yourself at home and hope to see you soon." "Okay," I said, feeling betrayed. I hung up. John had given me the impression that his niece knew we were going to be at her home. Now I was shocked to realize that he hadn't told her anything. I was mad too. I thought he had changed, but he was being the same person he had always been,

underhanded and downright untrustworthy. I went right over to him. He was sitting and watching television in the family room. He looked questioningly at me as I approached him.

"That was Faye on the line," I said, "and she thought I was still in Miami. I thought that you told her that we were coming here." *"She doesn't mind us being here, so what's the problem?"* "The problem is that we can't come to someone's home like that without letting them know." *"You worry too much. There is not going to be any problem."* "I still want you to call her and tell her what's happening." He shook his head and reluctantly got up off the couch to call her. I heard him as he explained the situation to Faye, and that was when I realized there was no apartment. We were going to be staying here at his niece's for a while, but who knew for how long?

I certainly didn't know. Why, oh way didn't I just collect my personal belongings and leave immediately? The answer is that I was a woman in love who seemed destined to receive the same pain inflicted upon her day after day, year after year. I wiped the one tear getting ready to fall from my eyes and began unpacking the essentials from the *U-Haul*.

Once Faye returned home, we lived at her place for a few weeks. She and the entire Johnsons family went out of their way to make us feel at home. But the problem was with us. We weren't going anywhere in life because John had not changed. He had the same lackadaisical attitude he had always had. I tried my best to live in harmony with him, but he wasn't working with me. John had made it clear to me that he didn't want to be married, and everything he did was to prove that he was right. Why had he called me that day to invite me to return to Orlando? Was the heat where he lived not strong enough, and was his bed too cold? Certainly his motive had nothing to do with love or a desire to be a good husband.

I was tired of living at Faye's place. She was the nicest person to me, but I needed my own place. I eventually moved out and found myself an apartment. Despite what was happening I still wanted John with me, but I knew he was practically gone yet again! God knows I tried my best to put on a strong front, but I kept having emotional breakdowns, which resulted in uncontrollable crying, and shouting matches. Truthfully, most of the times I was the only one in the fight, since John would just pick up the keys and out the door he went, returning many hours later, with no explanation given for the time he was gone.

It was so hard for me. I kept asking God why all this was happening and why I continued to live a miserable existence. What did I do? I mean I kept my weight down, and I cooked, cleaned and paid my half of the bills, sometimes even more because John didn't believe in getting broke for anyone. Never mind that I might have been down to my last dollar giving more than half the amount to cover the household. One of his mottos -- and he had a lot of them -- was *"They ain't gonna go broke if we don't pay them; they're just a bunch of crooks, so call and tell them we'll pay next month."* Unfortunately this vicious cycle went on throughout our entire marriage, and this one issue caused more problems than anything else. I finally got fed up and filed for divorce. I'm sure God and all the Heavenly Angels were applauding!

My divorce was finalized in 1999. I was sad because it ended, but I finally embraced a glimpse of God's promise for me when it came to marriage. He had given me enough signs for a deaf, dumb and blind person to understand that John was never the one God had for me. The hard lesson was finally learned, in the hardest way possible. But it was learned once and for all!

I'm happily married now, as I had stated in my Introduction. But how I got to that place of my life is another story, one I believe God may inspire me to write someday – soon!

You're probably wondering about my relationship with my daughter, Precious. Well, you know that my Mom was raising Precious while I took care of what I thought was the essential business of my life. My blinded love for John had robbed me of the common sense to see what was truly most important in my life. But, as they say, *"hindsight is always 20/20."*

When Precious was five years old, God impressed on my heart to go home and get her. It was like He said if I didn't get her now, I would lose her forever because she would never respect me as her mother. She would judge me as the no good mother who abandoned her, even if she formed a great relationship with Mom. Kids are far more perceptive than adults give them credit for.

As jacked up as I was back then, thinking only John mattered to me, I knew I didn't want to live the rest of my life with regrets. So I eventually called Mom and told her I was coming to get Precious and bring her to Miami to live with us. We were not married at the time, but at least she would be living with her father. I don't know if her presence hastened the date of our marriage, but John married me a year later. He never really wanted to get married, but said, *"I'm willing to try, and If it works, it works, and if it don't then it just don't!"*

I should have had the sense to know right there that I was subtly forcing him to do what he didn't want to do, and I paid a dear price for such stupidity. I can't tell you how many times I heard, *"Baby, I love you so much. I want to spend the rest of my life with you."* He played as many mind games with me as he wanted to, because I was literally a "fool" for love.

Our family was a big support for Precious. They loved and adored her. Mom really didn't want me to get Precious, but I knew I had to, and thank God I did. Still, because I had learned too well to hide my feelings and distrust some adults, my inability to connect, nurture, hug and tell my own child how much I loved her *did* affect her, and it took a very long time and a lot of prayer for to develop the closeness we have now.

Precious basically raised ME while she was growing up. I say this because Precious planned all of her school activities, signed all her school paperwork, and never lost focus the way I did all through school. She even transferred her 9th grade school year from an urban to a suburban high school from which she graduated. She was on the Varsity Cheerleading Squad, and did an excellent job, despite the fact that I never attended a game. She also planned ALL of her birthday parties, her high school and college graduations, and even her baby showers. Precious never locked me out of her life. I did that all by myself, and she forgave me for all of this, plus not being there for her when she gave birth to her first child.

Remarkably, Precious' main trait was resilience, which she definitely got from me. She found joy where there was none that I could see, and she grew strong, despite the dysfunction in her home life. Precious was always special, liked by everybody, and always a go-getter. She's doing well now – married with three beautiful kids named Austin, Katelyn and Haley, whom I love to life.

Precious was BORN to be a mother. She loves motherhood, while I had to pray and ask God how to connect with my child. Praise God, He answered my prayers. I marvel now, in retrospect, when I think of how numb I was to the world, while professing to be saved and full of the Holy Ghost. I had no idea that everything I was chasing after was with me all the time. Precious and I are very close today, and for that I thank God. She and I run and operate a Florida-based Nonprofit 501-c3 whose Mission is, *"The Empowerment of Women and Girls in the area of Personal Development and Entrepreneurship*." She also owns and operates a successful Daycare Center. In a nutshell, she's doing fine and her household services the one and only true God. I did something right ☺!

Today, I am thankful I can say, "My heart is full of light and love. My mind, sprit and soul are free and full of unlimited possibilities. God has truly "restored the years that the enemy stole from me." My love tank is full because I have unspeakable joy, hope and happiness. I love everybody – I have forgiven all and I love all. I no longer try to be HOLY. In other words I STOPPED TRYING TO DO WHAT WAS ALREADY DONE FOR ME. I simply started whole-heartedly believing what God said about me, and I can honestly say that I'm a happy, spiritually nourished and worthy woman!

THE END

How to Reach the Author

Veronica Nealy-Morris is a highly sought after Author, Entrepreneur, Professional Life Coach and Transformational Teach-Speaker. She is authentic, truthful, and very transparent. Veronica is held as a dynamic Communicator who speaks straight from her heart to yours with clarity and understanding. She uses her life experiences to help others begin their transformation, and subsequently evolve into the persons they were born to be.

Veronica realizes that life is not meant to be lived in solitary existence, but we are all part of God's "big plan." She says, " My path chose me and I had no say in the matter, but I was determined not to allow my path to control my future. I somehow knew God would bring me out on the other side, and God never disappoints!" She created a Dream Journal, *"Write the Vision Make it Plain,"* which she uses to encourage others to write their dreams and aspirations on paper (available lulu.com).

She can be reached for speaking engagements, book signings and readings, and as a member of panel discussions about moving from tragedy to triumph. Here is her contact information:

Veronicanealy@yahoo.com
407-953-5554